Published by Don Gillan - MMXVII

Copyright © Don Gillan, February 2018 – All rights reserved.

Manuscript created entirely in Libre Office,
the world's best *free* office productivity suite:
https://www.libreoffice.org/

Previous Publications in the "Scrapbook" series of vintage football histories:

Bradford City Season Scrapbook 1902/03-03/04: Changing Codes.
Bradford City Season Scrapbook 1907/08: Second Division Champions.
Bradford Park Avenue Season Scrapbook 1907/08: A Southern Adventure
Everton Season Scrapbook 1890/91: Anfield Champions in Blue
Leeds United Season Scrapbook 1919/20-20/21: From The Ashes.
Preston North End Season Scrapbook 1888/89: The Invincibles
Sunderland/Sunderland Albion Season Scrapbook 1891/92: The Mighty and the Fallen
The Wednesday Season Scrapbook 1889/90: Days of Alliance
Bradford City F.A. Cup Scrapbook 1911: How t'Cup Came Home to Bradford
Sheffield United F.A. Cup Scrapbook 1899-1902: The Three Cups
Tottenham Hotspur F.A. Cup Scrapbook 1901: 'Spurs First Cup

Rev. 1.03

Drink CADBURY'S (Registered) COCOA

GUARANTEED ABSOLUTELY PURE AND SOLUBLE.

BY ROYAL AUTHORITY.

Cadbury Bros. warn the public of those Dutch Cocoas and their English imitations, sold as pure Cocoa, to which about 4 per cent. of Alkali and other agents are added, to give apparent strength to the liquor, by making it a dark colour. This addition may be detected by the scent when a tin is freshly opened. No Cocoa can be stronger than Cadbury's, which is guaranteed **ABSOLUTELY PURE.**

A few of the many Good Reasons why CADBURY'S COCOA enjoys such World-wide Popularity.

It is guaranteed to be Pure Cocoa.
It is Soluble in boiling Milk or Water.
It is not reduced in value by the addition of Starch, Sugar, &c.
It is specially rich in flesh-forming and strength-sustaining principles.

It contains all the delicious aroma of the Natural Article, without the excessive proportions of fat.
It is delicious, nutritious, digestible, comforting, and a refined beverage suitable for all seasons of the year.

It is a gentle stimulant, and sustains against hunger and bodily fatigue.
In the whole process of manufacturing Cadbury's Pure Cocoa, the automatic machinery employed obviates the necessity for its being once touched by the human hand.

PRECAUTION & WARNING.—*Always ask for Cadbury's Cocoa. Always examine your Purchase. See that you have not been induced to accept an Imitation, and be wary of highly-coloured and drugged preparations offered as pure Cocoa. Anything of a medicated character associated with Cocoa proclaims at once that it is not pure.*

Introduction

In the summer of 1892, John Houlding, then president of the Everton Football Club and personal owner of it's Anfield ground, came into dispute with the rest of the Everton club committee over his demands for ground rental. With the two sides unable to reach any compromise, Houlding was voted off the Everton committee and the club departed Anfield to build a new home across Stanley Park at Goodison.

Left with an empty football stadium on his hands, Houlding took the pragmatic course of raising a new football club to play there, and Liverpool A.F.C. was born. Playing in blue and white, the new club spent a season in the Lancashire League before being elected to the Second Division of the Football League, winning both competitions at the first time of asking. This is the story of those two seasons, as reported by the press of the time with additional facts and commentary by the author. Every match in both seasons covered, stats and full period match report.

A Brief History of the Game

The origins of the game of football are short and precise, or ages long and impossibly diffuse, or anywhere in between – depending entirely upon your point of view!

The long version of the football story is that games involving a roughly spherical object knocked around by means of the perambulatory appendages have occurred in cultures all around the World since time immemorial. A roughly spherical object is an ideal appurtenance for involvement in all kinds of physical activity, competitive or otherwise, and can be manufactured in several ways from a range of materials - some ancient cultures even used the heads of their enemies sewn up (or not) in cloth or leather bags. As for propelling such an object, the feet are the ideal appendages for doing so without stopping to pick it up. The two seem, quite naturally, to fit together.

Boys are known to have kicked balls around on the streets of Ancient Rome. Cicero's law journals, for example, give a lurid account of a case involving a barber who accidentally, and fatally, sliced his customers throat open when he was struck by a ball kicked into his shop from outside. In Ancient Greek culture also, mosaics and pottery decorations have been preserved which seemingly depict the kicking of balls in some kind of sporting context. In Britain, ball games were banned during the great period of the wars with France between the 14th and 15th centuries because they distracted boys from dedicating the proper time to archery practice. King James I maintained the ban because the game acted more as "a meeter for lameing than for making able," in other words more likely to injure than promote fitness.

Just kicking a ball around haphazardly does not make it 'football' you say. Ah, then, but what is 'football' as we know it? Just one set of rules chosen from among many that were extant in 1863 (when the F.A. was formed). A set which, indeed, have in themselves evolved out of all recognition since then! Were any of those older games any less valid a progenitor of the modern game just because the sands of time have forgotten what the rules (if any) were?

The medium version of the story, so far as football in England is concerned, is that it originated in the great public schools of the South - Eton, Harrow, Winchester, Rugby and the rest – each of whom developed ball games with their own distinctive and carefully set down set of rules. Games which then escaped the public school confines into the Old Boys network when graduates from the schools wanted to carry on playing. Although these versions of the game were formalised, in most cases with documented sets of rules, they were still each different, representing several distinctly different variants of the game which yet needed to be brought together. Some of those ancient games persist to this day, albeit in a ritualised fashion, eg. the Eton 'Wall Game.' That first set of standard rules adopted by the F.A. were based upon the Cambridge Rules.

The short and precise version of the story is that the game of football as we know it today began in 1863, with the formation of the Football Association and the unification of the myriad different variants of the game under a single codified set of rules. Even then, the term "as we know it" is perhaps not the best choice since the 1863 version of the game would have looked very strange to the current day follower. The latter, for example, would no doubt howl "hand ball" every time the 1863 player made a "fair catch" with his hands before dropping the ball at his feet to carry on. He would have remonstrated with the referee for calling 'off-side' even when half the opposing team were playing the supposed 'offender' clearly on-side, or that 'offender' was in his own half of the field of play. And if he was upset by that he would have been apoplectic when the same player who played the ball into touch quickly picked it up and returned it back into play again. He would have wondered if he was even at the right venue where two unconnected wooden posts stood where each of the goal-frames should have been, and, perhaps most of all, he would have wondered where in heaven the two goalkeepers had got to.

In other words, that first set of rules laid down in 1863 described a game substantially different in several ways from the modern version. It would take several more years of amendments to the rules before it began to take on the shape of the game that is familiar to us today. Those changes came rapidly at first, as the game came to terms with itself, so that, by the period to which this book relates the game had already begun to take on a more modern appearance.

The position of the Goalkeeper, for example, with special dispensation to use hands to protect the goal, was introduced in 1871, although it was not until 1909 that the idea of varying the Goalkeepers kit to distinguish them from the rest of their team was introduced.

The Privileged South v. The Industrial North

Among the privileged public schools and public school old boys of the south there was a latent chivalric notion that sport, of any shade, was a high ideal to be entered into for it's own sake without thought of reward. Under that view, to take any form of payment for participating in a sporting activity sullied and demeaned it. It was idealists with this sort of viewpoint, the captains of several Old Boys clubs, that formed the Football Association, and thus defined a game that was intended from the start to be strictly amateur.

In the industrial north the situation was very different. There the clubs were mostly made up of working men, their very existence only having been made possible by the Factory Act of 1850. This, among other things, had decreed that the factories should close at 2 p.m. every Saturday, meaning that the average working man, for the first time in history, had a free afternoon of leisure time. Of course, lots of footloose young men with time on their hands and nothing to occupy it could, and initially did, result in a lot of trouble. But then the churches stepped in to encourage sporting activities as a way of promoting a healthy mind as well as body. The more forward thinking factory owners soon realised this was equally in their own interests and began to do the same, so that the first working men's clubs were generally formed around church and factory groups.

Land to play on was begged and borrowed, and kit was cobbled together, as an explosion of clubs were founded in all the great industrial centres. Crowds began to gather whenever these clubs played each other and it soon became apparent that the game had as much appeal for observers wanting to be entertained vicariously as it did for the players wanting to participate. Consequently, the club's began to raise funds by charging spectators.

The Northern[1] game rapidly grew in stature and what the Northern players may have lacked in flair compared to their Southern counterparts they made up for in organisation. The first Northern side to make a serious showing against the Southern clubs in the national cup competition were Darwen, who reached the Quarter-Finals in in 1879 and the Semi-Finals in 1881 – on both occasions being knocked out by the eventual winners (Old Etonians then Old Carthusians). In 1882, Blackburn Rovers lost to the Old Etonians in the final and a year later Blackburn Olympic went one better and defeated the Etonians in the final. After that, no 'Old Boys' club would ever win the competition again.

The Coming of Professionalism

As we have already seen, from the very formation of the F.A. professionalism had been banned in the game. As the game grew in the North, however, amateurism became an increasing problem. Working class players could not afford to take time off work to play the game, making it difficult to raise a team when a game had to be played in midweek[2], nor could the players spare much time to practice and develop their skills. Consequently a kind of 'shamateurism' arose around the Northern working mens clubs where players could be found jobs with sympathetic local businesses that not only paid unusually well but allowed plenty of time off for those particular individuals for playing and practising football!

It was this practice that first drew a horde of Scots south of the border and in so doing changed the very nature of English football. England had concentrated on the dribbling game until the Scottish invaders brought with them the fine art of passing which they had developed in their homeland. This new breed of dedicated, highly practised players and new style of football quickly overturned the dominance which the 'gentleman' players of the Southern 'old boys' clubs had held over the game. This also inevitably led to complaints from the Southern clubs, particularly after Cup ties, that the Northern sides that had beaten them were not true amateurs – complaints of which type led to the suspensions by the F.A. of both Accrington and Preston North End.

This was a step too far for the rest of the Northern clubs, however, who banded together in protest and threatened to withdraw from the F.A. and form their own Association unless the ban against professionalism was withdrawn. Realising that they would very quickly become a second rate organisation if the Northern power house went it's own way, the F.A. was forced to acquiesce in the matter, and in 1885 the professional game was born.

---

1 For 'Northern' read 'Northern and Midlands'.
2 Before floodlights midweek games had to kick-off before the end of normal working hours in order to finish before darkness fell.

Formation of the Football League

The Football League was the brainchild of William McGregor, a Scottish entrepreneur from Perthshire, who, after moving to Birmingham in pursuit of business interests, had become deeply involved with the Aston Villa club. He served the Villans for over 20 years in various capacities, including president, director and chairman. In that latter capacity he became frustrated at the annually repeated and bothersome ritual of arranging suitable fixtures for the club. The uncertainty of this process, the frequent cancellations, and the need to resort to too easy fixtures against lesser local teams to fill up the fixture list, all serving to confound his ambitions to establish the club on a more businesslike basis.

Consequently he conceived the notion of arranging a League of top clubs who would play each other annually, home and away, thus creating a guaranteed schedule of games against top quality opposition upon which each season's fixture list could be built. To that end he invited representatives of eleven of the most prominent clubs in the country to attend a meeting at the Anderton's Hotel in London, on Friday, March 22nd, 1888, to discuss the issue. After much debate, a proposal was carried to form a 'National Football Association League' and Mr. H. Lockett of the Stoke club was appointed secretary pro tem.

Following the meeting, the following circular was sent to the major clubs:

Dear Sir,

At a meeting of representatives of some of the leading clubs in the country, held at the Anderton Hotel, London, on Friday evening last, a strong feeling was evinced that something should be done to improve the present unsatisfactory state of club fixtures, and to render them more certain in their fulfilment and interesting character, and the following suggestions were made

(a.) That in order to secure a certain number of first class matches (irrespective of cup ties) the following twelve clubs shall be invited to a conference
  (1) to form a league, or union, for twelve of the most prominent clubs to play home and away fixtures.
  (2) to arrange dates for such matches; and
  (3) to decide upon rules and regulations for the same.
  The following are the names of the clubs:- Preston North End, Burnley, Accrington, Blackburn Rovers, Bolton Wanderers, Everton, Derby County, Notts County, Stoke, Wolverhampton Wanderers, West Bromwich Albion, and Aston Villa.

(b.) That all matches shall be played under the Cup rules of the Football Association, but any bona-fide member of a club shall be allowed to play, providing he has not played for any other club in the union or league during the same season.

(c.) That each club shall be expected play its full strength in all matches.

(d.) That the gross gate shall be divided in all matches. (This is not to interfere with reserves or stands, members, or season ticket holders.)

(e.) That the price of admission shall be at the option of the home club.

(f.) That the averages shall be taken from wins, draws, and losses, and not from the number of goals scored.

(g.) That the four (4) clubs having the lowest average shall retire, but shall be eligible for re-election.

(h.) That a meeting to consider the above shall be held at the Royal Hotel, Manchester, on Tuesday, April 17, at 6:30 p.m.; and that representatives of the above clubs are requested to be in a position, with dates, to arrange fixtures for the coming season.

I remain, yours truly, H. Lockett, Hon. Sec. pro tem.

As well as the original twelve, the next meeting was attended by representatives of the Nottingham Forest, Halliwell, and Sheffield Wednesday clubs, pressing their cases for inclusion on the basis that they were of at least equal standing with several of those clubs originally invited. Similar requests had also been received by post from several other clubs unable to attend.

After much discussion, however, the original twelve passed a resolution that due to the increased difficulties of arranging fixtures for a larger number twelve should remain the limit of the initial membership, so that no additional applications could be entertained. In a further resolution, Mr. Lockett was confirmed as Secretary and a date set at which the list of fixtures for each club would be finalised.

And so the Football League was born, the first round of fixtures being played in September, 1888. The basis on which the clubs were to be ranked was deferred for future discussion. That issue was settled at a further meeting of the club delegates at the Grand Hotel in Birmingham on 21st November, 1888, it being decided that points should be awarded for each match played on the basis of 2 for a win, 1 apiece for a draw and 0 for a defeat. The club accumulating the most points over the course of the season to be declared the winners. Where clubs had an equal number of points, goal average would be used to separate them (goals scored divided by goals conceded).

By that reckoning Preston North End then sat proudly at the head of the first ever official League table on 22 points (played 12, won 10, drawn 2, lost 0). Liverpool representatives Everton were fifth on 16 points (from 11 games), just ahead of West Bromwich on goal average.

How The Game Was Played

There were some significant differences in the way the Football was played in 1892/93 as compared to the current day. The Football Association had been in existence then a mere twenty seven years and Football, as an organised and regulated game, was still in it's relative infancy with the rules of play still set to undergo some major changes to evolve into the game we recognise today. To enable the reader to better understand the match reports reproduced in this publication, let me first summarise the more significant of these differences, particularly with reference to any terms which may be used in these reports that are not so common in the current day.

Formation – Tactics and playing formations were not so much a part of the game as they are today although by the end of the 1880's the "kick and rush" era had largely passed by and the Northern professional clubs in particular had begun to take a much more scientific approach to the game. The common earlier formations of 1-2-7 (copied from the handling game) and 2-2-6 had now largely been displaced by a still attacking minded 2-3-5 – a formation which would predominate in the game for many years ie.:

Outside Left – Inside Left – Centre Forward – Inside Right – Outside Right
(forwards)
Left Half – Centre Half - Right Half
(halves)
Left Back – Right Back
(backs)
Goalkeeper

Substitutes – match teams consisted of eleven players only, with **no** substitutes. Substitutes were not permitted in English League Football until the 1965-66 season. Prior to then, if a player was unable for any reason to continue to fully participate in the game then his team would have to play on a man short, or, in the case of the 'walking wounded', with the injured player switched to a less critical position - usually an outside wing where he would not compromise his teams defence and might still contribute to the attack with the occasional pass if the ball happened his way.

Players Kit – Players shirts bore neither numbers nor names for identification. This often led to misidentification in match reports.

Goalkeepers - Goalkeepers wore exactly the same strip as the outfield players of the same team. The rule requiring goalkeepers to wear distinctive tops (so they could be distinguished by referees in a melee of players) was not introduced until 1909. Many of the match reports mention the goalkeeper being made or 'forced' to use hands – this reflects that at the time, although handling was permissible on the part of the goalkeeper, the applicable ruling stipulated that he may do so only "in defence of his goal," i.e. to make a save. There was no specific limitation as to where on the field the goalkeeper might use his hands, although the latter stipulation effectively limited such use to the vicinity of his goalmouth.

Off-side – *A player was off-side if there were less than **three** opponents between him and the opposing goal line at the moment when the ball was played forward to him by a member of his own side – this applied anywhere on the field. The goalkeeper counted as, but needed not necessarily to be, one of the three. Prior to the beginning of the 1907/08 season, a player could be offside even in his own half of the field of play. The required number of opponents was reduced to two from 1925.*

Free-Kicks (including Corners) – *The distinction between 'direct' and 'indirect' kicks had not yet been made. All corners and free kicks at the time were 'indirect', ie. a valid goal could not be scored directly from either without the ball making contact with another player after the kicker.*

Match Ball – *Match balls were made of stitched leather panels and were much heavier than modern footballs made of lightweight synthetic materials. Furthermore, in wet conditions a ball could more than double in weight due to the leather skin becoming waterlogged.*

Charging (a.k.a. Shoulder Charge) – *A form of tackle wherein the tackler makes deliberate bodily contact with an opponent, leading with his shoulder against the opponents shoulder, in an effort to barge the opponent off the ball. Even the goalkeeper could be charged whilst in possession of the ball in an attempt to bundle him into the net. Charging was legitimate so long as each player had one foot on the ground at the time of contact, and the amount of force used was not 'excessive'. Charging remains in the rules today, but the idea of what is regarded as excessive is now applied so stringently that the forceful charging of old has gone from the game.*

Pitch Markings - *Differed substantially from the current day. When the rules of football were first laid down pitch markings were not required at all! Initially the only requirement was for four corner flags, the boundaries of play then being judged by line of sight between them. Some clubs began to improve upon this by painting lines on the pitch connecting the flags and this outer boundary line was subsequently incorporated into the rules from 1883. In 1887 a half way line was added, and further additions were made in 1891 to facilitate the incorporation into the rules of the penalty kick. Two new lines were then added in each half. A solid line 12 yards from the goal line indicated the area within which an appropriate offence should lead to a penalty kick, and an incomplete line 6 yards beyond indicated the distance which players other than the kicker and defending goalkeeper must retire whilst the kick was taken. The kick itself could be taken from any point along the 12 yard line. The double intersecting hemispheres indicating the arc of six yards from either goal-post from which a goal-kick could be taken also appears to have become standard*

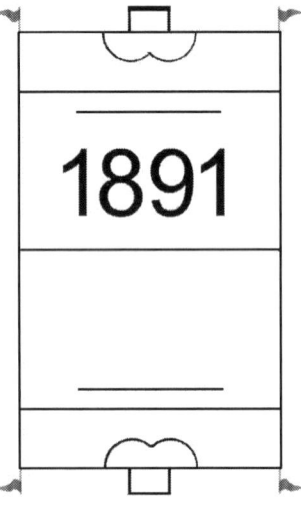

at this time, although since that rule was already well established this marking may have arisen earlier.

£ s. d. - U.K. Pre-decimalisation currency: pounds (£), shillings (s) and pence (d) where £1 = 20s : 1s = 12d. Allowing for inflation, the sum of £1 in 1894 would be worth approximately the equivalent of £121 at 2018 prices[3].

PLEASE NOTE: Since players did not wear names or numbers on their playing apparel at the time, proper identification of players depended greatly on the familiarity of the observer. Consequently it is possible, indeed likely, that a few at least of the scorers identified in the match reports reproduced herein may not necessarily correspond with the recognised tally.

NEWS REPORTS: Some factual errors in the newspaper reports reproduced in this book have been corrected by striking through the original text as printed in the report and adding the correction immediately afterwards contained in braces, ie. ~~erroneous text~~ {corrected text}. Where a word appears to have been omitted in the typesetting (not uncommon in early newsprint) a suggestion has been added followed by a question mark, all in braces.

3   Source: http://inflation.stephenmorley.org.

A Brief History of Liverpool A.F.C.

Liverpool F.C. were just one of literally thousands of Association football clubs, that arose in the industrial centres of the North and the Midlands during the latter half of the 19th Century. Most of these started out as amateur operations, but many turned professional after professionalism was legalised in the game after 1885.

Formed in 1892, as a professional outfit from the start, Liverpool were relative latecomers to the scene. Indeed, when Liverpool A.F.C. was first formed there were already three professional Association clubs operating in the City - Everton, Bootle and Liverpool Caledonians. Within a year, the latter two of these would fade out of existence, unable to meet the financial burden of operating on a professional level - leaving Liverpool and Everton to share the city alone. A fitting state of affairs since the two clubs origins are inextricably linked.

Like many other clubs, Everton's origins began with the Church – or, more specifically, a church, in this case the St. Domingo Methodist New Connexion Chapel, erected in 1871 at the junction of Breckfield Road and St. Domingo Vale (from which the Chapel took it's name). The New Connexion Methodists had previously worshipped in a premises at the rear of St. John's Market until that site was taken over by the corporation. Having tried other premises that proved unsuitable, the congregation resolved to build a new chapel, including spacious school-rooms. Designed by leading architects Hill and Swan (of Leeds), the entire project was completed at a cost of £6,800, and opened officially on 20th July, 1871.

It was quite common around that time for sporting clubs to arise out of church institutions and St. Domingo's was no exception. In 1877, newly appointed minister Reverend Ben Swift, assisted and encouraged in the creation of a cricket team as a healthy diversion for his parishioners. A year later, in 1878, a Football section was added to carry on activities throughout the winter months. Interest in the new St. Domingo's F.C. spread rapidly and soon outreached the chapel congregation. In light of this, and to continue to draw in members from a wider area than those attending the chapel, it was decided at a meeting at the Queens Head hotel in November 1879 to replace the name of the church with that of the surrounding area, and so Everton F.C. was born. The first match played by the club as Everton F.C. was against another church club, St. Peter's, in December 1879, Everton winning 6-0.

Matches at this time were played on a simple field in the south-east corner of Stanley Park which offered no changing rooms and no amenities for spectators. Even the goal-posts had to be taken down and stored away elsewhere after every match. Moreover, since it was public land, no admission could be charged – not that it would have generated much income from the meagre few that came along to watch in those earliest of days.

The renaming of the club, however, had the desired effect of enabling a much larger community of potential supporters to identify with the club, and within a very short time those meagre few that watched them every weekend grew into a multitude. The club also drew the attention of local Brewer and philanthropist Mr. John Houlding, a 'guardian' of the West Derby[4] Workhouse and Lunatic Asylum, whose home was at Stanley House, within the Park grounds where Everton were now playing. Houlding became deeply involved with the club, and the Sandon Hotel in Anfield, owned by Houlding, became the new venue for club meetings.

By 1882, Everton were testing their mettle against opposition from outside the city, and games at Stanley Park were drawing as many as 2000 non-paying patrons, whilst the club's finances remained fixed in the doldrums. Consequently it became clear that if the club was to continue to grow it needed an enclosed ground of it's own where admission could be charged. The answer was provided by William Cruitt, a friend of Houlding's, who arranged[5] for the club to have use of a piece of land in the vicinity of Priory Road.

There they established a semblance of a ground with primitive dressing rooms, a small stand for officials and perimeter fencing. Turnstiles at the entrances enabled them to charge spectators for admission, but the early takings were not what was hoped for, and the club had to resort to staging other activities by which to make money. Everton were yet to make their mark in the area, which they then did by winning the Liverpool and District Cup for the first time in 1884. Attendances, meanwhile, were steadily increasing, but while this was good for the club's finances, the noise and hubbub caused by the increasingly large crowds were not to the landowners liking, and after only two years at the site the club were asked to leave.

A new plot was found between Anfield Road and Walton Breck Road/Oakfield Road, on the site once used by the old Everton Cricket Club, only a few minutes walk from St. Domingo Vale. The club moved in 1884, proper covered stands were built, and their first game at 'Anfield,' was against Earlestown on 28th September, 1884. In fine weather a bumper crowd assembled to see Everton win by five goals to nil. Originally the land was leased from John Orrell, another friend of Houlding's in the brewing business, on the generous terms that the club maintain the walls, etc., enclosing the site and make an annual contribution to the Stanley Hospital in the name of Mr. Orrell. These terms were readily accepted.

When the F.A. were forced to back-down on the subject of amateurism and allow professionalism into the game Everton were one of the many Northern clubs who then chose to openly follow that route. Professional players meant a better class of football and better results leading to higher takings at the turnstiles.

Over the next few years the executive converted the ground at Anfield from a simple field surrounded by a brick wall to an international class ground with comfortable viewing facilities on all sides, and capable of accommodating over 20,000 spectators. By now also, Everton had become a much respected side and could draw opposition from across England and even Scotland to come and play them.

Consequently, in March 1888, Everton were one of those clubs invited to send representatives to the meeting at the Anderton's Hotel in London at which the Football

---

4   A Liverpool district east of Everton.
5   Modern research suggests the land actually belonged to local shipowner Thomas Seed, Cruitt's involvement in the arrangement, if correct, is therefore uncertain.

League was formed and thus became one of the twelve founder members. In their first season in that competition Everton finished eighth.

The Parting of the Ways

When Everton won the League Championship at the end of the 1888/89 season they were by then one of the richest club's in the land, the club's end of season account's showing a balance in hand of £1,792 8s. 1d. - including a massive profit on that one season alone of of £1,314 1s. 1d.!

It was precisely that issue, however, that led to a bitter conflict in the Everton club's ranks. John Houlding was a businessman who ran the club on businesslike terms and his own affairs likewise. Houlding had by this time bought out the land at Anfield with his own money, whereupon he had immediately begun charging the club a proper rent. He also charged the club for the use of his Sandow Hotel as the club's Headquarters and dressing rooms and possessed the sole rights to the sale of refreshments within the ground.

Some of the other members of the committee were already uneasy over the financial stranglehold Houlding appeared to have over the club, which came to a head when Houlding tried to link the ground rent to the club's profits (so that the amount charged in any year would include a percentage of the previous year's profit).

From Houlding's point of view, this was all simply good business, which, moreover, he knew the club could easily afford, but certain other members of the club committee began to accuse him of milking the club for his own financial gain. The situation reached crisis point when the previous landlords, the Orrells, claimed an easement[6] through the Anfield plot to reach additional land in their possession that would have necessitated the removal of the main stand. To avert this, the club would have had to rent that additional land also, but that, together with Houlding's demands, would have nearly tripled the clubs existing rent. The Committee then accused Houlding of knowing about this easement and of being complicit in the Orrells sudden enforcement of it.

Worse, neither Houlding or the Orrells were prepared to negotiate a term any longer than a single year, so that the 'ransom' could, potentially, have continued to be raised annually. The club then made an offer to buy up the land at 4s. 6d. a square yard, based upon a value that had been assessed by an independent land agent. Houlding and the Orrells, however, demanded 7s. 6d., which would have sent the club vastly into debt.

The dispute raged throughout the 1891/92 League season, whilst a sub-committee at the club had been raised to look into the possibilities of acquiring other land to which the club might relocate. The answer was provided by George Mahon, a leading Liverpool Chartered Accountant with the firm of Roose, Price and Co., who was church organist at St. Domingo's and a recent football convert, who revealed to the Committee that he had recently acquired an option on a piece of land just across Stanley Park.

---

6   Right of way - a right to cross or otherwise use someone else's land for a specified purpose.

The site, adjacent to Goodison Road, was of a good size to accommodate a football ground and had previously been a (plant) nursery.

A special general meeting was called which was held at the College, Shaw street, at which the members were told of the new site and that it's lease could be had for £50 a year (a fraction of the £370 Houlding and the Orrells were now demanding for Anfield), whilst the committee believed the cost to put it into condition for staging football would be around £1800. Consequently it was decided to make Mr. Houlding a final offer of £180 per annum for the use of Anfield (some members objecting that he had already refused that amount) and that that sum was to be dependent upon it's being written in to a ten year lease on the ground, and failing which the club would proceed with the option of moving to the Goodison Road site.

Houlding reacted quickly, the very next day, with the aid of two confederates from the Everton Committee, Messrs. Nisbet and Ramsey, forming The Everton Football Club and Athletic Grounds Company Limited, so that when the Everton Committee approached the Companies Registrar shortly afterwards they were told they could not register a company in the name of Everton Football Club because too similar an entity already existed. Houlding also tried to get his new company recognised by the F.A. and the Football League as the 'official' Everton F.C. but both bodies chose to back the majority of the Committee over the individual.

Accepting the inevitable, Houlding backed down and changed the name of his new company to "Liverpool Football Club and Athletic Grounds Company Limited," only to then meet with opposition from the local Rugby club, who already went by the name of Liverpool Football Club. This was overcome, however, by the insertion of the word "Association." A dispute with the old club over the ownership of the stands and properties was then resolved when an agreement was reached that Everton would take with them the turnstiles and treasurer's hut plus a settlement of £250.

And so Everton went off to develop Goodison into a ground worthy of their reputation whilst Houlding set about raising a new club to continue the game at Anfield.

A New Club

Houlding then received signal assistance in setting up the new club from Messrs. E. Berry, W.E. Barclay and John McKenna.

Berry was a prominent local legal practitioner who had acted as club solicitor for Everton during Houlding's tenure as president. He had also been hon. secretary of the Stanley Football Club that had a few years earlier been prominent in the city, playing it's matches at Walton Stiles.

Barclay had been Everton's first ever manager and one of Houlding's strongest supporters on the Everton committee, now remaining with him at Anfield as, officially, the new Liverpool club's first manager.

McKenna, was a self-made Irish businessman, who had likewise worked with Houlding on the Everton committee, and remained with him at Anfield when Everton left. As club secretary, McKenna would soon become the driving force behind the club as Houlding, having got the new club established, then faded into the background. In fact McKenna's control over all aspects of the administration of the club, including team and playing affairs, effectively relegated Barclay to an assistant role with McKenna himself being arguably the de facto *Manager*.

To get the new organisation established starting capital was needed and Houlding advanced the club the not inconsiderable sum of £500 – a loan upon which he said he expected no interest. The signing on of players then began in earnest, and an immediate application was made to join the Football League.

According to the Football League rules of the time, the bottom four clubs in the season's standings were automatically ejected, the vacancies thus created being available to old and new applicants, to be voted upon by the remaining members. At the League A.G.M., held that year in Sunderland on 13th May, however, it was proposed and carried that West Bromwich Albion, one of that season's bottom four, be exempted on the grounds of having won the F.A. Cup. As it had been decided to extend the League from fourteen teams to sixteen a total of five vacancies were thus made available for consideration.

Accrington, Darwen and Stoke, the three outgoing clubs, all applied for re-election, whilst delegates attended from Burton Swifts, Middlesbrough F.C., Middlesbrough Ironopolis, Newcastle East End, Newton Heath, Notts Forest, Sheffield United, Small Heath and The Wednesday to press their respective clubs claims. In addition Ardwick, Bootle, Liverpool and Liverpool Caledonians all applied by mail.

The clubs elected were: The Wednesday (10 votes), Notts Forest (9), Accrington (7), Stoke (6) and Newton Heath (6).

The meeting then moved on to the formation of a new Second Division of the League, the applicants being: Ardwick, Bootle, Burslem Port Vale, Burton Swifts, Crewe Alexandra, Darwen, Grimsby Town, Lincoln City, Liverpool Caledonians, Northwich Victoria, Sheffield United, Small Heath and Walsall Town Swifts. The representatives of the Newcastle and Middlesbrough clubs who were present at the meeting chose not to apply. Liverpool, who had no delegate present, had not submitted an application for the Second League. The size of the new League having been set at twelve clubs, all but one of the applicants were elected, the unfortunate exception being the Liverpool Caledonians.

Liverpool, along with the Caledonians, then turned their attention to the Lancashire League A.G.M. at Bury on May 21st, where both made application for membership. Both were accepted, along with Fairfield, as the League was extended from twelve clubs to thirteen - Witton and Heywood dropping out.

The Key Players

Most of the squad, and indeed every single one of the regular first team players in Liverpool's first ever season of Association football, were Scots. Indeed, out of 242 player appearances in the Lancashire League that season only 6 were made by players of other than Caledonian birth. Indeed, so many of the players names had the Scottish 'Mc' prefix that the supporters often humorously inserted it to those names where it did not belong, with cries of "play up, McRoss/McWyllie/etc."

Only players with at least 10 competitive appearances across the two seasons are included below:

Goalkeepers

Name	Date and Place of Birth	Previous Club	Country
Sydney Ross	08/06/1869 Edinburgh	Cambuslang	SC
Billy McOwen	??/04/1871 Blackburn	Darwen	EN
Matt McQueen	*see Utility*		

Sydney Henderson Ross was the regular goalkeeper from the inception of the club through most of it's initial season in the Lancashire League – until he was injured in a Lancashire Cup tie against Bootle in March, 1893, which caused him to be hospitalised. Utility player Matthew McQueen took over between the sticks when Ross was carried off in that match and retained the position in preference to reserve keeper **Billy McOwen** for the next few matches. McOwen managed only a brace of appearances in that first season but became the regular keeper in the second season, excelling himself as Liverpool went undefeated in League matches – McQueen again acting as deputy when McOwen was incapacitated. Ross never played for Liverpool again, but upon recovering from his injury returned to Scotland where he resumed his career with Cambuslang, Third Lanark and Clyde.

Backs

Andrew Hannah (c)	17/09/1864 Renton	Renton	SC
Duncan McLean	20/01/1868 Renton	Everton	SC

Andrew Hannah and **Duncan McLean** were each veterans of Everton's League Championship winning season of 1890/91, although McLean had made only a handful of appearances in that campaign. The following season Hannah returned to Scotland with his former club, Renton, whilst McLean then became a regular in the Everton side. At the end of that season, when Everton left Anfield for Goodison, McLean chose to remain with ex-Everton club president John Houlding, adding his services to the new team Houlding was founding to occupy the abandoned Anfield stadium, Liverpool A.F.C. This decision may have been influenced in McLean's case by the fact that he had been frequently criticised by the Everton Directors over his proclivity to foray too far up the field in support of the forwards. When Hannah was tempted back from Scotland to join the new club he and McLean formed one of the best full-back pairings in the League, unbroken in competitive matches throughout the whole of the first season and most of the second. Beyond his playing ability, Hannah was renowned for luck for his luck in regularly winning the coin toss to start matches.

Halves

John McCartney	??/??/1870 Newmilns	St Mirren	SC
James McBride	30/12/1873 Renton	Renton	SC
Joe McQue	11/03/1873 Springburn	Celtic	SC

The three Macs, McCartney, McBride and McQue were the primary centre-back combination throughout both of Liverpool's first two seasons. **John McCartney**, *who would go on to spend six years at the club, covering the transition to the now familiar red playing colours and playing in the First Division. Stockily built and uncompromising on the field, he was a hard man to pass although sometimes accused of being a little too rigorous in the tackle.* **Joe McQue**, *on the other hand, brought more science to the game than McCartney's brawn, reading the play and timing his tackles to perfection, then returning the ball cleverly to get his forwards on the attack. The third partner,* **Joe McBride**, *was different again, small and lightly built for a centre half, being sometimes described as a "wee stripling," he was fearless, fast and nimble – assets he turned to his significant advantage. He was capped for Scotland at the young age of 17.*

Forwards

Thomas Bradshaw	24/08/1873 Liverpool	Northwich Victoria	EN
Douglas Dick	09/07/1868 Kirktonholm	Glasgow Rangers	SC
Patrick Gordon	19/02/1870 Renton	Everton	SC
David Henderson	01/12/1868 Callander	King's Park	SC
Hugh McQueen	01/10/1867 Harthill	Leith Athletic	SC
Malcolm McVean	07/03/1871 Bonhill	Third Lanark	SC
John Miller	??/??/1870 Dumbarton	Dumbarton	SC
Tom Wyllie	05/04/1870 Maybole	Everton	SC
John 'Jock' Smith	19/12/1865 Kilmarnock	Sunderland	SC
James Stott	06/11/1870 Darlington	Middlebrough	EN

The arrival of centre-forward **John Miller** from Dumbarton was seen at the time as quite a catch for the new club. A proven goal-scorer North of the border, Miller's style of play was direct, fearless and unselfish, ready to serve his forward partners or take opportunities himself as circumstances demanded. He was the scorer of Liverpool's first ever goal, the first Liverpool player to score a hat-trick in a competitive match and set an early personal scoring record at five goals in a match. **Tom Wyllie** was a veteran of Everton's League Championship winning side at Anfield in the 1891/92 season, and was one of three players ever-present in the Lancashire League campaign (the others being Hannah and McLean) but then left the club to continue his trade in the Lancashire League with Bury. **Malcolm McVean** remained a regular in the side through both seasons and held the honour of scoring the club's first ever goal in League football (at Middlesbrough Ironopolis on the opening day of the 1893/94 season). Known for a being a mazy runner with an accurate shot. **Jock Smith,** a fast winger with great dribbling skills, was another high profile player that signed up for the club's initial season. Although in and out of the side he contributed his share of goals before leaving to join The Wednesday at the end of the initial season. **Hugh McQueen** was the younger of the pair of talented brothers whose name became almost synonymous with the early Anfield squad. Unlike his brother who could fill in anywhere on the field, Hugh specialised in the outside right position which he made his own. **Jimmy Stott** joined the forward line at the beginning of the club's second season and was one of the few English born players in the side but was raised in Scotland and started his footballing career there. Was the club's leading scorer in it's first League season with 14 goals in 16 games from the inside-right position before falling out of favour and losing his place to Givens late in the season. **Patrick Gordon** was one of football's early 'bad boys.' In three seasons at Everton he never reached his full potential or held down a regular first team place due to his frequent misdemeanours. A player of unquestioned talent, Liverpool jumped at the opportunity when Gordon was offered to them at the start of the second season and he proved a valuable assett in the chase for the championship. **David Henderson** joined Liverpool as first choice centre-forward for their second season. Not the most prolific of goal-scorers but his imposing presence created plenty of opportunities for others. **Thomas "Harry" Bradshaw** and **Douglas Dick** were Liverpool's reserve strikers during the first League season, both capable of performing well anywhere in the front line. Bradshaw became established in the side during the latter part of the season and would become a mainstay of the side for several seasons afterwards, whilst also in that time becoming the first serving Liverpool player to gain International honours (for England v. Ireland in 1897). He was also the first locally born player to turn out for the club, and had played with Everton reserves during the Toffees final season at Anfield.

Utility

Matt McQueen   18/05/1863   Leith Athletic   SC

McQueen (both seasons) was Liverpool's go to man when cover was lacking anywhere on the field. **Matt McQueen** *in particular could play in any department and almost any position on the field - including goalkeeper, centre-half and centre-forward!*

Players in Photograph (Next Page)

McOwen
McCartney, M. McQueen, Hannah --- McLean, Dick, Henderson
Gordon, McVean, McQue, McBride --- Bradshaw, Stott, H. McQueen

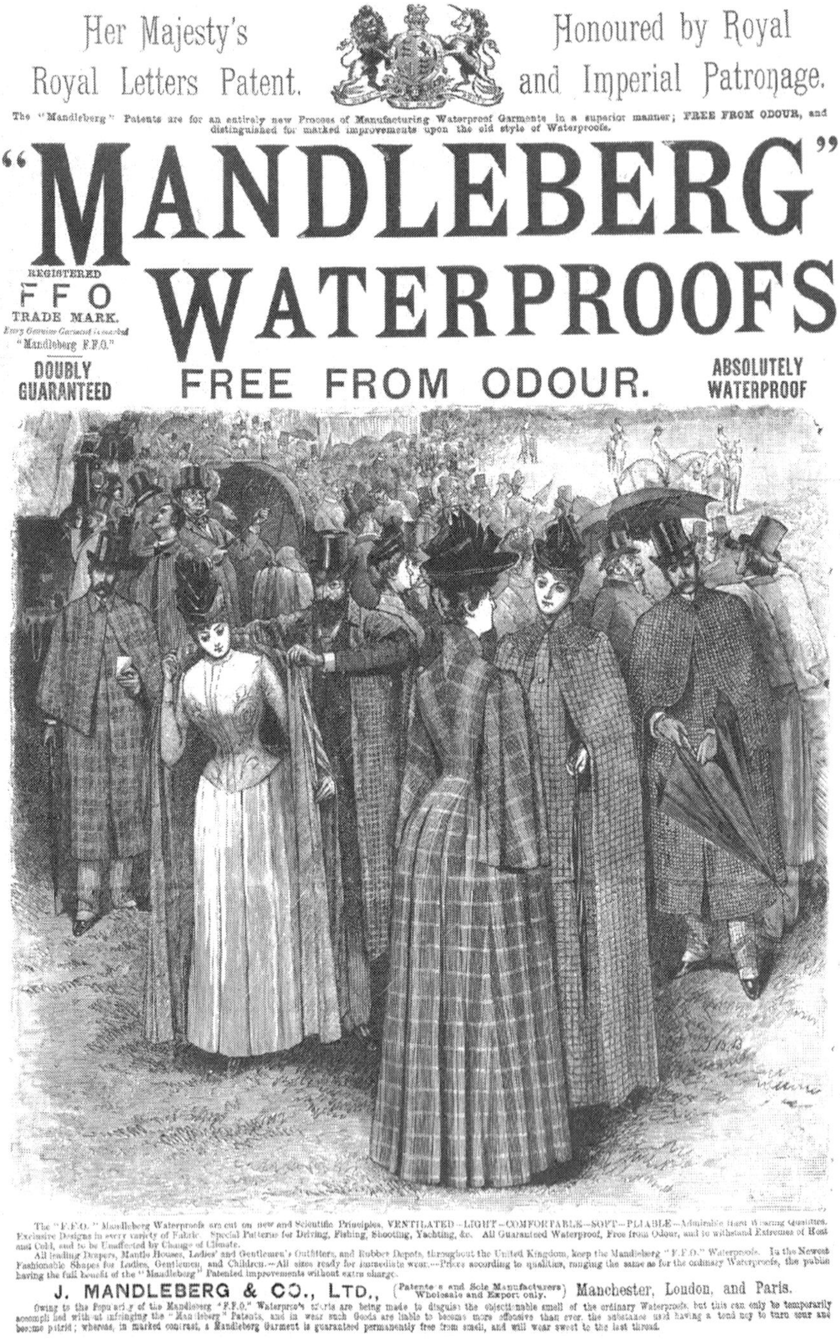

Her Majesty's Royal Letters Patent.
Honoured by Royal and Imperial Patronage.
The "Mandleberg" Patents are for an entirely new Process of Manufacturing Waterproof Garments in a superior manner; FREE FROM ODOUR, and distinguished for marked improvements upon the old style of Waterproofs.
"MANDLEBERG" WATERPROOFS
REGISTERED
FFO
TRADE MARK.
Every Genuine Garment is marked "Mandleberg F.F.O."
DOUBLY GUARANTEED
FREE FROM ODOUR.
ABSOLUTELY WATERPROOF
The "F.F.O." Mandleberg Waterproofs are cut on new and Scientific Principles, VENTILATED—LIGHT—COMFORTABLE—SOFT—PLIABLE—Admirable Hard Wearing Qualities. Exclusive Designs in every variety of Fabric. Special Patterns for Driving, Fishing, Shooting, Yachting, &c. All Guaranteed Waterproof, Free from Odour, and to withstand Extremes of Heat and Cold, and to be Unaffected by Change of Climate.
All leading Drapers, Mantle Houses, Ladies' and Gentlemen's Outfitters, and Rubber Depots, throughout the United Kingdom, keep the Mandleberg "F.F.O." Waterproofs. In the Newest Fashionable Shapes for Ladies, Gentlemen, and Children.—All sizes ready for immediate wear.—Prices according to qualities, ranging the same as for the ordinary Waterproofs, the public having the full benefit of the "Mandleberg" Patented improvements without extra charge.
J. MANDLEBERG & CO., LTD., (Patentees and Sole Manufacturers Wholesale and Export only.) Manchester, London, and Paris.
Owing to the Popularity of the Mandleberg "F.F.O." Waterproofs efforts are being made to disguise the objectionable smell of the ordinary Waterproofs, but this can only be temporarily accomplished without infringing the "Mandleberg" Patents, and in wear such Goods are liable to become more offensive than ever, the substance used having a tendency to turn sour and become putrid; whereas, in marked contrast, a Mandleberg Garment is guaranteed permanently free from smell, and will wear sweet to the last thread.

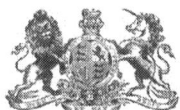

SEASON 1892/93
The Lancashire League

Athletic News - Monday 01 August 1892

The new Liverpool Football Club have spent a large sum of money in order to place a team in the field able to hold its own, and they have succeeded pretty well. Mr. W. E. Berkeley and his committee are old parliamentary hands, and know perfectly well that to do any good at all they must have a powerful team. Powerful teams nowadays mean a big salary list, and I shouldn't be at all surprised to find the Liverpool club paying more in wages than half the League clubs. However, if they are successful in their Lancashire League engagements, as I have not the least doubt they will be, there is little question about it being a paying concern. There is one thing for certain - they must have some money behind them, for they have not been limited to the £10 bonus, and have paid away some very large sums.

They have too good goalkeepers in Ross, of Cambuslang, and McOwen, of Darwen, while Hannah and McLean and quite clever enough at back. At half they are rather weak, but in McBride, of Renton, they have secured a splendid little player. Forwards there are strong with McVean (Third L.R.V.), Smith (Sunderland), Miller (Dumbarton), Wyllie (Everton), Brady (Renton), &c.; and on paper the team looks good enough for the task they have in hand, although such clubs as Bury and Blackpool are not disposed to hand over the championship right away - not quite.

Line Ups

In some cases it has not been possible to find the full line-up of both teams. Wherever possible in such cases the line-ups have been extrapolated from players mentioned in various alternative accounts of the match (verified) and/or from known line-ups in close chronological proximity to the game in question (unverified - shown in braces {}).

The new Liverpool club embarked upon it's first season with a team composed entirely of Scots. The first competitive match was a 'friendly' against Rotherham Town.

01/09/1892 OM: Liverpool v. Rotherham Town
Liverpool Mercury - Friday 2nd September, 1892

At Anfield-road, before a moderate attendance, Councillor John Houlding kicked off on behalf of Rotherham, Hannah having won the toss for Liverpool. At the outset play favoured the home side, who had the advantage of the wind, and once they got into their stride some pretty passing was shown by the forwards, Wyllie, Smith, and Miller especially being prominent. Shortly after the start the last named {**Miller**} scored the first goal of the season for Liverpool. **Kelvin** then broke through the visitors' defence, whilst a third was scored from a free kick {*anon*}. Following these reverses the Town played up much better, and several well-meant visits were paid to the Liverpool goal. The defence of the home backs and goalkeeper, however, was equal to the emergency, and the visitors were kept from scoring, although on at least a couple of occasions they were within a shade of doing so. ~~Everton~~ {*Liverpool*[7]} continued to have the better of matters, and for a long time Turner and Thickett had plenty to do to stave off repeated attacks of the Liverpool van. At length Leather led his forwards on, but they were well met by Hannah, and sending across to Kelvin, the latter player essayed at goal but his attempt went harmlessly over the bar. A moment later, however, Smith replied to the kick out from Wharton, and placed the leather over to Kelvin, who shot across the goal mouth, when **Wyllie** rushed up and registered goal No. 4. The ball hovered around the centre for a considerable time, when the Liverpudlians again bore down, and Smith tried a long shot, which Wharton easily cleared. Exchanges between the backs resulted in placing the home forwards well ahead, when **Wyllie** again got possession from his centre, and dodging Turner sent in a shot which Wharton failed to clear. From the centre kick the visitors got well down, and forced a corner, but the ball was quickly taken down the field, Wyllie and Smith working well together. Half-time was now called with the home team leading by 5 goals to nil.

On resuming, the visitors by strong combination raced down, and Ross had all his work cut out in clearing a hot shot from the opposing centre. With the wind in their favour the Rotherham forwards firmly held their position, but after the ball had twice gone behind Wyllie ran strongly down the right, but the venue was quickly changed, and after a hot pressure the leather only just missed the bar by the merest shave. Longden missed an easy chance a moment later, and for the next few minutes the home defenders had a very anxious time. Leather and Pickering in turn sent in capital shots, and the Liverpudlians were somewhat lucky in keeping their position intact. The monotony was broken by some smart play by Kelso, and following a clinking run down by the right pair, the ball was sent over to Kelvin, who made a poor attempt when the visitors' goal was at his mercy. After the goal kick, McBride rid himself of the ball under great difficulties, and the home lot were enabled to get into good position. The ball was safely worked away when the home line fairly swept down on their opponents' charge, but the final effort was luckily saved. A few minutes later **Miller** found himself without opposition, and easily brought up the total to half a dozen. **Wyllie** quickly placed another, and, from a corner, McQue sent in a stinger, which struck the crossbar. The

---

7 Evidently the reporter got a little confused over which match he was watching.

latter portion of the play was altogether in favour of Liverpool, though in the last minutes the visitors got well up and scored their first goal {*anon*}, retiring beaten by:

RESULT: Liverpool 7 – Rotherham Town 1

LIVERPOOL: Ross (goal); Hannah and McLean (backs); McBride, McQue and Kelso (halves); Kelvin [1], McVean, Miller [2], Smith and Wyllie [3] (forwards). [1 anon]
ROTHERHAM: Wharton (goal); Turner and Thickett (backs); Barr, Brown and Rodgers (halves); Longden, Cutts, Leather, Leatherbarrow and Pickering (forwards) [1 anon].

Liverpool's first match in the Lancashire League coincided with Everton's League season opener at Goodison, and with the two grounds literally only a short walking distance apart this inevitably had a significantly detrimental effect on the gate at Anfield. Consequently, whilst a crowd exceeding 12,000 packed in to Goodison to see the Toffees fight out a 2-2 draw with Nottingham Forest only a few hundred saw Liverpool's rampant annihilation of High Walton.

03/09/1892 LL01: Liverpool v. High Walton
Liverpool Mercury - Monday 5th September, 1892

This match was played on Saturday, at Anfield Road, before a few hundred spectators. The day was a dull one, showers of rain falling every few minutes, and this, combined with the great attraction at Goodison Park, no doubt accounted for the meagre attendance. The few lookers-on, a however, made up in the enthusiasm for what they lacked in numbers, and every bit of fine play received it's due share of applause. Owing to the late arrival of the visitors, some of whom had been driven to the Everton ground by mistake, the kick-off was deferred for nearly three quarters of an hour. The visitors won the toss, and elected to play with the somewhat changeable wind and an occasional sunshine at their backs.

In the absence of Miller, McVean set the ball in motion for the home side, and after some exchanges play was transferred to the visitors' end, and three corners and a foul came in quick succession, but they were all cleared with safety. McLean, slipping, gave the opponent's right a chance, but he quickly recovered himself and was soon kicking away in his usual style. Smith and McBride now came in for some cheering, the former breaking through the defence by smart dribbling, while the heading of the latter was unique. A raid from the Walton players was repelled, and after gaining two corners the homesters right rushed down, and some brilliant passing between **Smith** and Wyllie ended in the former registering the first point for his side in a league match, a feat which was greeted with great applause. Liverpool again assumed the aggressive, and McLean tested the fisting powers of Addison with a huge kick, and following up the advantage the home forwards swarmed round the goal. Exciting play now ensued. Shots after shot was cleared, and time after time the Walton goal hung in jeopardy. Finally **McBride** scored a second goal with a well directed effort. Walton now made strenuous efforts to get down the field, but although McLean missed his kick, Hannah could not be passed, and play was again taken to the visitors' quarters. Cameron had the goal at his mercy but failed to do the needful. However, by a pretty pass from the right wing, **McVean** scored again. After Walton had been repulsed the home right took the ball down, Wyllie passed right across the goalmouth, Kelvin shot, and from the rebound **Cameron** banged the ball through. From a corner **McQue**, who was playing a splendid game, scored the fifth goal with a daisy Cutter. Half-time found the homesters still attacking and the score:- Liverpool, five goals; Walton, nil.

After the interval the visitors pulled themselves together with an effort, but a foul against them changed the scene of action. Smith and Cameron both had good chances, but both failed to utilise them. At this juncture an accident occurred to one of the Walton men, and the game had to be stopped for a few minutes. The mischance, however, was nothing serious, and play was again resumed. After some good work by the forwards McVean shot over and a few minutes later again missed an easy chance of scoring. Shots rained in like hail, and from the ensuing scrimmage **Cameron** rolled the ball through. McQue made himself conspicuous by some clever heading and tackling, and the home half backs were feeding their forwards well, Enderby and Craven having plenty to do. An offside penalty relieved the pressure for some time. Liverpool, however, were not to be denied, and five corners were with difficulty rendered abortive. McVean gaining the ball affected a splendid run, and after being knocked down recovered himself, and secured the ball once more and travelled on. The ball was cleared out, and the combined rush by the visitors forwards was broken by McBride, who returned the leather again, **McQue** adding a seventh goal to the score. Towards the close Walton began to play up, but their efforts were futile, and Liverpool gained a corner, from which **Smith** scored. The whistle sounded shortly afterwards, leaving the score:

RESULT: Liverpool 8 – Higher Walton 0

LIVERPOOL: Ross (goal); Hannah and McLean (backs); McBride [1], McQue [2] and Pearson (halves); Wyllie, Smith [2], McVean [1], Cameron [2] and Kelvin (forwards).
HIGHER WALTON: Addison (goal); Enderby and Craven (backs); Gerrard, J. Law and Flintoff (halves); R. Law, Parker, Kay, Fowler and Heaps (forwards).

Liverpool's first away trip was to take them across country to the North East coast to take on Middlesbrough Ironopolis. "The 'Nops," as they were familiarly known, were the reigning Champions of the Northern League, and as such promised to offer a stiff test to the fledgling Liverpool side.

05/09/1892 OM: Middlesbrough Ironopolis v. Liverpool
Northern Echo - Tuesday 6th September, 1892

About 2,000 spectators assembled on the Paradise Ground, Middlesbrough, on Monday night to witness this match.

The 'Nops kicked off, and a few minutes after the start **Coupar** with a fine shot got the ball past Ross, thus scoring the first goal for the homesters. Some play in the visitors' quarters followed, when Smith, the Liverpool inside right, made a smart run down the field with the ball at his toe, but spoiled a good chance by putting behind. After this play was again transferred to the other end of the field, where a free kick being obtained for hands against the visitors, **Coupar** put the second goal through. A foul was given against the visitors in midfield some time later, and Elliott putting the ball well in a hot scrimmage took place in the Liverpool goal, which for some time was in imminent danger, the ball being eventually put over the bar. Very shortly after this the half-time whistle blew, with the score: Ironopolis, 2; Liverpool, 0.

On changing ends the 'Nops at once started to press, and within two minutes **Coupar** sent in a clinking shot, which Ross failed to negotiate, thus scoring the third point for the home team. Some end-to-end play ensued for about ten minutes, at the end of which the Washers again getting down Hill put across to **Coupar**, who, for the fourth time, did the trick with a smart shot. McReddie distinguished himself a little later by a fine run down the field, which resulted in a corner, and a minute after the same player passed to **Hughes**, who, eluding the custodian, registered the fifth point. The game ended without any further score being made.

RESULT: Middlesbrough Ironopolis 5 - Liverpool 0

LIVERPOOL: Ross (goal); Hannah and McLean (backs); Kelso, McQue and McBride (halves); Wyllie, Smith, McVean, Cameron and Kelvin (forwards).
IRONOPOLIS: Watts (goal); Elliott and Bach (backs); Seymour, Chatt and Nicholson (halves); Hill, Hughes [1], McCairns, Coupar [4] and McReddie (forwards).

Although this was Liverpool's first away venture, and the 'Nops were undoubtedly the best of the sides the Anfielders had faced so far, the scale of the defeat, after two such telling victories, was something of a wake-up call. The disparity between the two sides front lines was what settled the game. Coupar, for the 'Nops, it seemed, could not miss, while Liverpool's shooting was at best erratic and failed to take advantage of a defence lacking it's first-choice centre and left backs.

Liverpool's next visitor's were Barrow whose newly appointed honorary president was the wealthy shipping magnate and British M.P. Sir Charles Cayzer.

08/09/1892 OM: Liverpool v. Barrow
Liverpool Mercury - Friday 9th September, 1892

This friendly match was played at Anfield last evening, in pleasant weather, the attendance of spectators being about 600. Liverpool were without the services of Miller, whose place was filled by Cameron

Losing the toss. Cameron started against the sun for Liverpool, the same player a minute after causing Kennedy to fist away a lofty shot. For the first ten minutes the Barrow men were kept hemmed in their own quarters, their charge having some marvellous shaves. Pretty combination by the visitors brought them into close proximity to the home goal, Glen experiencing hard luck as he struck the crossbar. Getting smartly away the Liverpool men hotly pressed, Kennedy distinguishing himself as he cleared a grand attempt from McVean. From this stage to the interval both sides in turn tried to score, but nothing was done, the teams crossing over with clean sheets.

On resuming, the Liverpool forwards quickly took up the attack and hovered in front of the Barrow goal, success ultimately coming from the foot of **McVean**. Though showing splendid defence the Barrow men seldom became dangerous, owing to the capital defence of McLean and Hannah. After a lot of mid-field play **Wyllie** dribbled beautifully along on the line, and with a grand screw shot scored the second point for Liverpool. Play new became very 4 tame and uninteresting. Towards the finish the infielders taxed the Barrow defence to its utmost, but Steel and Fenton proved themselves a pair of worthy defenders and prevented further scoring, the game thus ending in favour of Liverpool by two goals to nil.

RESULT: Liverpool 2 – Barrow 0

LIVERPOOL: Ross (goal); Hannah and McLean (backs); Kelso, McQue and McBride (halves); Wyllie [1], Smith, Cameron, McVean [1] and Kelvin (forwards).
BARROW: Kennedy (goal); Fenton and Steel (backs); Stevenson, Conway and Shentaker (halves); Marshall. Poole, Peacock, Glen and Saddington (forwards).

The visit of Stockton pitted Liverpool against another Northern League side, who, whilst not as formidable as Ironopolis, were still a side not to be taken lightly. Although their star forward, Townley, was not available on the day, they still had accomplished goalscorers in the side whilst their Scottish keeper Ramsay was a hard man to pass.

10/09/1892 OM: Liverpool v. Stockton
Liverpool Mercury - Monday 12th September, 1892

Owing to the brilliant weather and the absence of the premier club from home, the Liverpool ground presented a lively appearance on Saturday. There were about 4000 spectators, and the frequent cries of "Play up, Liverpool," naturally called to mind the happiest days of Everton. The Stockton team was considerably altered from what was advertised, and people were asking in vain for the celebrated Townley. Miller was still missing from the homesters, and a new man was tried in Glen, who gave general satisfaction.

The visitors won the toss, and played with a blinding sun at their backs during the first half, which was no inconsiderable advantage. From the opening exchanges it was evident that a hard game was to be played. McVean was soon conspicuous with one of his dashing runs, and fine shots from the forward division severely tried the defence of Ramsay, Shaw, and McDermid, Smith kicking over the line amidst the greatest excitement. Liverpool were again making tracks for goal when Kelvin was ruled off-side, and the play was transferred to the other end, Ross just saving a swift low shot. McLung and Jones put in some pretty work and the visitors subjected the home goal to a heavy pressure of shots, but McLean managed to clear in time. The Liverpool left raced away and obtained a corner, from which **McVean** scored the first goal. This evidently put Stockton on their mettle, for in a few minutes **McLung** equalised with an easy shot, the ball rolling past Ross. Both goals were now visited in turn, McVean was working very hard in the front rank, and twice the ball was passed right across the goal mouth, but Smith and Wyllie were not at their posts. Half-time arrived, and found the score a goal each.

When McVean restarted, Liverpool were favoured by the sun, and great things were expected from them. A couple of fouls a few yards from the posts gave them a momentary advantage, but it could not be improved upon. The forwards had many good opportunities, but seemed to be unable to put on the finishing touch when required. Fine combination gave the ball to Wyllie, who put it in the crowd. Hannah returned the goal-kick, but McVean again put the ball over. Jones now ran down the wing and got the best of Hannah but McLean covered and cleared his lines. Kelvin received and passed to McVean, who shot, and from the re-bound **Wyllie** notched the winning point. The game now became fast and exciting, both goals escaping very narrowly, and although the teams made strenuous efforts to increase the score, the whistle sounded, and left Liverpool winners of a hard-fought game by:

RESULT: Liverpool 2 – Stockton 1

LIVERPOOL: Ross (goal); Hannah and McLean (backs); Cameron, McQue and McBride (halves); Wyllie [1], Smith, McVean [1], Glen and Kelvin (forwards).
STOCKTON: Ramsay (goal); Shaw and McDermid (backs); {Graham}, {Baillie} and {Hutton} (halves); {Atkin}, {Townley}, McLung [1], {Jones} and Cooper (forwards).
*Player names in braces {} are probable – **not** confirmed.*

Liverpool's next opponents were Grantham Rovers from Lincolnshire, who were then embarking on their first season as members of the Midland League. Grantham, on the whole, were a workman-like side but in Southwell, at outside-left, they had a free-scoring flying winger who, on his day, could wreak havoc in any defence.

15/09/1892 OM: Liverpool v. Grantham Rovers
Liverpool Mercury - Friday 16th September, 1892

This friendly game was played on the Anfield enclosure last evening, in fine weather and before 700 spectators. Liverpool tried a new full back (Fairly) in McLean's place. Both teams were strongly represented.

Losing the toss the visitors started the game, and McVean intercepting Edwards the Liverpool van at once took up the attack, Wyllie giving Broadbent a teaser to get rid of, which the Rover did in a finished style. The home lot continued to have the best of matters, but their play lacked finish, and a few good chances were thrown away. A free kick close in upon the Grantham goal, in favour of the Anfielders, was turned into account by **Glen**, as he beat Broadbent rather easily. So far the Rovers had done nothing, but on receiving this first reverse they showed better play, and gave both Hannah and Fairly plenty of work to protect their custodian. A strong lob from the former was taken up by the home van, and after some tricky short passing **McVean** scored another point for Liverpool. The visitors' half-back division was weak and easily beaten, thus causing the bulk of the work to fall upon Moon and Brittain, who for a while gamely defended their charge, but ultimately had to go under for the third time as **McVean**, from a centre by Kelvin, beat Broadbent with a lofty shot. From now until the interval Liverpool held the upper hand, but the score stood unaltered.

On resuming, play opened out more even, the Grantham front division putting more spirit into the game, Hannah and Fairly being put on their mettle to avert defeat. After Broadbent had twice saved, the visitors, by good combination, again troubled the Liverpool defenders, Ross conceding a corner from a straight shot by Chamberlain. The homesters rushed away in the centre, Kelvin and McVean both testing Broadbent. Smith followed with another which bothered the visiting custodian a great deal, he only clearing after the ball to all appearance had crossed the line. From this stage Liverpool held the upper hand, the Rovers' citadel having some narrow escapes. A clever bit of passing by Southwell and Pulling at last converted play to the home end, and a smart tip by the former across to **Chamberlain** enabled the latter to beat Ross with a real beauty. Liverpool again attacked strongly, and for a considerable time the Grantham backs were kept busy. Nearing the finish Liverpool still pressed, but no further scoring was done, the Anfielders thus retiring victors by:

RESULT: Liverpool 3 – Grantham Rovers 1

LIVERPOOL: Ross (goal); Fairly and Hannah (backs); Cameron, McQue and McBride (halves); Wyllie, Smith, McVean [2], Glen [1] and Kelvin (forwards).
GRANTHAM: Broadbent (goal); Moon and Brittain (backs); Rowe, McBarr and Geeson (halves); Southwell, Pulling, Edwards, Chamberlain [1] and Allen (forwards).

Despite scoring in only his second appearance, the triallist Glen left Anfield and made the short move across the City to Woodcroft Park to try out with the Caledonians, scoring half their goals in a 4-0 ordinary match victory over Chirk the following weekend.

Liverpool's debut in the Lancashire Senior Cup, a prestigious competition at the time, came in the form of a visit from Southport Central, the new club having to enter the competition in the Qualifying stage.

17/09/1892 LSC-Q1: Liverpool v. Southport Central
Liverpool Mercury - Monday 19th September, 1892

There would be fully 6000 spectators in the Anfield enclosure to witness this cup tie.

Liverpool kicked off, and had to face a brilliant sun. Wyllie was the first to make headway, but Robinson and Smith displayed excellent defence. Southport left then troubled Hannah. McQue was next prominent, and J. Gee had to clear. The game became very fast, and there was not much to choose between the teams until close upon half time, when Liverpool took a strong lead and kept the Southport custodian fully employed, shots from McBride, McVean, and Wyllie being successfully negotiated by Gee, who averted danger till change of ends and came in for quite an ovation on crossing over.

On resuming, Liverpool at once took up the running, and, after McKie had shot over, the Southport left broke away, and Ross had to handle. Play was stopped owing to McLean coming down heavily and dislocating his arm, but he pluckily returned and continued playing, the injured limb being strapped across his breast. This stoppage was followed almost immediately by another one, Platt being the victim this time. Kelvin got up too late to take advantage of a grand chance, and at length Liverpool gained the much longed for goal through the instrumentality of **Smith**. Southport rushed the game to the other end, and an excellent opportunity was thrown away, both Platt and Winstanley finishing badly. Wyllie had hard times at the top goal, the ball rebounding from the upright, and a flying visit was paid to the other end where captain Hannah cleared in the goal mouth, and the Liverpool right gained possession. **Wyllie** shot in, and from an exciting scrimmage Liverpool scored a second goal just as the whistle blew, the score reading:

RESULT: Liverpool 2 – Southport Central 0

LIVERPOOL: Ross (goal); Hannah and McLean (backs); Cameron, McQue and McBride (halves); Wyllie [1], Smith [1], Miller, McVean, and Kelvin (forwards).
SOUTHPORT: J. Gee (goal); Smith and Robinson (backs); C. Gee, McLaren and Mayor (halves); Platt, Fleetwood, Winstanley, Halsall and Miller (forwards).

The Anfielders were keen to recover some lost pride from their previous encounter in the return ordinary match against Middlesbrough Ironopolis. The 'Nops were without Coupar who had done so much damage to the Liverpool cause in the first game, the Scot having now thrown in his lot with Newcastle United.

22/09/1892 OM: Liverpool v. Middlesbrough Ironopolis
Liverpool Mercury - Friday 23rd September, 1892

A fair crowd assembled on the Anfield ground last evening to witness this friendly match. Owing to the absence of McLean and Hannah, Liverpool tried two local players to fill the back division.

Losing the spin, McArthur started for Ironopolis. From hands against Hughes Liverpool were able to make progress, Watts ultimately having to clear a slow shot from Wyllie. Some very pretty combination by the home right again put Liverpool in the visitors' quarters, and **Smith**, two minutes from the start, sent in a beauty which beat Watts rather easily. Liverpool were playing a splendid passing game, the forwards being kept well supplied by the half-back division. Elliott and Oliver were therefore kept busy dealing with the efforts of Wyllie, Miller, and McVean. Hill was the most prominent man in the Middlesbrough front division, he being very tricky and speedy in his touches. Getting away on the right, Hill was mainly responsible for **Hughes** making the score one goal all, with a low shot from a short range. From the restart McVean put in a dashing sprint, which met with cheers from the 2,000 onlookers, but he was smartly pulled up by McNair. Play now became even, but interesting. Just before the interval Ross was called upon to save a long attempt from McReddie, but the Liverpool custodian failed to get the ball away, and although McCudden had the goal at his mercy, he missed badly. Half-time score: Liverpool, one goal; Middlesbrough, one.

On resuming the Middlesbrough men at once attacked, and the Liverpool goal had indeed a lucky let off. The leather was put past Ross, but owing to that custodian being charged down before the ball crossed the line the point was disallowed, a decision which caused the ~~Everton~~ {*Liverpool*} contingent to give vent to their feelings. The visitors at this stage were seen to greater advantage, and for fully fifteen minutes they held the upper hand. The home backs were very weak in their clearances, thus giving their forwards little or nothing to do. Play continued chiefly in the home quarters and after Pearson and McCudden had had a hard tussle for possession **McArthur** rushed up and sent the leather through against the crossbar, it gliding through, Middlesbrough thus easing ahead. Owing to an injury Smith had to retire, leaving Liverpool with ten men. Ironopolis kept up the pressure until the end, but although Ross's charge was often in danger, no further scoring was done, a very moderate game thus ending in favour of Middlesbrough by two goals to one.

RESULT: Liverpool 1 – Middlesbrough Ironopolis 2

LIVERPOOL: Ross (goal); Pearson and McNally (backs); Stevenson, McQue and McBride (halves); Wyllie, Smith [1], Miller, McVean, and Kelvin (forwards).
IRONOPOLIS: Watts (goal); Elliott and Oliver (backs); McNair, Chatt and Seymour (halves); Hill, Hughes [1], McArthur [1], McReddie and McCudden (forwards).

Again, even without the deadly Coupar, the Nops had proven simply too strong, and too well organised, for the Anfielders.

The next visitors to Anfield, were Bury, who had finished the previous season not only as champions of the Lancashire League but also as holders of the Lancashire Senior Cup. The Buryites had suffered a significant loss since then, however. Their regular left-back, Thomas Cooper, who had come in for much praise during the course of that successful campaign, had been persistently chased by Aston Villa during the close season, but in a major coup for the club had re-signed for Bury instead. He was ultimately lost to the club just before the start of the season under altogether more tragic circumstances, however, when he met with a horrific death during the course of his full-time employment at Lucas's Hat Works by falling into a vat of boiling dye.

24/9/1892 LL02: Liverpool v. Bury
Liverpool Mercury - Monday 26th September, 1892

On Saturday afternoon the Liverpool Club had the well known Bury team at Anfield to fulfil their Lancashire League fixture. The visitors, since the season opened, had not tasted defeat. It was therefore naturally expected among the Anfielders that a great game was in store for them on Saturday. The day being beautifully fine there was a large turnout of spectators, numbering about 5000, among whom were over 500 from Bury, who during the course of the game did not fail to give vent their feelings. Both sides were able to place their full elevens on the field.

Losing the toss, Clegg commenced hostilities for Bury against a strong wind and sun. Liverpool, however, at once took up the attack, Wyllie having a couple of shies at goal without result. The home men came again, and after Baugh and Warburton were beaten Kelvin was given a clear course, but his final {*shot*?} went yards wide. From the goal-kick Bury lifted the hearts of their followers, as Plant and Bourn trickily brought about an onslaught upon the Liverpool goal, Hannah, however, eased matters by a timely clearance. The game became exceedingly fast and most interesting. After Ross had been called upon by Clegg, the Liverpool men sprinted along, and from a capital centre by Wyllie, **Miller** opened the scoring in favour of Liverpool. It was a pretty goal, and well deserved the applause which was given. Liverpool continued to show the better football, and Lowe on several occasions had to clear most difficult shots. McLean and Hannah were in great form at back, with the result that the well meant efforts of the Bury men were repeatedly blocked. Liverpool put in some beautiful combination, and sailing through the defence, **Cameron** found another entrance. From the midfield kick-off Liverpool again pleased their supporters immensely, as **McVean** with a lofty shot scored a third goal. Before the interval Bury tried hard to get through the home defence, but it was of no use, kept well posted by their backs and half-backs; the Liverpool van, just on half-time, beat Lowe for the fourth time {***Miller***}, thus crossing over with the score 4 to nil in their favour.

In the second half of the game, Liverpool, even with the wind and sun against them, stuck to their work manfully, and on one occasion Lowe certainly looked behind the line when he saved a beauty from Miller. Play was of a Sterling quality at this stage, it being quite a treat to witness the accurate passing of both teams. Bury in midfield were all that could be desired, but when their shooting power was tested they performed wretchedly. Wyllie was conspicuous as he speedily made tracks along the right, and finally sent a whizzer over the crossbar. Wilkinson had a clear way at the other end, but again bad shooting prevailed. Liverpool until the end of the game kept their opponents well in hand, no further scoring being done, a splendidly contested game thus ending in a win for Liverpool.

RESULT: Liverpool 4 – Bury 0

LIVERPOOL: Ross (goal); Hannah and McLean (backs); Kelso, McQue and McBride (halves); Wyllie, McVean [1], Miller [2], Cameron [1], and Kelvin (forwards).
BURY: Lowe (goal); Baugh and Warburton (backs); Pemberton, Jobson and Ross (halves); Wilkinson, Spence, Clegg, Bourn and Plant (forwards).

Liverpool travelled to the potteries to challenge a Stoke team who had been founder members of the Football League but who, in three seasons of membership, had not finished above the bottom two, and in the current season had won only one of their opening five League matches.

26/9/1892 OM: Stoke v. Liverpool
Liverpool Mercury - Tuesday 27th September, 1892

Played at Stoke, before about 2000 spectators. The home team, though without Dunn and Rowley, had the best of matters in the first half, **Evans** scoring four minutes from the start, but no further point was made up to half time.

After the interval, ten minutes from the finish, Liverpool equalised from a free kick {*anon*}. **Schofield** scored the winning point for Stoke right on time.

RESULT: Stoke 2 – Liverpool 1

LIVERPOOL: Not available – Scorers: [1 anon]
STOKE: Not available – Scorers: Evans [1], Schofield [1]

The next visitors to Anfield were the Dumfries based Queen of the South Wanderers (no connection with the current Queen of the South club). Liverpool gave a come-back trial to Alec Dick, who had been out of the game for two years since Everton dispensed with his services at the end of the 1889-90 season.

29/9/1892 OM: Liverpool v. Queen of the South Wanderers
Liverpool Mercury - Friday 30th September, 1892

Last evening Liverpool had the above Dumfries team as their visitors at Anfield. Owing to the weather being dull and showery, the attendance of spectators would not number more than 800. Alec Dick, the old Everton full-back, filled McLean's position in the home ranks. A new half-back named McLauchlan was also given a trial instead of Kelso. The Scotchmen had their full strength.

Miller started. During the first half of the game the play was remarkably even, and though slow was very prettily contested. Early on Wyllie put in a dashing run, and finished up well by screwing across the goal mouth, Miller having a very near thing with a shot which went over the crossbar. The Scotchmen followed with some smart combination, Hannah saving very luckily a capital attempt by Robson. Before the interval Liverpool tried hard to find an opening, but no scoring was done.

The second portion opened much faster, both goals in turn being warmly attacked. The Scotch full backs showed grand defence, and the pair repeatedly, by some powerful kicking, drove the Liverpool van back into their own quarters. McBride, the home left-half, was also conspicuous in dealing with the movements of the "Queen's" right wing pair. Liverpool now pressed, and twice sent over the crossbar, and then Collins had to save a warm shot from McVean. After a lot of midfield play Liverpool got the upper hand from a straight attempt by **Miller**, which was the only goal scored in the match.

The Wanderers, who, by the way, include a few very young players, are a fairly good team, and during the course of the game showed some pretty combination. They have a capital pair of backs in Harding and Glendinning, for, although they are both lightly built, they nevertheless showed strong kicking powers. Their trio of halves all worked hard and fearlessly. The Liverpool team played a good game, though they never specially exerted themselves. Alec Dick made a passable reappearance.

RESULT: Liverpool 1 – Queen of the South Wanders 0

LIVERPOOL: Ross (goal); Hannah and Dick (backs); McLaughlan, McQue and McBride (halves); Wyllie, Cameron, Miller [1], McVean, and Kelly (forwards).
QoSW: Collins (goal); Harding and Glendinning (backs); Grierson, Craven and J. Glendinning (halves); Bedford, Kennedy, Robson, Shankland and Sharpe (forwards).

Having been drawn away to West Manchester in the Second Qualifying round of the Lancashire Cup the following weekend, Liverpool's Lancashire League fixture against the Mancunians took on the nature of a preparation for the main event. Notable among the visitors was top class multi-sportsman Frank Howe Sugg. Sugg had played County cricket for Yorkshire and Derbyshire and was currently serving Lancashire and England as a right-handed batsman. On the football field in his prime he had, on separate occasions, captained The Wednesday, Derby County and Burnley and had played for Everton at Anfield during the inaugural season of the Football League!

01/10/1892 LL03: Liverpool v. West Manchester
Liverpool Mercury - Monday 3rd October, 1892

This fixture was played on the Anfield ground on Saturday afternoon. Owing to the weather being so unfavourable the attendance of spectators would only number about 1000. The visitors, who by the way are drawn against the Liverpool club in the ~~English Cup~~ {Lancashire Cup} tie, to be played at Manchester next Saturday brought their strongest eleven, including Frank Sugg, who took up his position at right full back. The homesters were also well represented.

Punctually at 3.45 Bogie started the ball for Manchester, and crossing over to his left wing, Hannah had to intercept Bridge as he was making for goal. The Liverpool van smartly took up the running, only, however, to be pulled up by a strong lob by Sugg. Play then settled down in midfield, and for a considerable time was of a give-and-take nature. Both defences were occasionally taxed, Entwistle being conspicuous as he safely dealt with a beauty from Wyllie. The visitors settled down to their work and showed some capital combination, with the result that Hannah and McLean were both pressed, the former only easing by conceding a corner kick to Bogie. This was safely got rid of by Ross, and McBride placing among his forwards, the Liverpool van took up a strong position, Entwistle experiencing a warm five minutes as Wyllie, Miller, Kelvin, and Smith all tried to effect an entrance. Pretty passing was now indulged in by both teams, Miller on the one side and Bogie on the other leading their men in fine style. Gradually gaining ground, West Manchester ultimately forced the home defence back into goal, and try as they would neither Hannah nor McLean could make an effectual clearance. Six corners in succession were taken by the Manchester men, and had it not been for the stubborn defence of the homesters they certainly must have scored. The Liverpool front division at last got away, and, after Miller had been driven back by Pickering, Wyllie drove the leather hard against the net on the wrong side. Bogie took up a fine pass from Allison, and, racing past the home halves, gave Ross a teaser to manipulate. Two more corners were forced by the visitors, and a clear opening was thrown away by Walsh. Just before the interval the Anfielders broke away, but, like their opponents, success was denied them, half-time coming with no score by either side.

On resuming, the Liverpool men shook off the loose tactics which they had shown during the first half, and at once got into their proper stride, causing both Sugg and Russell a deal of exertion to stem their determined attacks. A powerful drive by the latter landed the ball at Bogie's toe, and the visiting centre getting his men into Line parted to **Bridge**, who neatly evaded Hannah and drove past Ross, thus scoring a well earned goal - the first of the match. This undoubtedly brought the home men to their senses, as from this stage they performed grandly. Wyllie, on the Wing, had a severe tussle with Russell, and then drove over the crossbar. Not to be denied, down upon Entwistle's charge the Liverpool men went, and after a sharp bit of pretty combination Kelvin sent over to **Wyllie**, who in turn made the score one goal all with a rasping shot. Called upon by the spectators, the home men fairly made rings round the Manchester defence, and although the latter gamely resisted defeat, **Smith**, after a scrimmage, sneaked through a second point. With only a minute to play the ball was centred in midfield, and McVean from a lob by McQue filled Entwistle's hands and the latter only partially clearing, **Miller** pounced on the leather and added a third goal, amidst great cheering, Liverpool thus winning an exciting game by:

RESULT: Liverpool 3 – West Manchester 1

LIVERPOOL: Ross (goal); Hannah and McLean (backs); Cameron, McQue and McBride (halves); Wyllie [1], Smith [1], Miller [1], McVean, and Kelvin (forwards).
W. MANCHESTER: Entwistle (goal); Sugg and Russell (backs); Spiers, Pickering and Allison (halves); Bridge [1], Iddon, Bogie, Walsh and Leigh (forwards).

Liverpool's stiffest test to date came in a trip to Glasgow to take on the Rangers at Ibrox. The Rangers team were not yet the force in Scottish Football that they were soon to become but already included two legendary players who have since been inducted into the Rangers hall of fame – John McPherson, described at the club's 50th year jubilee as the finest player to turn out for them in that time, and Jock Drummond, then a recent arrival from Falkirk but soon to become one half of a legendary full-back pairing with Nicol Smith (who joined Rangers the following season). Both were Scots Internationals, the latter was renowned for wearing a cloth cap into action!

06/10/1892 OM: Rangers v. Liverpool
Scottish Referee - Friday 7th October, 1892

At Ibrox Park, in wet weather, and before 5,000 spectators. The Liverpool were without Smith, who is suffering from an injured ankle.

Rangers lost the toss, and Martin (Northern) led off by a side kick to J. McPherson. Kelso sprang in and deprived the latter of the ball, and kicking over to Cameron the speedy left-winger of the visitors dribbled down the field, till smartly tackled by Gow, who by a huge kick sent the ball well into goal, and Kerr kicked over. D. McPherson got on to the goal kick, and attempted to dribble past McBride, but the old Renton man outwitted him, and crossed the ball over to the left wing, where a desperate bout occurred between Marshall and Kelvin, the Kilmarnock man all but defeating the Ranger. The Rangers, warming to their work, got within shouting distance of Ross, and **Kerr** shot. The effort, from the Press Box, looked as if it had skiffed the post, but the referee allowed a goal - his decision being received with murmurs of dissatisfaction by the visitors. Liverpool now worked together with a will, and Wyllie dribbling grandly defeated Mitchell and Drummond and sent in a scorching shot, which took Haddow all his time to save. An accident to McPherson and Cameron caused the game to be stopped for a few minutes. they were both attempting to head the ball at the same time when their heads met. The Rangers by close concerted action wended their way past the visitors' halves, and but for the grand defence of Hannah would have scored. The visitors' left wing by pretty passing outmanoeuvred Gow and looked like equalising, but Drummond headed out. Nerved by the narrow shaves they were experiencing at goal the visitors redoubled their efforts, and **Cameron**, receiving an accurate pass from Wyllie, lost no time in shooting past Haddow. Within a minute from the centre-field kick the Rangers scored their second goal, **H. McCreadie** having the honour from a pass right across goal mouth from Kerr. Nearing the interval, the visitors exerted themselves to the utmost to again draw level, and Cameron all but accomplished this - his effort missing by inches. Right from the goal kick the home forwards, by beautiful passing, fairly wandered the visitors, and Martin booting strongly in, **Kerr** followed up, and amid great excitement put the ball through for the third time. Keeping up the pressure even against the stiff breeze, the light blues hovered in front of Ross and frequent shots were sent in, which, however, were saved by Hannah and Ross. A. McCreadie, evidently desiring to emulate the great feat of Doyle a month ago, dribbled the ball nearly the entire length of the field, and crossing to his brother {**H. McCreadie**}, the latter shot true as an arrow, and beat Ross for the fourth time. In the second half it looked long odds on the Rangers winning comfortably, for they crossed over leading by 4 goals to 1.

{no second half commentary}

The play of the visitors, seeing they are a new organisation, was watched with much interest, and while they are not up to first class form, time and practice may work wonders in their ranks. Individually they are a powerful lot - in fact, almost the cream of Scottish talent - to wit, Hannah, McBride, Wylie, &c. Kelso assisted the Liverpool to-day, and played with much his old agility and ability. The best of the half-backs in the visitors' ranks was McBride. Wyllie and Cameron shone conspicuously in the front rank, but Miller, the old Dumbartonian, was slow, and evidently out of form. On the Rangers' side every man played well, and therefore it would be unfair to particularise. The back division did all that was wanted of them, while the forwards played splendidly together. In fact, on to-day's form the Light Blues, barring desertion and injury in their team, will make a bold struggle to top the League record. The proceedings were enlivened by the strains of Dr Guthries Edinburgh Industrial School Band, which played various musical selections during the afternoon. The saving of Ross during the closing moments of the game was particularly fine, and called forth the plaudits of the spectators.

RESULT: Rangers 6 - Liverpool 1

LIVERPOOL: Ross (goal); Hannah and McLean (backs); Kelso, McQue and McBride (halves); Wyllie, McVean, Miller, Cameron [1], and Kelvin (forwards).
RANGERS: Haddow (goal); Gow and Drummond (backs); Marshall, McCreadie and Mitchell (halves); Kerr [2], D. McPherson, Martin, J. McPherson and H. McCreadie [2] (forwards). [2 anon].

Liverpool's second match in the Lancashire Senior Cup competition saw them travel away to antagonise the West Manchester club, in Stretford, whom they had beaten 3-1 at Anfield the previous Saturday. Not far away, at Salford, in the other Lancashire Cup competition (Rugby), a major battle was being fought out between the homesters and Swinton.

08/10/1892 LSC-Q2: West Manchester v. Liverpool
Manchester Courier - Monday 10th October, 1892

On the ground of the former, at Brooks's Bar. Not withstanding the counter attraction at Salford, there were 2,500 persons present.

Miller started for Liverpool who immediately got the leather into close quarters but "West" receiving the ball out of close play took it out of danger, and shortly afterwards received a free kick for a foul. Walsh shot, but Ross saved and kicked out strongly. Liverpool followed out and play settled in midfield. The visitors charged down the field, and after repeated efforts **Miller** shot a fine goal. Nothing more was scored up to half-time.

After the interval "West" had the best of the game at the beginning and they rushed the ball through from a corner *{anon}*. **Miller** shot the second goal for Liverpool, and just before time was called ~~Kelso~~ *{**Kelvin**}* shot the third goal.

RESULT: West Manchester 1 - Liverpool 3

LIVERPOOL: Ross (goal); Hannah and McLean (backs); Cameron, McQue and McBride (halves); Wyllie, Smith, Miller [2], McVean, and Kelvin [1] (forwards).
W. MANCHESTER: Entwistle (goal); Sugg and Russell (backs); Spiers, Pickering and Allison (halves); {Bridge}, {Iddon}, {Bogie}, Walsh and Leigh (forwards). [1 anon]
*Player names in braces {} are probable – **not** confirmed.*

Liverpool were away in Cup competition for the second week in succession, but this time in the National competition against Cheshire side, Nantwich. Liverpool had made overtures to the Cheshire side to switch the venue of the game to Anfield but had then baulked at their demands for £60 to do so. John McCartney, a new signing from St. Mirren, made his Liverpool debut. Notable amongst the homesters was goalkeeper Champion, a fine custodian who had played in Liverpool with the Earlestown club.

15/10/1892 FAC-Q1: Nantwich v. Liverpool
Athletic News - Monday 17th October, 1892

The newly-formed Liverpool club journeyed to Nantwich, an excellent game resulting. A perfect storm of rain continued during the whole of the game, which gave the burly Scotchmen the advantage over their lighter opponents, and their four goals were scored in the last twenty minutes of the game. Up to that time the home team had quite as much of the game as Liverpool, and missed two or three easy chances of scoring, and on dry ground it would nave troubled Liverpool to win at all.

RESULT: Nantwich 0 – Liverpool 4

LIVERPOOL: Ross (goal); Hannah and McLean (backs); McCartney, McQue and McBride (halves); Wyllie [1], McVean, Miller [3], Cameron and Kelvin (forwards).
NANTWICH: Champion (goal); Shenton and Keay (backs); Critchley, Crawford and Hitchen (halves); Cartwright, Bull, Hope, Garnett and Hollowood (forwards).

Most period newspapers, including the Liverpool Mercury, published the score at the time as being 3-0 to Liverpool. As such information was generally syndicated to the press at large from a single source it is easy to see how such a mistake could spread across much of the network.

Liverpool travelled to Higher Walton, near Preston, for their return Lancashire League fixture confident of a third successive victory in light of the 8-0 drubbing they had given the homesters at Anfield.

22/10/1892 LL04: Higher Walton v. Liverpool
Liverpool Mercury - Monday 24th October, 1892

Liverpool journeyed to Higher Walton on Saturday to tackle the home club in the return match of the Lancashire League.

Miller kicked off, and the visitors, with a crosswind slightly in their favour, immediately made matters look ominous for Addison. After a little finessing and an excellent centre by McBride, **Miller** secured, and easily placed a goal to the credit of Liverpool, McVean directly afterwards having the hardest of lines in not scoring with a terrific shot which struck the bar and rebounded into play. Forrest on the home right then headed a forward movement, but McLean interposed and gave to Wyllie, who ran the ball out. Still continuing in the enemies quarter, the visiting forwards found the home backs and goalkeeper an enormous amount of work, and to their credit they did their shares exceedingly well. From a capital clearance by Enderby Forrest again got off, and forced a corner from McLean. This caused Ross an anxious few minutes, but having cleared in splendid fashion a stinger from Parker, he was not again seriously troubled throughout the game. From one of McCarthy's throws the visiting forwards had a very good chance, but dallying too long, the opportunity was missed. Just on half-time Wyllie, receiving the ball from McCartney, raced past all opposition, and giving **Miller** the sphere that player easily headed through the second point for Liverpool.

Upon the restart Liverpool still showed improved football, and by the grand play of the three halves kept the home defence "on the move" continuously, two exciting scrimmages under the bar warming up both players and spectators, for in a short time the visitors had increased their lead by two goals, one each by **Miller** and **Wyllie**[2], who later on secured the fifth, Liverpool thus running out victors;

RESULT: Higher Walton 0 – Liverpool 5

LIVERPOOL: Ross (goal); Hannah and McLean (backs); McCartney, McQue and McBride (halves); Wyllie [2], McVean, Miller [3], Cameron and Kelvin (forwards).
HIGHER WALTON: Addison (goal); Enderby and Craven (backs); Gerrard, J. Law and Flintoff (halves); Forrest, Livesey, Booth, Howarth and Parker (forwards).

In the Second Qualifying round of the national Cup competition Liverpool welcomed to Anfield the town club from Newtown in Wales. Newtown's first round tie had been at home to Tranmere Rovers, Liverpool's near neighbours from across the Mersey, but the Welshmen had been awarded a walk-over when the Rovers had been unable to send a team the 80 miles distance. Newtown had seemingly found reversing the journey no insurmountable obstacle, however, to contest the tie at Anfield. Liverpool were strengthened by two more new signings in the Scottish brothers Hugh and Matt McQueen from Leith Athletic. The talented brothers had previously been approached by the Liverpool Caledonian club but when the 'Callies' were held up by financial difficulties the Anfielders had snatched them away instead.

29/10/1892 FAC-Q2: Liverpool v. Newtown
Liverpool Mercury - Monday 31st October, 1892

At Anfield, in presence of 4000 spectators. The Liverpool team was further strengthened by M. and H. McQueen late of Leith athletic.

Worthington opened the play, and for a few minutes the Welshmen put on a bold front. The Liverpool team, however, soon settled down, and subjected the Newtown defence to some severe pressure, and after some stubborn resistance Edwards was rather easily beaten by a lobbing shot from **McCartney**. Once or twice the Reds made strenuous efforts to get down, but were never dangerous, and after a bit confined themselves strictly to defence. It availed little, however, as **Wyllie** put on number two. Townsend placed one through his **own goal**, and **McVean** wound up the first half by scoring number four.

Change of ends brought no relief to the visitors, and Liverpool were always attacking. **McVean** notched a fifth point, and **Wyllie** got a sixth with a flying shot, **H. McQueen** making the score into seven goals during the next minute. Newtown played up desperately under these reverses, and Morgan and Pryce-Jones initiated raids to the other end, only to find the defence far too strong for them. **Wyllie** got the eighth, and **Cameron** piled on the ninth goal at which total the score stood when the whistle blew, and Liverpool were loudly cheered on leaving the field.

RESULT: Liverpool 9 – Newtown 0

LIVERPOOL: Ross (goal); Hannah and McLean (backs); McCartney [1], M. McQueen and McBride (halves); Wyllie [3], Cameron [1], Miller, McVean [2] and H. McQueen [1] (forwards). [1 og]
NEWTOWN: Edwards (goal); Taylor and Townsend (backs); Tucker, Chapman and Read (halves); Pryce-Jones, Evans, Worthington, Thomas and Morgan (forwards).

The attendance of 4,000 was a magnificent one for Liverpool, especially in light of the other cup tie being played in the city on that day. Just two and a half miles away, at Hawthorne Road, Bootle were entertaining the Caledonians in an intriguing north versus south of the city encounter, the 'Callies' winning a tremendous battle 3-2.

Liverpool next made their first trip to the Fylde coast to take on a Blackpool that, like themselves, had a perfect record of four wins in their opening four Lancashire League fixtures. Consequently a stiff game was expected, but with Liverpool's League goals tally standing at 20 to Blackpool's 11 there was good reason to be optimistic!

05/11/1892 LL05: Blackpool v. Liverpool
Liverpool Mercury - Monday 7th November, 1892

The first meeting of these teams took place at Blackpool on Saturday. As each club had equal points, great interest was manifested in the game. Blackpool had their full team, but Liverpool were short of Smith and McBride.

Hannah won the toss, and Marsden kicked off, before 4000 spectators, with the sun and wind against them. The opening manoeuvres were highly exciting and quite sensational, Miller took Marsden's initial kick, and he and McVean broke away, but when becoming dangerous were sent to the right about by Morgan, and Parkinson forced a corner off McQueen. This was nicely placed, but was eventually cleared. The relief was only temporary, as by most determined play the home team ran up and crossed to **E. Parkinson**, who shot a grand goal after five minutes play. Three minutes had hardly elapsed when from another centre by the home right **Pittaway** headed the second point for the home club, the spectators showing their pleasure at this unexpected result by frantic cheers. From the kick off Miller and McVean got away, and, after eluding the halves, McVean was sent spinning by Parr, while Morgan sent the sphere travelling towards Ross. For a time the play was fairly even, but Blackpool gave Liverpool no rest, and after the visitors had given an exhibition of pretty combination, in which Wyllie's final effort just topped the bar, the homesters, by an individual effort of Tyrer, brought the game back again into the visitors' half, where an error of judgment on the part of Hannah let in Pittaway, who gave to **Parkinson**, and that player easily added the third goal. Play now eased down, and after testing Wright with rather slow shots, half-time was called, with Liverpool pressing.

The play was all in the home half on the recommencement. Following the style of their opponents, the visitors now put more go and work into the game, and this, assisted by accurate passing, kept the home team entirely on the defence, Wright having several warm handfuls to deal with; but the fates were against Liverpool, and try as they would they could not score, McQueen on the left and Wyllie on the right both having very hard lines with their centres and shots. Cameron missed an excellent chance after a beautiful run about half the length of the field by Miller, McVean, and McQueen. Tyrer now changed the venue, and Ross saved in grand fashion a scorching shot from Marsden, and so the game went on, Liverpool having the best of the play, but not making the most of their opportunities, and the whistle blew leaving the result:

RESULT: Blackpool 3 – Liverpool 0

LIVERPOOL: Ross (goal); Hannah and McLean (backs); McCartney, McQue and M. McQueen (halves); Wyllie, Cameron, McVean, H. McQueen and Miller (forwards).
BLACKPOOL: Wright (goal); H. Parr and Morgan (backs); Stirraker, Davy and F. Parr (halves); J. Parkinson, Tyrer, Marsden, Pittaway [1] and E. Parkinson [2] (forwards).

Liverpool made a quick return to the Fylde coast, this time to face Fleetwood Rangers, hoping to make good the defeat they had suffered the previous week. The Rangers were so far unbeaten in the Lancashire League and had just returned from a triumphal southern tour, whereon they had defeated Chatham (6-1), Millwall (4-1) and Royal

Arsenal (2-1) in successive days. After a week's rest, however, Liverpool would be fresher than their opponents for the game at hand.

12/11/1892 LL06: Fleetwood Rangers v. Liverpool
Liverpool Mercury - Monday 14th November, 1892

Liverpool undertook another journey into the Fylde district on Saturday, and, smarting under the reverse at Blackpool, there was an air of determination with the team that boded no good for Fleetwood. McBride and Smith were again in their places and they materially improved the play all round.

Liverpool started uphill with the wind, but Fleetwood were the first aggressors, Brogan mulling a fine opportunity when in a good position. The Liverpool forwards then got away, and from McVean's pass **Miller** safely steered the ball into the net. Fleetwood again bore down, and to make amends for his previous non-success, **Brogan** banged a terrific shot through, thus putting the teams level after five minutes play. But it was evident even at this stage of the game who were the better team, and the methodical style of Liverpool soon asserted itself, and **McVean**, brushing past all opposition, put on number two. By McLean lying too far up the field, Brogan and Hogan, the home right, raced away and centred, and although McQueen saved in a critical moment, the homesters made a strenuous claim for the ball being through, but the referee decided against them. Again the visiting forwards got away, and Miller, McVean, and McQueen gave an excellent display of combination, **McVean** finishing the effort by scoring the third point for Liverpool, which left the game at half-time 3 to 1 in their favour.

In the second half Liverpool, keeping themselves well together, severely tested Chapman, and to his credit he did his work exceedingly well, and assisted by two reliable backs, ~~Colby~~ {Colley} and Bibby, Liverpool, although mostly in their opponents' half, could not increase their score. Ultimately **Smith**, by a sharp screw shot, did the trick, and a pleasant and fast game ended in a victory for Liverpool:

RESULT: Fleetwood 1 – Liverpool 4

LIVERPOOL: Ross (goal); Hannah and McLean (backs); McCartney, M. McQueen and McBride (halves); Wyllie, Smith [1], Miller [1], McVean [2] and H. McQueen (forwards).
FLEETWOOD: Chapman (goal); Colley and Bibby (backs); {Dempsey}, {Yates} and {B. Robinson} (halves); Hogan, Brogan [1], {Craven}, {Wilson} and {R. Robinson} (forwards).
*Player names in braces {} are probable – **not** confirmed.*

A trip to the West Midlands next brought a prestigious friendly encounter with Aston Villa, who, as well as being founder members of the Football League, were former F.A. Cup winners and the previous season's beaten finalists. The Villans fielded a significantly weakened side from their regular League eleven, which no doubt accounted for the small gate - 2000 being only one-sixth of the number that had packed in to see the League match against West Bromwich two days earlier. It was a decision, however, they may subsequently have come to recognise as a mistake!

14/11/1892 OM: Aston Villa v. Liverpool
Birmingham Daily Post - Tuesday 15th November, 1892

A friendly match between these teams was played at Perry Barr before about three thousand spectators. The visitors were well represented, but the Villa were without Devey, Athersmith, Dowds, G. Campbell, and Evans. Their places were taken by L. Campbell, Davis, Stokes, Woollaston, and Burton.

The Villa kicked off uphill, and for the first few minutes had the balance of play, the Liverpool goalkeeper having to stop a fine shot from Hare. Then, however, the Villa were pressed, and during the next five minutes the visitors scored twice to the no small astonishment of the home team {*anon²*}. The latter, recognising that they had a difficult task before them played up better; but their form was very much below its usual standard and the back play was very indifferent. The result was that **H. McQueen** soon headed a third goal. The visitors well deserved to score for they passed splendidly and their half-backs were very smart. In the few minutes that remained the Villa gave an improved display but they failed to score and at the interval were three goals in arrear.

On restarting the visitors went away with great dash, and Denning had much difficulty to stop a shot from Miller. He managed to turn the ball out however, and it was transferred to the other end of the field. A good attack was made, and after an exciting tussle **L. Campbell** scored the first point for the Villa. Stimulated by their success they played up brilliantly, and kept up a perfect bombardment upon the Liverpool goal. It, was, however, grandly defended and successfully resisted capture for a long time. About three minutes from the finish the Villa made a fine attack, and **Davis** beat the goal-keeper with a capital shot. No further, goals were scored, and the visitors thus won by:

RESULT: Aston Villa 2 – Liverpool 3

LIVERPOOL: Ross (goal); Hannah and McLean (backs); McCartney, M. McQueen and McBride (halves); Wyllie, Smith, Miller, McVean and H. McQueen [1] (forwards). [2 anon]
VILLA: Dunning (goal); Wollaston and Russell (backs); Stokes, Cowan and Burton (halves); Brown, Davis [1], Hare, Hodgetts and L. Campbell [1] (forwards).

For the Third Qualifying Round F.A. Cup tie at Northwich Liverpool chose to grant the McQueen brothers, who had important business elsewhere, a leave of absence due to a question over their eligibility. F.A. rules forbade any player who played during the close from figuring in the following season's F.A. Cup competition. The brothers had in fact played with their previous club in Scotland where there was no close season, but as they had not been subject to English F.A. jurisdiction at the time (then still being registered with the Scottish F.A.) there was a question as to whether the rule applied. The brothers had already played in the earlier cup tie at Newtown but as the Welshmen had not complained the point had not been tested! Liverpool had tried to induce the Vics, for a financial consideration, to switch the venue to Anfield – but without success. On arrival at the Drill Field, the Liverpool party found the pitch to be in a deplorable condition and objected on those grounds to the match proceeding as a cup tie.

19/11/1892 FAC-Q3: Northwich Victoria v. Liverpool
Liverpool Mercury - Monday 21st November, 1892

This game was played at Northwich on Saturday, in wretched weather, rain falling heavily most of the time. The ground was a perfect quagmire, pools of water, intermixed with sawdust and mud, being the prevailing features, and Liverpool lodged a protest. Through some doubt as to the qualification of the brothers McQueen, the Liverpool Committee left them out, McQue and Kelvin taking their place.

Bradshaw started the game, and the home team were the first aggressors, a foul in front of goal giving them an excellent opportunity, but Crozier put the ball through. Wyllie then raced up the right, but Scanlon cleared in grand style. McLean returned, and after a most exciting "bully" in goal the ball was put out to **Wyllie**, who shot through, after about ten minutes play. Miller and McVean then made a pretty run, but Miller slipped when getting into position. Postles next gave to Ramsay, that player putting in a grand shot, which Hannah only partially cleared. McLean came to the rescue, and Smith threaded his way through his opponents, only to be robbed by Scanlon, through sticking to the ball too long. Fecittt, who had given Hannah some trouble previously, ran down on the left. McCartney pulled him up and passed to Miller, but Crozier was too quick for him and shot over to his right wing, Hargreaves slipping past McLean like an eel, and **Fecitt**, lying handy, safely put the ball into the net from Hargreaves centre. This unexpected success was greeted with frantic cheers by the crowd, as up to this point Liverpool were by far the better team, and had most of the play. Cheered on by the shouts of their supporters the home team were again hovering around Hannah, McLean, and Ross. Eventually McVean and Kelvin relieved by a good run on the left, but Kelvin's final shot was extremely weak. By long passing and sharp following up Hargreaves fastened on to the ball and centred, and an exciting scrimmage was formed in the Liverpool goal, from which **Fecittt** landed goal number two. This second success gave the home team an incentive to play up, and the game became fast and furious. Wyllie, Miller, and Kelvin giving Gow, the home custodian, several hot shots, which he successfully cleared. Again Liverpool bombarded the home goal, McBride putting a teaser in, and Wyllie supplementing with one which just topped the bar. From a pass by McBride Miller scored a capital goal, but Mr. Lewis gave him offside. Postles, the back, played the ball, but the referee was too far away to be sure of it, and consequently Liverpool lost a legitimate point. As time drew near each team made strenuous attempts to score, the play becoming most exciting as Gow fisted out shot after shot, and then Ross doing ditto at the other end. Urged on by the onlookers the home team much improved during the last few minutes, and kept Liverpool from being dangerous, and so a fast and fiercely contested game ended in a win for Northwich:

RESULT: Northwich Victoria 2 – Liverpool 1

LIVERPOOL: Ross (goal); Hannah and McLean (backs); McCartney, M. McQue and McBride (halves); Wyllie [1], Smith, Miller, McVean and Kelvin (forwards).
NORTHWICH: Gow (goal); Scanlan and Postles (backs); Ramsey, Crozier and Stanley (halves); Hargreaves, Finnerhan, Bradshaw, Macbeth and Fecittt [2] (forwards).

The absence of the McQueen's had severely affected the team's combination play and no doubt played a significant part in the result. The brothers private business, meanwhile, had seen them make a temporary return to Scotland where Hugh was getting married! After the match Liverpool made their protest over the state of the ground official by lodging the necessary deposit with the F.A. At a meeting of the committee the following Wednesday, however, after hearing the evidence of the referee, the protest was disallowed. Ironically, Northwich were then drawn in the next round away to Liverpool Caledonians[8], so that Liverpool were deprived of what could have been a lucrative local derby.

In a return to Lancashire League fare, Liverpool next travelled to Waterfoot in the Rossendale Valley to contest for points with the Rossendale Club[9]. Liverpool were again without the McQueen brothers, who had not yet returned from their leave of absence.

26/11/1892 LL07: Rossendale v. Liverpool
Liverpool Mercury - Monday 28th November, 1892

This match was played at Rossendale. Liverpool were again weakened by the absence of the brothers McQueen, Hugh becoming a Benedict[10] on Saturday last. The ground was fearfully heavy and sloppy, and when Brown started the game there would be about 1500 spectators.

Play was fairly even at the start, but the smarter combination of the visitors' enabled Kelly to try his shooting powers, but he made a very poor use of the chance offered. Weir received the kick off and gave to his left, Sharples, the inside player, dodged Hannah, and had the goal at his mercy, but although close under the bar Ross managed to clear his very weak attempt, and McCartney put in a beauty at the other end, which, if it had been properly followed up, would have been improved upon without a doubt. Garner and Sharples, on the left, raced up and gave Brown an opportunity, who banged across, but that player was at his best, and cleared gallantly. McLean, with a huge kick, gave to the visitors right wing, who travelled towards Holden, Wyllie finishing up with a grand shot, which was with difficulty cleared.

Upon restarting a most sensational piece of play occurred. **Miller** gave the initial kick to McVean, and by alternate passes and re-passes the two players alone ran clean through their opponents and scored, not an individual touching the ball but themselves. This decided the game, for now Liverpool's passing improved, and before long **McBride** had added a second, although the home team pressed severely in the last few minutes, Hannah and McLean played so well that they held the Rossendale forwards in check, and when the whistle blew Liverpool had secured two more points by this victory.

RESULT: Rossendale 0 – Liverpool 2

---

8   In fact in their short co-existence the two clubs never met. Despite both being members of the Lancashire League the 'Callies' folded before their fixtures against each other could be contested.
9   Not connected with the more recent Rossendale United club who were based at nearby Newchurch.
10 Benedict (archaic) – a man who married after a long bachelorhood (ie. a man who married later in life than the norm).

LIVERPOOL: Ross (goal); Hannah and McLean (backs); McCartney, M. McQue and McBride [1] (halves); Wyllie, Smith, Miller [1], McVean and Kelly (forwards).
ROSSENDALE: Holden (goal); Blears and Davis (backs); Whiteside, W. Brown and Weir (halves); R. Brown, Garner, Sharples, Radcliffe and Duckworth (forwards).

Liverpool welcomed Fleetwood Rangers for their return Lancashire League match back to full strength, looking for another win to try to make back ground on leaders Bury.

03/12/1892 LL08: Liverpool v. Fleetwood Rangers
Liverpool Mercury - Monday 5th December, 1892

Played at Anfield on Saturday, before 3000 spectators. Liverpool were fully represented, having the same team which had defeated the Rangers at Fleetwood by four goals to one.

Hannah won the toss and defended the Oakfield Road goal. Wilson commenced hostilities, and immediately Leadbetter and Robinson created a diversion on the right. Hannah repulsed them, and after some indiscriminate kicking on both sides Smith and Wyllie brought the ball well up, but Wyllie shot over the bar. Good defence by Bethel Robinson and Bibby kept Liverpool at bay, and it was some time before **McVean** found an opening. This success, combined with the fact of having a strong wind behind them, caused Liverpool to be continually on the aggressive, and before half-time **Miller**[3] had added three goals to Liverpool's score, making the game 4 to nil in their favour.

Upon resuming the game was more open, Chapman first conceding a corner, and Ross following his example immediately afterwards. McLean again came in for a round of applause for saving in a critical moment and bringing the ball down to Hugh McQueen, who raced off and centred, the ball hovering in dangerous proximity to Chapman; but **Miller** put an end to the doubt by scoring the fifth goal. A quick run and centre by Smith and **Miller** culminated in the sixth being headed by the latter, while **M. McQueen** completed the score by a grand shot from half-back, which altogether nonplussed the goalkeeper, and the whistle blew leaving the homesters winners of their seventh league match by:

RESULT: Liverpool 7 - Fleetwood 0

LIVERPOOL: Ross (goal); Hannah and McLean (backs); McCartney, M. McQueen [1] and McBride (halves); Wyllie, Smith, Miller [5], McVean [1] and H. McQueen (forwards).
FLEETWOOD: Chapman (goal); B.Robinson and Bibby (backs); Craven, Dempsey and Yates (halves); Hogan, Brogan, Wilson, Leadbeater and R. Robinson (forwards).

Miller, who was already the first Liverpool player to have scored a hat-trick in a competitive match, now set the bar even higher by becoming the first to score five goals in a game. The Liverpool Mercury in it's general editorial shared the acclaim for Miller's achievement with Smith and McVean for their splendid support play. Before the match the McQueen brothers were accorded an ovation on their return, the Anfield faithful keen to congratulate Hugh on his happy event. Matt celebrated by scoring his first goal for the club.

The next being a Cup weekend, Liverpool's expulsion from the national competition left them free to fulfil a 'friendly' match at Heywood Central, whom they were yet to meet in a Lancashire League fixture.

10/12/1892 OM: Heywood Central v. Liverpool
Manchester Courier - Monday 12th December, 1892

Played at Heywood before 1000 spectators.

The visitors commenced with the incline against them, and at once they were forced on the defensive. Webster gave Ross two stiff shots, and some time afterwards the homesters got a free kick in the Liverpool goalmouth, but it availed nothing. Excitement ran high with when the Central peppered away at the visitors' goal but could not find an inroad. At half-time neither side had scored.

On the resumption the visitors soon became dangerous, and Sharples luckily saved a shot from Wyllie. The "Centralians" then returned to the attack, and Jones and McWhinnie grazed the Liverpool crossbar with magnificent shots. Liverpool again attacked and **Miller** notched a beautiful goal, but the homesters equalised from the foot of **Horsfield**. Both teams tried hard for the mastery, and the backs on each side gave a brilliant exhibition, but nothing further was scored, and the result was a draw of one goal each.

RESULT: Heywood Central 1 – Liverpool 1

LIVERPOOL: Ross (goal); Hannah and McLean (backs); McCartney, M. McQueen and McBride (halves); Wyllie, Smith, Miller [1], McVean and H. McQueen (forwards).
HEYWOOD: Sharples (goal); {Pearson} and {Evans} (backs); {Halpin}, {Scholes} and {Reagan} (halves); Jones, McWhinnie, Horsfield [1], {Allan} and {Webster} (forwards).
*Player names in braces {} are probable – **not** confirmed.*

In the cup on that day, Northwich Victoria defeated Liverpool Caledonians 3-2 at Woodcroft Park, thus becoming single-handedly responsible for knocking three of the four professional Liverpool clubs out of the competition – Bootle, Liverpool and Caledonians.

In the return Lancashire League match against Blackpool, Liverpool were looking to put matters to rights after their earlier defeat by the seasiders on the Fylde coast.

17/12/1892 LL09: Liverpool v. Blackpool
Liverpool Mercury - Monday 19th December, 1892

This important fixture was brought off on Saturday at Anfield, and the interest was so great that fully 6000 spectators watched the game.

Both teams were as advertised, and when Marsden started against the wind the excitement rose to a high pitch. Wright was early called upon, and it looked as though it was going to be a nice thing for the home team, as first Wyllie, then Miller and McQueen all had capital shots. Stirraker cleared the danger, and his left wing by pretty passing troubled Hannah, who when nearly beaten saved in excellent style, and again Miller and the wings were swarming round Wright, and Morgan gave a corner. After a severe bully in the visitors' goal the ball was put out to Parkinson, who outpaced McLean and sent smartly across to **Pittaway**, who finely scored the first point. Liverpool, by good half-back play, were again in dangerous vicinity to Morgan, Parr, and Wright, but their vigorous defence allowed of no dallying, and they cleared time after time when a goal seemed imminent. Marsden was next conspicuous for a dashing run, winding up with a shot, which, being well followed up, made matters look awkward for Ross, but McLean cleared. So again the ball was brought back, and Wyllie missed an easy chance, an unfortunate piece of business that Smith repeated.

Upon resuming, Blackpool soon asserted themselves, while Liverpool fell off, but Hannah and McLean put in some big kicks. Miller then got nicely down and dribbled through his men, but the final attempt was cleared. Blackpool were to the fore once more, and being more fortunate than their opponents **Marsden** tricked Hannah and scored a second point. Liverpool now seemed to realise their position, and put an immense amount of spirit into their play, but Blackpool were equally determined to hold their advantage, although Wright must be voted somewhat lucky in negotiating several of the shots sent in from the left wing, and also those from McBride and McQueen, that of the latter looking almost a certainty; and so right up to the finish Liverpool commanded the play, but could not get the ball, and so a grandly contested game ended in a second win for Blackpool by:

RESULT: Liverpool 0 – Blackpool 2

LIVERPOOL: Ross (goal); Hannah and McLean (backs); McCartney, McQueen and M. McBride (halves); Wyllie, Smith, Miller, McVean and H. McQueen (forwards).
BLACKPOOL: Wright (goal); H. Parr and Morgan (backs); Stirraker, Davy and F. Parr (halves); Parkinson, Pittaway [1], Tyrer, Marsden [1] and Parkinson (forwards).

A second defeat by the seasiders enabled the latter to move two points clear of the Anfielders in the League table, second to leaders Bury by two points.

For the second weekend in succession Liverpool entertained opposition from Blackpool, this time the South Shore club being the visitors to Anfield.

24/12/1892 LL10: South Shore v. Liverpool
Athletic News - Monday 26th December, 1892

Liverpool have not been doing so well of late, and will not take the championship so easily as they anticipated; in fact, if they do not pull up they will have to be content with third place, as Blackpool had beaten them in both their matches, and Bury are showing considerable improvement. On Saturday the Liverpudlians journeyed to Blackpool to cross swords with South Shore, and although they manage to score in the first five minutes from a good shot by **Wyllie**, they could not again break through the Shoreites defence in the remaining eighty-five minutes, although during that time their defence was impregnable.

RESULT: South Shore 0 - Liverpool 1

LIVERPOOL: Ross (goal); Hannah and McLean (backs); McCartney, McQueen and M. McBride (halves); Wyllie [1], Smith, Miller, McVean and H. McQueen (forwards).
SOUTH SHORE: {Parker} (goal); {Rose} and {Naylor} (backs); {Atherton}, {Daley} and {Baldwin} (halves); {Birchall}, {Pratt}, {Mather}, {McNab} and {Taylor} (forwards).
*Player names in braces {} are probable – **not** confirmed.*

The Liverpool Caledonians match at Higher Walton on that day was cancelled owing to the Caldonians having resigned from the League on the grounds of the club being wound up.

---

*The **Liverpool Caledonian Football Club** had been formed at the beginning of the 1891/92 season by a group of Liverpool based Scots under the direction of Mr. Robert Kirkland. They were based at the Woodcroft Park ground near Wavertree Station in the South of the city, and their their inaugural game was at this ground on 21st September, 1891, when Everton kindly consented to provide the opposition. Although initially formed as an amateur club, the committee had quickly realised this philosophy would not work to meet their ambitions and so had taken the bold move of turning professional, thus forming, along with Everton and Bootle, a triumvirate of professional clubs then operating in the City. At the end of the season the club was incorporated as the Liverpool Caledonian Company Limited and applied to be included in the newly formed Second Division of the Football League. In the latter they were unsuccessful, however, and, along with the newly formed Liverpool A.F.C., joined the expanding Lancashire League instead. At the start of the new season hopes were high, and although the club's books showed a significant negative balance (largely due to the wages bill and expenditure on developing spectator facilities at Woodcroft Park) only £2 on each of the 300 £5 shares sold by the club upon incorporation had so far been collected, leaving the club with a sum of as yet unrealised investment that far exceeded it's debts. To all outward appearances, therefore, the club had done exceedingly well in it's first year and indications seemed to point to a bright and successful future. That early promise seemed to be augmented when the Caledonians easily won their first Lancashire League fixture 4-1 at Southport Central.*

In the background, however, the storm clouds were already gathering! Certain of the club's creditors were clamouring for payment and, although the club was rich in prospect, tomorrow's income cannot pay today's debts and the club had little in the way of immediate cash. When attempts to speed up the schedule for the payment of the remaining share balance failed to produce any significant amount of immediate extra capital the club's debts began to weigh heavily upon them. Consequently, by early November the club found itself in dire straits. At a crisis meeting of the shareholders on 14th December, 1892, it was revealed that one of the club's major creditors had initiated proceedings for compulsory liquidation over a debt that the club could not, at that time, afford to pay. Accordingly, after a vote, it was unanimously agreed by the shareholders that the company be wound up voluntarily. Consequently, the club resigned from the Lancashire League and it's results were expunged from the official record. For Liverpool F.C. meant the loss of the Christmas Day and New Years

For the "Callies" it had been a short but stellar existence. In a lifetime that lasted a mere sixteen months they had tested their mettle successfully against some of the best exponents of the Association game in the North-West and had played as far afield as Royal Arsenal and Airdrieonians. Unfortunately, they had reached too far too quickly, and made the fundamental mistake of spending too much capital before it had actually been raised, and that had been their undoing.

Liverpool's next visitors were Sheffield United, who shared an unusual distinction with the Anfielders - both clubs having been founded to make use of an empty stadium after another club had moved out! In the visitors case it was Bramall Lane, which had been regularly rented by the Sheffield Wednesday club until they established their own ground at Olive Grove. Up to that time Sheffield United had been the management company that owned and rented out the stadium but had no team of their own to play there. Following Wednesday's departure, Sheffield United Football Club had been formed to fill the void, and, like Liverpool, their early history had been nothing less than meteoric. Now in their fourth season, they had started the current campaign as one of the founder members of the new Division Two of the Football League.

26/12/1892 OM: Liverpool v. Sheffield Utd
Liverpool Mercury - Tuesday 27th December, 1892

This match was played at Anfield yesterday, before 6000 spectators. The weather was delightfully fine, but the slippery nature of the ground made the players very careful at times. Hannah won the toss and defended the Oakfield Road goal.

Hammond started, and the visiting right made tracks for Ross, and for a time the game was confined to the Liverpool quarters. Miller eased the pressure and gave to Wyllie, who raced away from his opponents and tested Howlett, who was all there. Still continuing to have somewhat the best of the argument, McVean and M. McQueen really deserved to score with two capital attempts. Hammond and Brady were next prominent, and caused Hannah to display his defensive powers, and, with McCartney's assistance he pulled up the left wing in splendid style. At this juncture Drummond was transferred to the left wing, and in co-operation with Brady they proved a most dangerous pair, giving the home defence much annoyance. Two fouls from Cameron created a diversion for a few minutes, but otherwise Liverpool had by far the best of it, for they obtained two corners, and Miller was almost too strong for Hallett with one of his fast shots. The play now became most exciting, both goals being visited in turn, and both Hammond and Croxen had fruitless shies. The Sheffield forwards were now livening up to their work, and a keen race took place between Hannah and Brady, in which the former proved victorious. Half-time found the visitors' attacking, and the score nil on both sides.

Upon resuming Wyllie got away on the wing, but 'hands' spoiled a possible chance. Strong half-back play by the United enabled the visiting forwards to cause Ross to become wide awake, and he used his hands with good effect. McLean eventually relieved with a huge punt, and Wyllie securing dribbled beautifully on the right, and finished up with a grand shot, which under ordinary circumstances would have scored. Having slightly the best of the game Liverpool kept up a fusillade of shots, Miller on one occasion just missing when close in. Following the kick off Hammond ran down the centre and passed over to Drummond, who obtained a corner, which proved fruitless. M. McQueen gave Miller a good opening, but weak play by Smith threw the chance away. An exciting bully in goal immediately afterwards looked ominous for the United, and how the goal was saved was remarkable. An accident to Croxen, who fell heavily when charging McLean, caused a slight stoppage. A foul, well taken by Hannah, resulted in a goal kick, and then the visitors' by a series of throws in made considerable headway, but McQueen's grand half-back play nipped most of their well meant efforts in the bud. The play became very exciting as both goalkeepers were visited, and by their saves they deserved the lavish applause accorded them. Miller now became very conspicuous by neat dribbling and effective passing, and from a centre by Wyllie was unfortunate enough to head over the bar. As time drew near the home team maintained the upper hand, McCartney, McQueen, and McBride being too good for the forwards, and on McQueen, whose fine play throughout elicited loud commendation, at last led an attack, and Miller passing to **Wyllie** that player scored for the home team with a difficult screw shot. Right up to the finish Liverpool pressed, and a capital game ended in a win for the home team by:

RESULT: Liverpool 1 – Sheffield United 0

LIVERPOOL: Ross (goal); Hannah and McLean (backs); McCartney, M. McQueen and M. McBride (halves); Wyllie [1], Smith, Miller, McVean and H. McQueen (forwards).
SHEFFIELD UTD: Howlett (goal); Whittam and Cain (backs); Howell, Hendry and Waller (halves); Croxen, Drummond, Davies, Brady and Hammond (forwards).

Although the scoring was limited to a single goal, this was generally regarded as being the best game the young club had played so far on it's home ground.

Ahead of either of their Lancashire League fixtures, Liverpool next made the short trip up the coast to Southport to test the mettle of the Centralians in an ordinary match.

27/12/1892 OM: Southport Central v. Liverpool
Liverpool Mercury - Wednesday 28th December, 1892

This friendly match was played at Southport yesterday, in beautiful weather. Both teams were short of their full strength, Hannah and Miller being absentees from the Liverpool side, while Dodd, Platt, and Watkinson failed to put in an appearance for the homesters.

Cameron kicked off, before a poor muster of spectators, and Forshaw at once made play on the home left. Wyllie replied with a short run, but found Gee in a good humour. C. Gee robbed Cameron, and Devonport shot over the crossbar. Immediately following Hamer tested Ross with an awkward shot, and after a period of desultory play the Liverpool forwards came away nicely, and Wyllie just missed. Not to be denied, **Hamer** put in a beauty which struck the upright and rebounded through, thus scoring the first point for the Central. Within less than a minute **Wyllie** equalised with a fast low shot. After this Liverpool had the best of the game, and if their left wing had been given more to do the score would certainly have been increased. After half an hour's play **McVean** dribbled through his opponents, and added the second point to the visitors.

Nothing further was scored up to half-time, and on resuming McVean missed two easy chances, especially one given him by Cameron, but he made amends by nearly doing the trick when in a nasty position. Devonport and Lofthouse changed the venue, and Ross was caught napping by a straight long shot from **Devonport**, which struck the crossbar and tumbled into the net. Forshaw came in for a round of applause for a rapid sprint up the left, and Ross had a few anxious moments, but eventually McQueen cleared, and McVean tried a long one without success. Smith then came in for an ironical cheer for sticking to the ball and being neatly upset, and as a fact his whole performance was not by any means up to concert pitch. Joe Lofthouse was next conspicuous for capital centres and obtaining three corners in succession, and the back play of Smith and Rimmer materially assisted to keep up the pressure on the visitors' goal. Wyllie momentarily relieved but Smith was robbed, while the Central rushed up and "Kenny" put over the bar. Up to the finish the homesters had slightly the better of the argument, a run by McQueen and Cameron, and a shot by McVean being the only items of importance for Liverpool, and a good and exciting match ended in a draw:

RESULT: Southport Central 2 – Liverpool 2

LIVERPOOL: Ross (goal); M. McQueen and McLean (backs); McCartney, McQue and McBride (halves); Wyllie [1], Smith, Cameron, McVean [1], and H. McQueen (forwards).
SOUTHPORT: J. Gee (goal); Smith and Rimmer (backs); C. Gee, Mayor and Ripley (halves); Lofthouse, Devonport [1], Melrose, Hamer [1] and Forshaw (forwards).

Liverpool ended the year with a visit from Heywood Central. Liverpool were much in need of a win to try to chase down Bury at the top of the table but Heywood were a strong side, who had held Liverpool to a draw in their ordinary match a couple of weeks earlier.

31/12/1892 LL11: Liverpool v. Heywood Central
Liverpool Mercury - Monday 02 January 1893

The first meeting of these clubs in a League match took place at Anfield on Saturday, before nearly 2000 spectators. The clubs had met a fortnight ago in a friendly game, the result being a draw, and consequently great interest was evinced as to how the home team would shape against the club who on Boxing Day overwhelmed Bury by 5 goals to 1.

Miller started the game, and, putting out to the right wing, Wyllie and M. McQueen (who played vice Smith) cantered up the field and secured a corner, which, being nicely put in by Wyllie, was neatly converted by **Miller**. This success gave confidence to the home team, and they played with remarkable vigour and precision. McQueen and McVean roused an enthusiastic cheer for a most brilliant run, but Sharples ran out and cleared. Webster was given possession, and rushing past Hannah had a clear field before him, but McLean raced across, and tackling successfully gave the leather to Wyllie, who combining in splendid fashion with McQueen overcame all opposition and centred, but the strong, defence of Pearson and Evans relieved the danger for a while. Shortly afterwards McQue judiciously gave to **Wyllie**, and that player obtained the second goal, while immediately he {*Wyllie*} put a third through. Heywood, in no way disheartened, played very strongly, and **Pearson** scored. **McVean**[2] then became noticeable in scoring two fine goals, while McLean was also brought into unenviable prominence by deliberately fouling close into goal, and **Jones**[p] scored from the penalty kick. Just on time the two McQueens put in a splendid piece of work {*M. McQueen scored*}, and were deservedly applauded; and an interesting game resulted in a victory for Liverpool by:

RESULT: Liverpool 6 - Heywood Central 2

LIVERPOOL: Ross (goal); Hannah and McLean (backs); McCartney, M. McQue and McBride (halves); Wyllie [2], M. McQueen [1], Miller [1], McVean [2] and H. McQueen (forwards).
HEYWOOD: Sharples (goal); Pearson [1] and Evans (backs); {Halpin}, {Scholes} and {Reagan} (halves); Jones [1p], {McWhinney}, {Horsfield}, {Allan} and Webster (forwards).
*Player names in braces {} are probable – **not** confirmed.*

Liverpool began the new year with a trip to Droylsden to visit the new ground of the Fairfield club. Fairfield had made bold moves at the start of that season, joining the Lancashire League, launching as a limited company, and securing a new ground on Gransmoor Road close to the Gransmoor Hotel. On the field, however, their results had been on the poor side of mediocre, leaving them languishing just below mid-table in the Lancashire League standings.

02/01/1893 LL12: Fairfield v. Liverpool
Liverpool Mercury - Tuesday 03 January 1893

This Lancashire League match was played at Manchester yesterday, in cold but fine weather, before 3000 spectators.

The opening stages of the game were very erratic owing to the frozen snow lying upon the field. Hannah, with his usual good fortune, won the toss, and for the first quarter of an hour midfield play prevailed. Liverpool at last began to assert themselves and from a well-placed free kick, taken by McBride, **Miller** opened the score for the visitors. They were not long allowed to hold the lead, however, as from a fierce scrimmage in goal the ball was rushed through, and the score equalised {**anon**}. The game still continued in the same ding-dong fashion, but before half-time **Wyllie** had given the visitors the lead by a capital oblique shot. Having to face a slight wind, Liverpool, on the restart, were pressed, but so safe was the defence of McLean and Hannah that all attacks were repulsed, and from a capital bit of combination between McQueen, Miller, and McVean, **McQueen** again scored. This reverse, together with the fierce calls of the spectators caused the homesters to rouse up, and Handford, Egan, and Doughty came dashing down the field in grand style, and Ross for a few minutes had a warm time, but McQue got in a big kick, and Miller and his supports were again causing trouble to the Fairfield defenders, **Cameron** with an awkward curling shot, increased the score of Liverpool to

4, and with this result the game ended in a decided victory for Liverpool by 4 goals to 1, and once more the Anfield club head the Lancashire League.

RESULT: Fairfield 1 - Liverpool 4

LIVERPOOL: Ross (goal); Hannah and McLean (backs); McCartney, M. McQue and McBride (halves); Wyllie [1], Cameron [1], Miller [1], McVean and H. McQueen [1] (forwards).
FAIRFIELD: Slater (goal); Bennett and Handford (backs); Dought, Ramage and Stuart (halves); Doughty, Hodgkinson, Egan, Handford and James (forwards). [1 anon]

Another trip east, this time to the north of Manchester, took Liverpool to Heywood for a quick return against the Centralians from Heywood. Meteorologically, the day was a poor one, with a persistent strong wind blowing the length of the length of a field which was inches deep in uncleared snow, the conditions being such that good play was practically impossible.

07/01/1893 LL13: Heywood Central v. Liverpool
Liverpool Mercury - Monday 9th January, 1893

This return match was played at Heywood on Saturday. Considerable local interest was aroused, as the home supporters were anxious to see the team who had so soundly thrashed their players the week previous. Hannah lost the toss, and had to face a stiff breeze.

The homesters at once pressed, and early on secured a corner, which was cleared by McBride. Webster obtained possession and requisitioned Ross's defensive powers, but that ubiquitous individual was ever on the alert, and displayed his capabilities with undoubted effect. The pressure being eased Liverpool paid a visit to Sharples, but H. McQueen was unfortunate in shooting over, a feat which Wyllie repeated a little later. Pearson relieved and gave his forwards possession, and McWhinnie suffered hard lines in grazing the upright. Again was the Liverpool goal in jeopardy, as Heywood infused a great amount of dash into their play, and unsuccessfully claimed a goal for the leather being over the line when Ross finally cleared. Playing with redoubled energy the Heywood team were at last rewarded, as for a very questionable foul given against Liverpool **Woolfall** notched the first point. Although maintaining the advantage in play, the home team had not increased their score up to half-time.

Liverpool, who now had the assistance of the wind, attacked strongly, but the defence of Evans and Pearson was exceptionally fine, and for a spell all the efforts of the visitors were neutralised. Then Hannah had to exhibit remarkable promptness and agility to save his goal, but gradually the visitors were assuming the upper hand, and before long that most prolific scorer of the team, **Wyllie**, had notched his usual goal. After this success the Liverpool players continuously peppered Sharples from all positions, and it appeared as though life and the fates were going to defy all attempts to lower his citadel; but **McBride**, who had sent in several magnificent shies, was at last rewarded in seeing one of the curlers completely baffle the home custodian. From the outset the visitors held full command of the game, but were unable to increase the score, and thus maintained their position at the top of the league by:

RESULT: Heywood Central 1 – Liverpool 5

LIVERPOOL: Ross (goal); Hannah and McLean (backs); McCartney, M. McQue and McBride [1] (halves); Wyllie [1], M. McQueen, Miller, McVean and H. McQueen (forwards).
HEYWOOD: Sharples (goal); Pearson and Evans (backs); Woolfall [1], Scholes and Reagan (halves); Jones, McWhinnie, Horsfield, Allan and Webster (forwards).

A third successive away match in the Lancashire League took Liverpool to West Manchester. Conditions for the game were even worse than the previous week, again spoiling any prospect of good football.

14/01/1893 LL14: West Manchester v. Liverpool
Liverpool Mercury - Monday 16 January 1893

This return fixture was played at Manchester on Saturday before 3000 spectators. A severe frost on Friday night following the thaw in midweek had covered the ground with sheets of ice, which had been covered with a sprinkling of sand. The state of the ground, together with a fierce biting windy which blew across it, totally spoilt the game, from a spectators point of view.

Miller kicked off, but the homesters were first to the front with a corner. McLean headed out and McCartney raced up the right and gave to Wyllie, but that player's final shot was yards wide. Heavy kicking by both sides predominated for some time, till at length Bridge roused the spectators by a grand individual effort on the home right, finishing up with a capital centre, which Bogie ought to have converted, but placed high over the bar instead. McQue then fed Miller, who with McVean and McQueen confined the play in the home half, a shot by Wyllie just topping the bar.

In the second half the homesters became more decided in their attack, and Ross had to deal with several queer shots which came curling in with the crosswind, but the Liverpool custodian, with one exception, was very clean with his saves. Towards the close it looked as though Miller was going to repeat his performance of the first match, for he got through in capital style, but was blocked by Russell in the act of shooting. Both sides were visited in turn, and Suggs height enabled him to clear a capital corner by McCartney, and then McBride was applauded for saving at a critical moment. A pleasantly contested game ended in a draw.

RESULT: West Manchester 0 – Liverpool 0

LIVERPOOL: Ross (goal); Hannah and McLean (backs); McCartney, McQue and McBride (halves); Wyllie, M. McQueen, Miller, McVean, and H. McQueen (forwards).
W. MANCHESTER: Sugg (goal); Burrows and Russell (backs); Spiers, Pickering and Allison (halves); Bridge, Walsh, Bogie, Iddon and Waring (forwards).

Liverpool next indulged in a trial of strength against one of their championship rivals, facing the Bury club in an ordinary match at Gigg Lane. Matt McQueen filled in for Hannah who had taken a knock in the previous game.

21/01/1893 OM: Bury v. Liverpool
Liverpool Mercury - Monday 23 January 1893

At Bury, before 4000 spectators. Liverpool won the toss, and took advantage of a strong wind. The visitors showed superior tactics, but were very weak in shooting. Bury, on the other hand, put in more attempts, but McLean defended well.

The play during the second half was very even, and neither side gaining any advantage the result was a draw, neither side having scored.

RESULT: Bury 0 – Liverpool 0

LIVERPOOL: Ross (goal); M. McQueen and McLean (backs); McCartney, McQue and McBride (halves); Wyllie, Smith, McVean, Miller and Kelvin (forwards).
BURY: not available.

A tragic incident occurred when, shortly after the end of the match, a young man was seen to climb a hoarding at York Street, about a mile from the Gigg Lane ground, and then cast himself into a body of still water at a site known locally as 'Old Charley's Lodge'. Police were summoned by a witness but arrived too late, the subject having already drowned. Upon recovery of the body, the victim was identified as Joshua Ashworth, aged 26, a labourer for Bury Corporation who was due to have been married the following week. He had collected his weekly wages on the morning of the match, but from the absence of cash and presence of betting slips in his pockets it appeared he had lost the whole amount betting on his favourites to win. Despair at this loss and it's consequences was believed to be the reason for his suicide.

In the first round proper of the Lancashire Senior Cup Liverpool were drawn at home to Darwen. The Darreners had lost their place in the Football League at the end of the previous season but had then been elected as founder members of the new Division Two, in which competition they were now doing well. The Darreners were also accomplished cup fighters, having some years earlier been the first Northern side to reach the semi-finals of the national competition. Hannah returned to the side despite being less than 100% match fit.

28/01/1893 LSC-R1: Liverpool v. Darwen
Liverpool Mercury - Monday 30th January, 1893

The appearance of the Liverpool ground at Anfield on Saturday reminded one of the days when large crowds wended their way thither. Fully 8000 spectators assembled in anticipation of witnessing a closely contested game, in which they were not disappointed. The ground was in capital going order, and as both teams had undergone extra preparation, the excitement became intense as McKenna kicked off to time.

Darwen had the best of the opening exchanges, Entwhistle, on the visitors' left, being early noticeable for a fast sprint, but Hannah interfered, and enabled McCartney to put across to McQueen, who, being tackled by Leach, judiciously crossed to the right wing, where Wyllie forced a throw in from McAvoy. This McCartney sent well in, and a corner resulted, which, being grandly placed, was easily converted by **McVean**. This unlooked-for success inspired the Liverpudlians to greater efforts, and for a time they were masters of the situation, but the exceptionally fine defence of Orr and Leach allowed of no dilatory action, and from one of the formers tremendous kicks Wade and Campbell got into a telling swing, which left McLean in a dilemma, and danger seemed imminent, but Hannah interposing just in time, McQue, who was playing a skilful game, passed over to the right, and Smith and Wyllie outmanoeuvred all, and scored a corner. The ball was well placed and bobbed about in tantalising fashion. McVean missed when his partner had attended to the goalkeeper. Again the visitors forwards, fed by Maxwell, went rushing towards McQueen in formidable array, Entwhistle and the right wing being the most dangerous, and from a shot by the former McQueen had to be remarkably smart to save a downfall. Half-time arrived with Liverpool leading by a goal, but having to face a strong wind which had been of material assistance to them during the first portion of the game.

Miller recommenced operations, and McVean and McQueen brought the leather well up on the left, but had the misfortune to run over the line. Darwen retaliated, and Matthew McQueen deservedly earned a round of applause for robbing Wade, by a supreme effort, in the act of shooting. Liverpool delighted their supporters by their form, and, though playing against the wind, had as much of the game of their opponents. Fortunately, McLean and Hannah improved as the game went on, and, with discreet play by their halves the visitors were kept at bay. Miller then executed a pretty dribble down the centre, and put out to McQueen, but Wyllie just missed the desired space by a shave. Towards the end Liverpool pressed severely, and shots by McVean, Smith, and Wyllie were deserving of a better fate than they received. When Mr. Stacey blew his whistle on completion of time, leaving Liverpool winners by one goal to nil, the cheering was most hearty, and the team received the congratulations of all.

RESULT: Liverpool 1 – Darwen 0

LIVERPOOL: Ross (goal); Hannah and McLean (backs); McCartney, McQue and M. McQueen (halves); Wyllie, Smith, Miller, McVean [1] and H.McQueen (forwards).
DARWEN: Kenyon (goal); Leach and Orr (backs); Fish, Maxwell and McAvoy (halves); Wade, Campbell, Sutherland, McKenna and Entwhistle (forwards).

Darwen objected over eligibility of McQueen brothers on the grounds they had played in Scotland during the close season. The objection was subsequently overruled.

Liverpool's next visitors were Stoke, founder members of the Football League but whose experience in that competition so far had been less than stellar. In three campaigns in that competition they had twice finished bottom and once second from bottom. This season, however, was showing a marked improvement.

04/02/1893 OM: Liverpool v. Stoke
Liverpool Mercury - Monday 6th February, 1893

This friendly game was played at Anfield on Saturday, in the presence of only about 1000 spectators, the smallness of the number being due to the great attraction of the English cup tie[11] in the immediate neighbourhood. Both teams were strongly represented, Underwood and Hannah being the only absentees.

Miller kicked off, and, after a few exchanges, Naughton and Dickenson made headway on the Stoke right, and the home backs bungling, **Naughton** was enabled to score a rather easy shot within three minutes. This unlooked-for reverse appeared rather to nettle the home team, as they livened up considerably, and a judicious pass by Miller to McQueen, who in turn centred accurately, was the means of menacing danger to Rowley, but the international took matters very coolly, and easily cleared. Dickenson was making off at top speed when McBride interposed and robbed him in a magnificent manner, putting in to the goalmouth, so that **Miller** was given a chance to equalise, which he took full advantage of. Up to half-time the game was earnestly contested, Liverpool having slightly the most of the play; Wyllie and McQue putting in two capital shots for them, while Brodie and Schofield were very near doing the trick for Stoke.

In the second half, Stoke increased the pace, and rapid sprints by Schofield and Naughton were a source of danger to Ross, but the home custodian was in good form, and it was only when hampered by his own side and opposing forwards that **Baker** was allowed to secure a second point for Stoke with a high shot. Just on time Smith and Miller made brilliant individual efforts to score, and Rowley decidedly lucky in dealing with a header from Smith. Immediately afterwards the whistle was blown and Stoke were victorious:

RESULT: Liverpool 1 – Stoke 2

LIVERPOOL: Ross (goal); M. McQueen and McLean (backs); McCartney, McQue and McBride (halves); Wyllie, Smith, Miller [1], McVean and H. McQueen (forwards).
STOKE: Rowley (goal); Clare and Bateman (backs); Christie, Proctor and Brodie (halves); Naughton [1], Dickenson, Baker [1], Schofield and Evans (forwards).

Liverpool travelled to Gigg Lane for a top of the table clash that looked certain to have a huge impact on the championship race, Bury's slip up at Southport the previous week week having left the championship race tighter than ever. The reporter's contention that this match "practically settles the championship" was somewhat premature, however, as subsequent events would prove.

---

11   Everton v Nottm. Forest at Goodison.

11/02/1893 LL15: Bury v. Liverpool
Liverpool Mercury - Monday 13th February, 1893

This match which practically settles the championship of the League took place at Bury on Saturday. Recognizing the importance of the game a large crowd, numbering fully 8000, assembled round the enclosure. Liverpool were without their smart left winger, Hugh McQueen; who, unfortunately, is laid up with an injured thigh. This necessitated the inclusion of Hannah, who has not by any means recovered from the injury to his toe-joint, while M. McQueen filled his brother's place. Punctually the teams lined up.

Miller kicked off, while Smith took up the pass, but Jobson intervened and gave to his left wing, Platt and Bourn, who, outwitting McCartney, centred quickly, and Wilkinson tested Ross with a spanking shot within a minute of the kickoff. Liverpool replied, with a smart run up on the left by McQueen, which resulted in a corner, which proved of no avail. The high wind greatly interfered with play, and, after a period of high kicking, Clegg earned applause for neatly robbing McQueen, but he in turn was dispossessed by McBride. And then pretty combination was shown by the visitors, in which all the forwards took part, but the vigorous play of Warburton removed the danger, and Plant sent in a long shot which, by the help of the wind, nearly took effect. McLean headed clear, only to see Spence shoot hard in, but Rose was ever ready, and saved in a remarkable manner. The next item was a series of corners gained by the homesters, and it was surprising how Plant on one side and Wilkinson on the other managed to gauge the wind to such a nicety, for only two corners of theirs were put out during the whole game. Thanks to Ross and McLean, danger was staved off for a time, but the long kicks of the home half-backs, and the swift rushes of Barbour and his wings were a constant source of trouble. Another series of corners accrued, and Plant placing finely **Barbour** headed through, after 35 minutes play. This success roused unbounded enthusiasm, and, urged on by the cries of their supporters, the "Shakers" penned Liverpool pretty well during the remainder of the first half, but did not increase their score.

Liverpool opened well on changing ends, a splendid attempt by McQueen being only a trifle high. Bury, who were now facing the wind, put a lot of dash into their play, and before long were swarming around Ross. McLean and Hannah generally stopped the shots, but allowed the homesters to gain several corners, from one of which **Plant** headed through the second point. This virtually settled the game, as Liverpool were playing now in a listless fashion, which contrasted very unfavourably with the play of their opponents. Again the inevitable corner was obtained, and after being fisted out twice by Ross, it was returned and scrambled through before Ross could recover himself {*anon*}. Play now became of a scrambling nature, both teams seeming to have lost their temper, and the referee had to award several free kicks for fouls on both sides. When time was called, what should have been a good game ended in an easy win for Bury.

RESULT: Bury 3 – Liverpool 0

LIVERPOOL: Ross (goal); Hannah and McLean (backs); McCartney, McQue and McBride (halves); Wyllie, Smith, Miller, McVean and Kelvin (forwards).
BURY: Lowe (goal); Warburton and Holt (backs); Clegg, Jobson and Rose (halves); Plant [1], Bourn, Barbour [1], Spence and Wilkinson (forwards). [1 anon]

Liverpool next travelled to South Yorkshire for the return ordinary match against their opening day and, indeed, first ever opponents – Rotherham Town.

11/02/1893 OM: Rotherham Town v. Liverpool
Sheffield Independent - Monday 13th February, 1893

There were between 2000 and 3000 spectators on Clifton Grove Ground, yesterday, to witness a friendly match between the above clubs. The visitors put their full strength into the field, whilst Rotherham were without Pickering and Cutts, whose places were taken by Leather and Cross.

Losing the toss Rotherham kicked off towards the park, facing the sun and a strong wind. Liverpool had the best of the exchanges for the first 20 minutes, but were well kept at bay by the capital back play of the Rotherham men, Watson and Thicket (full backs) being especially prominent. McKaye, too, negotiated several difficult shots. At length McKean placed the ball in the net, but an appeal for infringement of the off-side rule was successful. Still the visitors pressed, and had a couple of fruitless corner kicks. After 35 minutes had expired, the Liverpool forwards made a neat run, and, in the scrimmage in the home goal, **M. McQueen** put on the finishing touch. From the free kick the home left wing ran down, and there was a hot scrimmage in the Liverpool goal, and further attacks from the same wing enabled **Longden** to equalise just before half-time.

When ends were changed the wind had modified somewhat, but the Rotherham men kept the leather well in the Liverpool quarters, and they had several times hard luck. Longden, Leather, and Leatherbarrow worked finely together, and once the former struck the upright. Fifteen minutes after the interval **Leather** neatly added a second goal for his side. From the centre kick the visitors ran down, but McKean shot across the home goal and the ball went out. Then from the goal kick the Rotherham left wing worked close in and forced Ross to concede a corner, and a second and third similar advantage occurred in succession. In eight minutes the visitors had equalised, Cameron shooting in, and Thickett attempting to clear headed into his own net {***own goal***}. On the restart Rotherham resolutely attacked, but they had hard lines, McCormick struck the crossbar. Ross just intervened in a capitally judged shot by Cross, Leather with a fine run looked like scoring, and there were repeated scrimmages in the visitors' goal. Once, however, the Liverpool men broke away, and at a dangerous moment Rodgers saved splendidly. But the pressure continued at the Liverpool goal, and a hard fought game resulted in a tie.

Rotherham Town 2 – Liverpool 2

LIVERPOOL: Ross (goal); Hannah and McLean (backs); McCartney, McQue and McBride (halves); Wyllie, M. McQueen [1], Miller, McVean and Cameron (forwards). [1 og]

ROTHERHAM: McKaye (goal); Watson and Thickett (backs); Barr, Brown and Rodgers (halves); Longden [1], Leather [1], Leatherbarrow, Cross and McCormick (forwards)

Next came a trip to Nelson to take on the League's wooden spoonists. The North Lancastrians had taken only five points from fifteen Lancashire League fixtures, leaving them firmly affixed to the foot of the table – a position brought about more by deficiencies in defence than attack. Whilst their forwards were scoring as freely as many of the teams above them, their backs were shipping goals at an alarming rate, providing the Liverpool forwards an ideal opportunity to recover their goalscoring form!

18/02/1893 LL16: Nelson v. Liverpool
Liverpool Mercury - Monday 20th February, 1893

The first meeting of these clubs took place at Nelson on Saturday. Although rain fell continuously a large and excited crowd assembled.

Miller kicked off against the wind, but with a slight incline in the visitors' favour, and immediately H. McQueen and McVean carried the leather into the corner, but the former placed the sphere on the net. The home right made an effort to get through. McBride interposed, and for a time Nelson were placed entirely on the defence, but weak shooting by the Liverpool forwards lost many chances. Splendid judgement by Almond allowed the homesters a look in, which, being well followed up, gave a few anxious moments to Ross; but McLean came rushing through, and **McVean** obtaining possession, dribbled past all opposition and scored. By Half-time Liverpool were leading by two goals, the second point coming from the toe of **Miller**.

Turning round, the Nelson team quickly added two goals and equalised {**Fairbairn & Almond**}, the Liverpool team taking matters too easy; but with the possibility of a defeat facing them they improved in their play, and **Miller**, by one of his brilliant efforts, placed his side in front, and having most of the remaining portion of the game Liverpool were recorded winners:

RESULT: Nelson 2 - Liverpool 3

LIVERPOOL: Ross (goal); Hannah and McLean (backs); McCartney, McQue and M. McBride (halves); Wyllie, M. McQueen, Miller [2], McVean [1] and H.McQueen (forwards).
NELSON: Matthews (goal); Leach and Craven (backs); Mack, McGuffie and Almond [1] (halves); Sanderson, Lightbown, Brown, Rushton and Fairbairn [1] (forwards).

For the second time in three weeks Liverpool entertained Stoke in an ordinary match at Anfield. Stoke having won the first encounter, and one at Stoke earlier in the season, the Liverpudlians were looking for some level of requital.

23/02/1893 OM: Liverpool v. Stoke
Liverpool Mercury - Friday 24th February, 1893

This return friendly match was played last evening at Anfield before a muster of about 1500 onlookers. Both teams were indifferently represented, Stoke being short of Schofield and their usual three half-backs, while Liverpool at the last moment found that Hannah, McQueen, and Smith were unable to assist them through injuries, and to make matters worse for the homesters, Kelvin, one of the substitutes, played but poorly.

Baker kicked off, and the opening stages were decidedly in favour of the visitors, their forwards being much more combined than those of Liverpool. Strong kicking by McLean gave temporary relief, and allowed McVean to get off with a tine run, but Miller misjudged the pass and put the ball over the touch line. Again the Stoke forwards threatened danger, but this was nullified by Dunn and Edge not taking up a pass from their right wing. Then McQue threaded his way down the field, and Clare only just saved when hard pressed. Long kicking by both sides prevailed for some time, a want of cohesion being evident among the Liverpool forwards, but Ross a little later on created some enthusiasm by a grand save under great difficulty. The game livened up somewhat at this stage, and Naughton and Dickenson kept McBride and McLean well on the move to avert danger. Ross was called upon to save from the former, and did so smartly, and then the home team had a look in, McQueen causing Rowley to use his hands, a feat which Wyllie and Miller repeated shortly afterwards. Timorous play by Kelvin lost a good opening for Liverpool, and then the whole of the visiting forwards executed a pretty movement which ended in the ball rolling harmlessly over the line. Half-time arrived and …

Miller restarted. At once he and his forwards moved towards Rowley, Underwood giving a corner to avert further danger from Wyllie. Again Liverpool were to the front and Clare and Underwood had to exert themselves to stave off defeat. Weak play by Wyllie gave Draycott a chance and giving to his left wing they outpaced MCartney and shot across to Naughton, who promptly gave Ross a very warm one to deal with, and be was rightly applauded for a grand clearance. McBride next brought himself into prominence for successfully tackling his opposing wing and giving to McVean, and that player when in the act of shooting being charged from behind, was awarded a foul, which, however was badly utilised. Liverpool now had slightly the best of the game, and with the many chances accorded them ought without a doubt to have scored. Miller, who played an unselfish game throughout now got through, and passed over to McQueen, but again Wyllie missed a possible opportunity. As time approached, the game became exciting and the players allowing discretion to fly to the winds "went" for each other in anything but scientific style, and fouls became frequent. But strive as they would neither side could score, and a rather uninteresting game resulted in a draw, no goals being scored.

RESULT: Liverpool 0 – Stoke 0

LIVERPOOL: Ross (goal); McCartney and McLean (backs); Cameron, McQue and McBride (halves); Wyllie, McVean, Miller, H. McQueen, and Kelvin (forwards).
STOKE: Rowley (goal); Clare and Underwood (backs); Thomson, Littlesales and Draycott (halves); Naughton, Dickenson, Baker, Edge and Dunn (forwards).

Liverpool next entertained Southport Central who the previous week had parted company with their veteran player-coach – the famous ex-Blackburn Rover and England International Joe Lofthouse. Lofthouse was suffering from the beginnings of a lung infection that would, in a few weeks, see him confined to bed and lead to several newspapers across the country, on May 16th that year, carrying the story of his sad demise. Those stories were greatly exaggerated, however, Lofthouse pulled through and even returned to football with the Walsall Town Swifts.

25/02/1893 LL17: Liverpool v. Southport Central
Liverpool Mercury - Monday 27th February, 1893

The first meeting of these clubs in the Lancashire League competition took place on Saturday, at Anfield, before 3000 spectators.

McCabe started on behalf of Southport, and immediately Devonport obtained a foul off McLean, but the ultimate aim was not successful. C. Gee then stopped McQueen and gave to Halsall, but McBride stepped in and judiciously passed to McQueen, and after some pretty exchanges and passes between them and **McVean**, the former completely baffled the Southport custodian with a fast high shot. The play of the home team now wonderfully improved, and they literally swarmed around Gee. McVean got through once very nicely, and gave to Miller, but Smith blocked the ball as the centre-forward was in the act of shooting. McCabe then obtained the leather from a goal kick, and put out W. Hastings, who darted off at top speed past Hannah, and Ross had to run out to save. Again the home team were in the old spot, and after **McQueen** had shot hard in twice over, persistency brought its reward, and he nonplussed Gee with a splendid shot. Wyllie then had hard luck with a capital header, which Gee only just managed to put over the bar. McVean sent sharply across the goalmouth, but the chance was not taken advantage of. Half-time found Liverpool leading by two goals, and after an uninteresting display in the second portion of play the result remain the same.

RESULT: Liverpool 2 – Southport Central 0

LIVERPOOL: Ross (goal); Hannah and McLean (backs); McCartney, McQue and McBride (halves); Wyllie, M. McQueen, Miller, McVean [1], and H. McQueen [1] (forwards).
SOUTHPORT: J. Gee (goal); Smith and Fairhurst (backs); C. Gee, Muir and Dodd (halves); Halsall, Devonport, McCabe, Winstanley and Hastings (forwards).

Anfield was next given over to the staging of the Grand Theatrical Football Gala, in benefit of the Stanley and Northern Hospitals, which had become an annual event at the ground during Everton's tenure there. The event included foot and bicycle races and other sporting events between the theatrical gentlemen whilst the ladies mingled with the crowd selling cigarettes, buttonholes, bon-bons, etc. The highlights of the event were two football matches; the first between teams of pantomime artistes representing Liverpool and Manchester, the players appearing in their full pantomime costumes; and the second between the Liverpool first eleven and an eleven of the Lancashire County Cricket Club, put together by the famous footballer and cricketer Frank Sugg.

03/03/1893 CH: Grand Theatrical Football Gala
Liverpool v. Lancashire C.C.
(also Liverpool Artistes v. Manchester Artistes)
Liverpool Mercury - Saturday 4th March, 1893

The fifth annual theatrical football gala, which originated with a committee of gentlemen in Liverpool, and is still carried on under that committee, was held yesterday afternoon at the grounds of the Liverpool Association football club, Anfield.

The weather and the fact that this gala was the second of the season[12] militated considerably against its success, there being only a moderate assembly. Arrived there the fun of the day began, and it must be said that one and all worked with a will to gain the smiles and the money of the spectators. The host of pantomimists - both ladies and gentlemen - from Manchester also assisted in no small degree to make matters lively. The reappearance of the "coster" and his "donah" (Messrs. Austin Harford and E. McKernan), assisted by an "undertaker" and a "Gringoire," was a signal for the opening of pockets, and "gags," songs, and the sale of "buttonholes," oranges, and cabbages brought in a considerable sum. The ladies with cigarettes, sweets, photographs, and other unconsidered trifles also succeeded in coining large amounts. Special calls were made on the committee box, in which were the Mayor (Mr. R.D. Holt), Mr. J.A. Willox, MP, Mr. Alderman Ruddin, Dr. Whitford, Dr. Flinn, Messrs. T. McCracken, J.H. Dunne, J a holding, H. Bruce, the Brownsville, Austin Taylor, Woods, Byrne, and others. The entertainment of the afternoon opened with various races for stagehands, ladies, gentlemen, and others, and considerable excitement and amusement were caused by the contest.

The great attraction of the afternoon was the match between the Liverpool and Manchester Pantomime Gentleman, and it must be said that, though both were playing in earnest there were many comical occurrences and situations, every one of which was fully appreciated by the onlookers. The Liverpool came out best by two goals to one, while in the tug of war Manchester succeeded in lowering the colours of the Mersey city. In the match between the Liverpool League team and the County Cricket XI also, there was plenty of amusement combined with a considerable amount of excitement, the final result being a draw of two goals each. Though there was not a great "gate," there can be no doubt that the opportunities offered were taken full advantage of, and, if expenses were heavy, there is every prospect of a substantial

---

12 Everton F.C. also staged an event.

sum being realized for the benefit of the Stanley Hospital, the Infirmary, and the children of the late Mr. Alfred Smith (the originator of the sports), in whose aid the match was arranged.

During the afternoon the band of the 12th Royal Lancers gave a selection of music. Prior to the opening of the grounds the committee were entertained by Mr. McCracken and Mr. Dunne at the Sandou hotel. Subsequently Mr. McCracken, in the name of the subscribers, made a presentation to Mr. John Houlding, in acknowledgement of his work on the committee and also of his attention to the wants of the Stanley Hospital. Mr. Houlding, in accepting the testimonial, which took the form of a silver punch bowl, said that it had always been his endeavour to serve the interests of the Stanley Hospital, as it was doing such good charitable work among the poorer classes of the north end.

RESULT: Liverpool 2 – Lancashire C.C. 2

LIVERPOOL: Exact line-up not known
LANCASHIRE C.C.: Not known

Some weeks later, the balance sheet for the event was published as follows:

INCOMINGS		OUTGOINGS	
Gate Money	£82 12s 0d	Printing/posting etc.	£73 15s 7d
Ladies Sales	£74 3s 0d	Gate Expenses	£5 11s 0d
Ticket Sales	£68 6s 6d	Rail Fares etc.	£53 2s 6d
Donations	£22 11s 0d	Band etc.	£14 4s 11d
Programme Advertising	£17 10S 3d	Sundries	£5 18s 6d
		Northern Hospital	£36 0s 0d
		Stanley Hospital	£36 0s 0d
		Children of A. Smith	£40 14s 7d
TOTAL	**£255 7s 9d**	**TOTAL**	**£255 7s 9d**

The next visitors to Anfield were Nelson, who the previous weekend had climbed off the bottom of the Lancashire League standings by thrashing fellow strugglers Higher Walton (who then took over as wooden spoonists) 11-2 at Nelson – the then bottom club thereby becoming the first Lancashire League club to reach a double-figure score in a League fixture that season! Inspired by that success the players had then been promised a bonus of 10 shillings a man to win at Anfield – the money being pledged by a local publican (5s. a man), the Club Committee (2s. 6d. a man) and Alderman Robert Hartley of the Nelson Town Council (2s. 6d. a man). Alternatively the players would receive 2s. 6d. each for a draw!

04/03/1893 LL18: Liverpool v. Nelson
Liverpool Mercury - Monday 6th March, 1893

These clubs met at Anfield on Saturday, to play the return engagement in the Lancashire League competition, before 2000 spectators.

Hannah won the toss, and are R. Brown (late of Stanley) kicked off against a strong wind and facing a glaring sun, but at once the home team, materially assisted by the elements, attacked strongly and within five minutes **M. McQueen** had drawn first blood for Liverpool. Still continuing to have much the best of the game, the home team, with few exceptions, were never out of the enemy's quarters, but so exceptionally fine was the defence of Matthews in goal, aided by Leach and Craven at back, that the Liverpool forwards failed to find another opening during the first portion of the game, although splendid attempts were made by Miller, McQueen, and McVean.

A lead of one goal was not a great advantage, considering the home team had to face the wind. However, realizing the position, Miller and his wings forced the play, and Wyllie, who seemed entirely out of form, missed a golden opportunity. Directly **M. McQueen** threaded his way through his opponents and scored with a magnificent shot, which Matthews had no possible chance with; and from a corner taken by Wyllie later on the same player headed against the crossbar. Almond relieved, and Sanderson was the means of obtaining a corner for Nelson, which was safely headed away by McLean. Again Liverpool were pressing, and from a foul taken by McLean, **Hugh McQueen** added a third goal for the Anfielders. This being the final point of the game ended by Liverpool winning:

RESULT: Liverpool 3 – Nelson 0

LIVERPOOL: Ross (goal); Hannah and McLean (backs); McCartney, McQue and M. McBride (halves); Wyllie, M. McQueen [2], Miller, McVean and H.McQueen [1] (forwards).
NELSON: Matthews (goal); Leach and Craven (backs); Mack, McGuffie and Almond (halves); Sanderson, {Lightbown}, Brown, {Rushton} and {Fairbairn} (forwards).
*Player names in braces {} are probable – **not** confirmed.*

By all accounts the Nelsonian's backs at least were inspired to heroic efforts in this match but were let down by their forwards who showed no sign of the lethality in front of goal that had inspired their committee's largesse. In any event, they all had good cause to rue the contributions of the McQueen brothers which had cost them dear –

10s. a man to be precise! Sanderson gamely played to the end despite breaking a finger in his left hand.

Liverpool entertained Aston Villa in the return ordinary match at Anfield – the turnout being a relatively poor one for a club of Villa's calibre. As in the first match, however, Villa fielded an essentially reserve XI, with only a handful owning any significant first team experience.

09/03/1893 OM: Liverpool v. Aston Villa
Liverpool Mercury - Friday 10th March, 1893

This game was played at Anfield last evening, before 2000 spectators.

Hannah won the toss, and played with a strong wind at his back. This great advantage caused the home team to be constantly on the aggressive, and during the first ten minutes the visitors were entirely confined to their own quarters. Excellent half-back play by McQue and McBride was responsible for **McQueen** gaining the first point, the visiting goalkeeper making but a very amateur attempt to save. Again the home forwards swooped down upon Benwell, and McVean narrowly missed scoring. Strong half-back play by Cowan and Brown gave Hodgetts and his partner a chance, but Hannah intervened and allowed M. McQueen to have another shy, which unfortunately for his side he sadly missed. From the kick off A. Brown obtained possession and ran past McLean, but McQue met his centre and cleared. Again the visitors right wing forced the play and passed to Hodgetts, who in turn gave to Woolley, and that player shot in splendidly, but the ball went over the goal line. Danger was only temporarily relieved, for again Hodgetts and Woolley were conspicuous for grand play, and the latter centring, **Skea**, appearing to be under the post and in an offside position, shot in and equalised. Liverpool retaliated, and McQueen was given two golden opportunities, but shot too high, and after McVean and McQueen had menaced the visitors citadel Baird gave relief, and the game became more open. Half-time was called, the teams having played only 30 minutes.

Miller restarted, and immediately McVean and his partner forged their way ahead, but the latter put out. Play now became very open and interesting, and after a period of midfield exchanges Hodgetts kicked strongly forward, and a bully was formed in the home goal mouth. McBride cleared, but **Skea**, a promising recruit, got hold of the leather, and by a long shot placed the Villa further ahead. The game had hardly been restarted when the same player {**Skea**} was fortunate to add another point, and although Liverpool had several chances later on, the weak play of the forwards failed to increase their score, and a pleasant game resulted in a win for the Villa:

RESULT: Liverpool 1 - Aston Villa 3

LIVERPOOL: Ross (goal); Hannah and McLean (backs); McCartney, M. McQue and McBride (halves); Wyllie, M. McQueen, McVean, H. McQueen [1] and Miller (forwards). [2 anon]

VILLA: Benwell (goal); Wollaston and Baird (backs); J. Brown, Cowan and Russell (halves); A. Brown, Skea [3], J. Devey, Hodgetts and Woolley (forwards).

In the Second Round of the Lancashire Senior Cup competition, Liverpool faced the short trip to Hawthorne Road, less than three miles North, to face Bootle in a local derby. Although Everton were away at Preston in the same competition, cheap specials for that match from Liverpool Exchange Station provided a counter attraction, as did an intriguing match at Goodison between Everton's second eleven and the famous St. Bernard's team from Edinburgh. Even so, sufficient local interest was centred in the match at Hawthorne Road to set a new record for gate receipts at Bootle in the sum of £219 1s. 6d.

11/03/1893 LSC-2: Bootle v. Liverpool
Liverpool Mercury - Monday 13th March, 1893

The meeting between these clubs had been looked forward to with great interest since they were drawn together in the Cup competition. About 8000 spectators lined the enclosure at Hawthorne Road, and excepting a strong wind everything tended towards an exciting game, Hannah, whose luck in tossing is proverbial, had the choice of ends, and availed himself of the no mean advantage of the aforesaid breeze and dazzling sun. Liverpool were the first to put in an appearance, and were met with a great cheer, but upon the home team showing up they received a great ovation, and were decidedly the favourites.

Punctually to time Grierson gave the initial kick, and at once Bootle were the attacking party, and when a foul occurred close to the Liverpool goal, the home supporters made themselves *en évidence* in an unmistakable manner. McCartney relieved, and McQueen nearly scored with a shot which skimmed the bar. Splendid defence by Arridge and the Bootle halves, combined with strong kicking, gave the leather to Montgomery, who dribbled into the centre of the field and then passed forward to Clarkin, who, rushing past McLean, sent in a fast shot, which Rose cleared, but **Gallocher** met the return, and banged the ball into the net. This well deserved success nearly drove the home supporters wild with delight, the cheering being terrific. Miller recommenced, but Hughes was too sharp for M. McQueen, and gave to his right, McQue intervened, and by a long shie gave the Liverpool forwards a chance, but they were too slow to take advantage of it. Arridge sent up the field with a big kick, and Grierson fisted out to Gallocher and Clarkin, and a weak attempt by McLean brought trouble upon Ross, the Liverpool goal having a very narrow escape. The venue of the game now changed, and Liverpool were found attacking strongly. A foul by Montgomery was well taken by McCartney, but only a fruitless corner resulted. McBride met the kick off, and a splendid shie by him was placed yards wide by M. McQueen. Another glorious opportunity was offered to the visitors by Hutchinson fouling close in goal, but McLean made very poor use of the chance. Montgomery caused a diversion on the home left by breaking away, but McLean stepped in and gave to H. McQueen, who was lavishly applauded for a grand shot, which McLachlan just managed to save. Timorous play by Wyllie lost an almost certain chance. The Bootle forwards livened up, and Hannah was severely pressed, being compelled to give a corner to avert danger. Robertson successfully tackled McVean and H. McQueen, but McBride took up his pass to the forwards, and tricking Grierson sent to Miller, who was not successful in his endeavours to get through for a shot. As half-time drew near excitement became intense, as after a long spell of pressure by Liverpool a cry of goal was taken up, but the shout was entirely wrong, as was seen after a few moments of suspense.

Immediately upon restarting a long kick by Arridge caused Ross to handle. Not to be denied, however, the home forwards, who were conspicuous for rare dash, swooped down upon the Liverpool defence, and after the visiting custodian had partially cleared a shot from Lafferty, he was unfortunately injured, and **Gallocher** had no difficulty in adding a second point for Bootle. The result was now counted upon as a foregone conclusion, as, with only ten men, and having to fight again wind and sun, the chance of Liverpool wiping out the two points against them seemed very remote. Matthew McQueen, "the utility man," was placed between the sticks. Upon resuming, Hughes was prominent for clever half-back play, while a foul by McCartney looked dangerous for Liverpool, but Clarkin eased the suspense by missing a grand chance given him by the home left. Two fouls against Booth carried the ball into their quarters, and Miller missed by the nearest shave. McQue met the kick off, and by a long punt forward enabled Miller and Wyllie to exercise a pretty piece of combination, which culminated in a good shot by Miller, but the ball glanced off the bar, and **H. McQueen** rushed up and scored for Liverpool. The visitors now played desperately for another point, and the game became very fast, neither side being able to claim any advantage. Grierson broke away nicely once or twice, but failed in shooting, and then McQueen brought off a marvellous save from what appeared to be a certainty from Montgomery. Fouls became rather frequent, Robertson, McEwan, and H. McQueen coming under the notice of the referee. Towards the end of the game Liverpool rushed up again, and it was only due to the determined back play of Arridge and Hutchinson that disaster was prevented at this critical period of the game. Neither side increased their score, and an exciting game ended in a win for Bootle:

RESULT: Bootle 2 – Liverpool 1

LIVERPOOL: Ross (goal); Hannah and McLean (backs); McCartney, M. McQue and McBride (halves); Wyllie, M. McQueen, Miller, McVean, H. McQueen [1] (forwards).
BOOTLE: McLachlan (goal); Hutchinson and Arridge (backs); Robertson, Hughes and McEwan (halves); Clarkin, Gallocher, Grierson, McLafferty and Montgomery (forwards).

Goalkeeper Ross had, in fact, badly broken his leg in a collision with Lafferty in the process of thwarting that player's attempt on goal – in injury which would keep him out of action for the remainder of the season and, in the short term, was serious enough to confine him to Stanley Hospital! In fact, Ross would never play for Liverpool again.

In the absence of Ross the versatile Matt McQueen took over again between the posts for the visit of Fairfield. Before the game Liverpool trailed Bury by a single point at the top of the League standings on 18 games each (from 22). With two home Lancashire League games in three days (during which period Bury had none), it was an ideal opportunity for Liverpool to put themselves clear at the top!

15/03/1893 LL19: Liverpool v. Fairfield
Liverpool Mercury - Friday 17th March, 1893

The return fixture between these clubs took place last evening at Anfield. Liverpool were minus the services of were Ross and Smith, the former being seriously ill from an injury received last Saturday.

Hannah won the toss, and Fairfield started against a stiff wind. Fairfield were the first to show up, but ere long superior skill, assisted by the elements, became ascendant, and the home team had much the best of the game. A foul near the Fairfield goal resulted in **McLean** scoring off one of the visitors', and by half time **Miller**[2] had obtained two other points, and made the game three goals to nil in favour of Liverpool.

Upon resuming, the home players, who showed a refreshing amount of vigour, were early to the fore, and Miller was not long in calling upon the visitors custodian to handle. Although playing with the wind Fairfield did not seriously threaten the home goal; and McCartney, McQue, and McBride (the Liverpool half backs), being in good form, the home forwards were given many chances, and from a clever piece of combination, which resulted in a corner, **Wyllie** scored the fourth goal, which was later on followed by another from a **McQueen** - a grand header - which the goalkeeper had no chance with, and the game ended in a decisive win for Liverpool:

RESULT: Liverpool 5 – Fairfield 0

LIVERPOOL: M. McQueen (goal); Hannah and McLean [1] (backs); McCartney, M. McQue and McBride (halves); Wyllie [1], McVean, Miller [2], H. McQueen [1] and Kelly (forwards).
FAIRFIELD: Slater (goal); Bennett and Handford (backs); Whatmough, Campbell and Stuart (halves); Platt, James, Handford, Egan and Doughty (forwards).

The destruction of Fairfield moved Liverpool into first place, now, with the season rapidly drawing to an end a similar result against South Shore could extend their lead to three points!

18/03/1893 LL20: Liverpool v. South Shore
Liverpool Mercury - Monday 20th March, 1893

This match was the attraction at Anfield on Saturday. South Shore were fully represented, whilst the home team were without Ross, their clever goalkeeper, but Smith, after a lengthened absence, reappeared.

Winning the toss the Blackpoolites defended the Oakfield goal, and promptly to time Miller gave the initial kick before fully 2000 spectators. Liverpool were the first to show up, Miller, Smith, and Wyllie putting in some pretty exchanges, and when the game was but five minutes old **Wyllie** had pierced his opponents defence. Following the kick off Taylor and Mather carried the ball into Liverpool quarters, and the home goal was threatened. McQue relieved and gave to Smith, who passed on to McQueen, and that player dribbled rapidly down the left, and centred so accurately that **McVean** was enabled to add a second point. Still maintaining a fierce fusillade, the home team, with the exception of occasional bursts away by Helliwell, Birchall, and Mather, kept Rose and Naylor fully employed, and by half time **Miller** had supplemented the score by a clever piece of work.

On turning round the home team fell away in their play, and went in for too much short passing, which generally resulted in losing the ball. South Shore profiting by this found Hannah and McLean much more work to do than previously, and before long McLean, through lying too far up the field, left Hannah to himself, who being determinedly tackled cleared in a very feeble style, which let in **Birchall**, who put in a terrific shot in McQueen's hands, which that player could not hold. This reverse caused the home team to put more effectiveness into their play, and **Miller** scored twice, but had the misfortune to have one goal disallowed. No further score accrued, and an interesting and fast game resulted in favour of Liverpool:

RESULT: Liverpool 4 - South Shore 1

LIVERPOOL: M. McQueen (goal); Hannah and McLean (backs); McCartney, McQue and M. McBride (halves); Wyllie [1], McVean [1], Miller [2], Smith and H. McQueen (forwards).
SOUTH SHORE: {Parker} (goal); Rose and Naylor (backs); {Atherton}, Helliwell and {Baldwin} (halves); Birchall [1], {Pratt}, Mather, {McNab} and Taylor (forwards).
*Player names in braces {} are probable – **not** confirmed.*

Liverpool next made their first appearance in the Liverpool Senior Cup, organised by the Liverpool and District F.A. and competed for by the eight leading clubs affiliated to that organisation. In the first round Anfielders had been drawn away to Chester F.C., but in return for a guarantee of £40 the Cestrians had been induced to switch the venue to Anfield.

22/03/1893 LiSC-1: Liverpool v. Chester
Liverpool Mercury - Thursday 23 March 1893

This tie which was originally fixed to be played at Chester, was decided at Anfield road last evening. Chester played their full strength[13], including Deighton and Wilson, late of the Caledonian's, whilst Liverpool were without Ross and Smith, neither of whom has yet recovered from his injuries. About 2000 spectators lined the enclosure.

Ashton started, and after the opening exchanges Liverpool settled down in the visitors' quarters, and when ten minutes had elapsed McQue placed the ball well into goal, and the home forwards rushed up and scrimmaged the first point through {***anon***}. Still keeping up the attack the homesters gave the Cestrians defence no rest, and corner after corner followed in quick succession. Hays saved a dangerous one, well put in by McLean, and giving to Ashton that player called upon McQueen to use his hands, who cleared in a most brilliant fashion. Liverpool again returned to the attack, and after good combination, McVean passed over to **McQueen**, who, having a possible chance, promptly banged the leather into the net. Chester then opened out somewhat and a series of exchanges took place between Hannah and McLean for Liverpool, and Porter and Wilson for the visitors', and when the half-time whistle blew Liverpool were found in the enemies quarters.

---

13 *Apart from the absence of their influential namesake right-back, Chester Powell.*

The second half opened in a spirited fashion, Chester being the first to the front, but only succeeded in crossing the goal line. Not to be denied, the visitors came again, and subjected the home goal to some severe pressure, and McQueen only saved amid great difficulty, a feat he was loudly applauded for. This did not suit the home team, and again they were masters of the situation, and dashing play by the forwards allowed the visitors' no rest, and a foul occurring close into goal, **Hannah** was enabled to score a third point by judicious placing of the ball. The play of the Cestrians here improved, especially in the forward division, and the game became more open than hitherto, but so solid was the defence of McQue, McBride, and McLean, that danger was generally relieved before reaching McQueen, although Hays gave the latter a scorching shot which deserved to score. During the last few minutes of the game McVean, Miller, and McQueen worked in a most determined manner, and **McVean** obtained a fourth goal, while McQueen struck the crossbar with a terrific shot, which point ought to have had a better fate. When time was called the home team had won their way into the semifinal.

RESULT: Liverpool 4 – Chester 0

LIVERPOOL: M. McQueen (goal); Hannah [1] and McLean (backs); McCartney, M. McQue and McBride (halves); Wyllie, McVean [1], Miller, Cameron and H. McQueen [1] (forwards). [1 anon]
CHESTER: Pay (goal); Owen and Wilson (backs); Astbury, Porter and Carter (halves); Deighton, Fleming, Ashton, Hays and Lewis (forwards).
Referee: Mr. Armitt.

Liverpool next joined with Bootle to give a benefit game for David Kirkwood, a player who had never figured with either club! Kirkwood was well known to Liverpool Club founder and President John Houlding, however, having been Everton's regular left-half in their League Championship winning season of 1890/91 - during Houlding's presidency of the 'Toffees'. Released midway through the following season Kirkwood had then returned to his native Scotland with the Broxburn club, but had then been tempted back to Liverpool at the start of the current season to play with the Caledonians. It was whilst playing for the "Callies" in a Lancashire League fixture at South Shore towards the end of November, 1892, that Kirkwood had suffered a compound leg fracture in a collision with the Shoreites centre-forward, Mather, that had brought an end to his footballing career. That was less than a month before the Caledonians club had folded, and consequently Houlding and Liverpool had stepped in to provide him a much needed benefit.

23/03/1893 BM: Liverpool v. Bootle
Liverpool Mercury - Friday 24th March, 1893

This friendly game, by the kindness of the executives of the competing clubs, took place at the Anfield enclosure last evening, before 2000 spectators. Seeing the great favourite this unfortunate player was, it seems inexplicable that a much greater number were not present to show their sympathy with him in his distress. From the money taken at the gate, together with the expected sale of tickets, it is computed that the Liverpool secretary will be enabled to hand over, when all accounts are paid, about £50. When the teams lined up it was seen that both sides were not at their full strength, the most noticeable absentees being Ross and McCartney on the Liverpool side, and McEwan and Mc Lafferty of the Bootle team.

The game opened rather tamely, but after some heavy kicking by both pairs of backs the Liverpool team settled down into some very pretty passing, and working with more method than their opponents they were the first to attack, Smith putting in a great effort to reduce the Bootle goal. McVean followed with a rattling shot which, had it been more correctly directed, could not have failed in its desired object. Montgomery next had an attack, and Jones, a second team player, who throughout the game showed to good advantage, finished up with a nicely judged shot, which the home custodian as cleverly cleared. After Brandon had followed with another hot shot, the homesters gave a fine display of combination, and a curious decision on the part of the referee gave them a corner, which McBride skied over the bar. Selfishness on the part of Wyllie lost the home team a chance, and then Brandon, Jones, and Montgomery got away in characteristic style, but when danger was imminent Montgomery spoilt the previous good effort by shooting wide of the post. Hughes met the goal kick and tipped to his right wing but McBride pluckily tackled Clarkin, and Smith obtaining possession, compelled Whitehead to fist out. Bootle returned to the attack, and were pressing at half-time.

Bootle reopened in capital style, good defence by Arridge and Hughes keeping the Liverpool forwards at bay, and McQueen had to negotiate several shots from Brandon, Jones, and Gallocher. At length Hannah cleared effectually, and McVean and Wyllie sprinted up the right wing, the latter sending across in magnificent fashion, but the home left failed to utilise the opportunity. Splendid play by the Liverpool halves now confined the game in their opponents quarters; Miller sending in to Whitehead, who saved in nice style when hardly pressed. A rapid burst away by Jones and Montgomery, and Hannah only just nipped in in time to save what looked like a certain goal. McBride then showed good judgement, and dropped ,the leather in front of Whitehead, and before he could effect a clearance **Miller** and McVean rushed the ball through, thus scoring the first point for Liverpool. Nothing daunted, Bootle played up with great dash, but the home team if anything maintained the advantage to the finish, and won a clever game by a goal to nil.

RESULT: Liverpool 1 – Bootle 0

LIVERPOOL: M. McQueen (goal); Hannah and McLean (backs); Cameron, M. McQue and McBride (halves); Wyllie, McVean, Miller, Smith, H. McQueen (forwards).
BOOTLE: Whitehead (goal); Hutchinson and Arridge (backs); Robertson, Hughes and Grierson (halves); Clarkin, Gallocher, Brandon, Jones and Montgomery (forwards).

Liverpool entered into their penultimate Lancashire League fixture, and the last at Anfield, with the championship of that competition still hanging very much in the balance. Liverpool led Bury by three points in the standings, but the Shakers had two games in hand, enough to leap-frog the Anfielders if they maintained a perfect record. After playing three games in the previous seven days, however, Liverpool could not raise a full eleven of fit men for the visit of Rossendae. Consequently, rather than play a man short or risk injury to a man only half-fit, trainer Wally Richardson, who earlier in life had played football in the military, made up the numbers at left-half. On the same day, Everton were contesting Wolverhampton Wanderers in the Final tie of the F.A. Cup, and as the tie was being staged at the Fallowfield Stadium in Manchester much of the City had made the relatively short journey.

25/03/1893 LL21: Liverpool v. Rossendale
Liverpool Mercury - Monday 27th March, 1893

This, the last of the Lancashire League fixtures at Anfield, was played before about 2000 spectators on Saturday. Rossendale were fully represented, and included Alexander (late of Accrington), but the home team were short of Ross and McCartney.

Ireland set the ball in motion, and by dashing play the Rossendale forwards carried the leather in close proximity to McQueen, and before long the latter had to use his hands twice. Liverpool did not appear to be able to pull themselves together for a bit, and it was owing to the stubborn defence that the visitors' did not score. Then Miller led up an attack, and the ball remained in the vicinity of the visitors' goal, and McQue, getting a chance, placed the leather nicely in, and McVean and Miller rushed up and scored {**Smith**[14]}. After Liverpool had maintained a long bombardment of their opponents' goal, **Ireland** sprinted down the centre of the field, and a mistake by McLean, who otherwise played a fine game, allowed the former an opening, which he immediately took advantage of, and equalised. Liverpool scored again from a well placed corner by McQueen, **McVean** being the operator, and a hard fought game resulted in a win for Liverpool:

RESULT: Liverpool 2 - Rossendale 1

LIVERPOOL: M. McQueen (goal); Hannah and McLean (backs); Richardson, M. McQue and McBride [1] (halves); Wyllie, Smith [1], Miller, McVean [1] and H. McQueen (forwards).
ROSSENDALE: Holden (goal); {Blears} and Davis (backs); {Alston}, {Weir} and {Spencer} (halves); Radcliffe, Ireland [1] {Duckworth}, {Sharples}, and {Alexander} (forwards).
Player names in braces {} are probable – **not** confirmed.

Liverpool began their Easter programme with a return ordinary match against Darwen on Good Friday. The previous Saturday the Darreners had ended their Football League Second Division campaign with a crushing 6-1 victory over a strong Grimsby Town outfit. Like Liverpool, the Darreners had been contenders for their championship for most of the season, but in the final accounting had finished only third.

31/04/1893 OM: Liverpool v. Darwen
Liverpool Mercury - Saturday 1st April, 1893

The fixture played at Anfield proved to be a good attraction, as fully 5000 spectators turned out to witness a second edition of the Lancashire Cup tie, played on the same ground some time ago. Darwen, turned out as advertised, while the home team had to dispense with the services of Ross. Punctually the teams lined up.

---

14 Other sources attribute Smith with the goal.

McKnight gave the initial kick against a slight wind and after a brief attack by the Darreners, effective play by McQue carried the ball into the visitors' goalmouth, an abortive foul occurring early on in the game. Judicious play by Miller led up to a strong assault, and Leach and Orr were called upon to exert themselves, and, a second foul being awarded against the visitors', the excitement rose as a probable chance of scoring accrued. Kenyon, however, used his hands with great effect, and then Rennie eased the abnormal pressure by a pretty run, in which Hannah showed to great advantage, in nipping in and taking up the latter's pass and so removing the source of danger. Liverpool returned to the attack in taking style, and often looked like scoring, but the vigorous defence of Orr, Maxwell, and McEvoy neutralised the efforts of the Liverpudlian's time after time, but the persistence of the home team was at last rewarded, for Hannah, tackling Sutherland in nice fashion, gave to Miller, who, having no opening himself, passed on to **Wyllie**, and that player opened the score with a swift low shot. The game continued to be of the same hard going stamp, both sides striving at every nerve, and Darwen twice over had rather hard luck in not equalising, although the home team commanded most of the play.

Upon the reopening the visitors asserted a slight superiority, but McQue, with Hannah and McLean, eventually wore the attack down, and, after the Anfielders had essayed to get through, the previous keenness of the players fell away, and both sides slowed down. After a period of indifferent play, Liverpool by a sequence of throws in again were the assaulting party, but, try as they would, they could not get through the grand defence of Darwen. Towards the end both sides seemed to be reinvigorated and several escapes of both goals passed by, but the backs were so exceptionally good that the danger was repulsed, and a most interesting and hard fought game ended in a win for Liverpool by:

RESULT: Liverpool 1 – Darwen 0

LIVERPOOL: M. McQueen (goal); Hannah and McLean (backs); McCartney, McQue and McBride (halves); Wyllie [1], Smith, Miller, McVean and H.McQueen (forwards).
DARWEN: Kenyon (goal); Leach and Orr (backs); Fish, Maxwell and McAvoy (halves); Wade, Campbell, Sutherland, McKnight and Rennie (forwards).

Liverpool's second Easter fixture took them to the North East for a return ordinary match against Stockton, who themselves had been in Liverpool the day before for a Good Friday fixture at Bootle (the latter winning 2-1).

01/04/1893 OM: Stockton v. Liverpool
Liverpool Mercury - Monday 3rd April, 1893

This game was played at Stockton on Saturday, in fine weather, before 2000 spectators.

Hannah, having won the toss, elected to play with a strong breeze, and Thompson kicked off for Stockton. Immediately Miller and Wyllie forged their way through, and sending out to **McVean**, that player rushed off at full speed and scored with a splendid fast shot. Immediately upon restarting the visitors centre almost repeated the trick, and then Liverpool assumed a distinct advantage, and Stockton were sorely pressed. Before long **Miller** put another goal to the credit of the visitors', which caused the homesters to liven up, and Jones, McLung, and Townley all had shies at McQueen, who was, however, very safe. Liverpool now took matters are very quietly, and half-time arrived with Liverpool leading.

When the game recommenced Stockton besieged McQueen, but it was some time before **Jones** headed through, and just when time was about to be called **McLung** sent through and equalised, the match thus ending in a draw.

RESULT: Stockton 2 - Liverpool 2

LIVERPOOL: M. McQueen (goal); Hannah and {McLean} (backs); {McCartney}, {McQue} and {McBride} (halves); Wyllie, {Smith}, Miller [1], McVean [1] and {H.McQueen} (forwards).
STOCKTON: {Ramsay} (goal); {Shaw} and {McDermid} (backs); {Willocks}, {Cochrane}, {Hutton} (halves); {Atkin}, Townley, McLung [1], Thompson and Jones [1] (forwards).

This match indirectly led to something of a furore in the North East since Stockton had in fact been instructed by the Cleveland F.A. to meet Darlington at Middlesbrough on this date to replay the Final of the Cleveland Professional Cup – the clubs having drawn 2-2 in the original encounter. Having already arranged the friendly with Liverpool, the Stockton Committee, immediately after the drawn game, had advised the Cleveland F.A. of their prior commitment for April 1st and consequent unavailability to play the replay on that date, but the latter had then ordered them to proceed with the replay on that one date anyway. Stockton had then written back "We cannot give up our Liverpool engagement and throw away a good 'gate', and if you persist in having the game played on the 1st there will only be one team there." Fine testimony to the drawing power of the Anfielders that their visit should promise to be so lucrative as to be preferred to a Cup Final, albeit a local one! Stockton had then stuck to their guns and entertained Liverpool at Stockton, but as a consequence of their refusal to play in the Final, the Cleveland F.A. had awarded the cup to Darlington and suspended the Stockton club for the remainder of the season!

Next visitors to Anfield were the London Corinthians, it being quite a coup for such a new club to earn a date in the famous southern amateurs Easter tour. The Corinthians included several Internationals, including: Humphrey Percy Jones, the famous 14 times capped Welshman; Robert Cunliffe Gosling who had scored for England against Scotland just two days earlier; and Hugh Harrison who had gained his first cap in that match.

03/04/1893 OM: Liverpool v. Corinthians
Liverpool Mercury - Tuesday 4th April, 1893

This important fixture took place at Anfield last evening, before 3000 to 4000 spectators. The visitors had two of the International team who had represented England against Scotland on Saturday last. The university men turned out somewhat early. Hannah with his proverbial luck, won the toss, and this caused the Corinthians to defend the Anfield goal against a blinding sun.

Gosling commenced the game, and the visitors were at once to the front. Alexander putting in a rather wide shot. Liverpool then took up the running, and McBride put in a rattling shot, which McVean was just too late to convert. The visitors then had a turn, and, from a judicious pass by Wilson to Humphrey Jones, the latter player sent in a rather puzzling shot, which Hannah saved, but Kelly, meeting the ball, returned with such good effect that amidst the scrimmage formed in goal, the ball was nearly headed through. This state of affairs did not seem to suit the Liverpool team, and they carried the ball to the other end, from which resulted a fruitless corner. Still continuing on the attack, McVean got in with a grand sprint, and but for the timely interference of Pelly, who stepped in with a terrific sprint, calamity would have befallen the Corinthians. Liverpool then did too much passing and re-passing, which did not gain ground, while remarkable precision was shown by Dewhurst, Gosling, and Alexander in a pretty combination down the centre, in which the former brought McQueen to his knees in saving. The home team, by clever combination, brought the leather again to Wilkinson, McBride being especially prominent in bringing up the opposing forwards, and sending home with good effect. From one of his efforts a grand chance was offered, but Harris came to the rescue with a fine rush and cleared in capital style. But, still being on the aggressive, Smith led up a fine attack, which culminated in **Miller** scoring a capital goal, which success was greeted by enthusiastic cheers. The Corinthians followed this up with a splendid rush, and Gosling shot in with almost a successful effect. Even play then succeeded for a long time, and half-time arrived with Liverpool leading by one goal.

When the sphere had been restarted, the three inside Corinthian forwards showed nice passing, and then Liverpool assumed command, and Miller propelled a straight one, which nearly came off. Shortly afterwards a foul occurred in the visitors' quarters, which, being well taken by McLean, was turned into account by a rush of the forwards, **McQueen** giving the final touch, the only decent point in his play of the day, and thus an interesting and clever game resulted in a win for Liverpool:

RESULT: Liverpool 2 – Corinthians 0

LIVERPOOL: McQueen (goal); Hannah and McLean (backs); McCartney, McQue and McBride (halves); Wyllie, Smith, Miller [1], McVean and H.McQueen [1] (forwards).
CORINTHIANS: Wilkinson (goal); Harrison and Pelly (backs); Lawrence, Humphrey Jones and Wilson (halves); Stanborough, Dewhurst, Gosling, Alexander and Pryce Jones (forwards).

A first visit from 'overseas' opposition (albeit the Irish Sea!) came in the from of Cliftonville from that district of Belfast, Northern Ireland. With regular steam crossings between Belfast and Liverpool and both clubs grounds being within easy reach of the relevant docks, Liverpool was an ideal focal point for the Irishmen's short English tour. Again Liverpool faced a side boasting several Internationals, namely Crookston and Stansfield, although their Irish International, Clugston, was indisposed.

04/04/1893 OM: Liverpool v. Cliftonville
Liverpool Mercury - Wednesday 5th April, 1893

This fixture which on paper promised to be an interesting game, took place at Anfield last evening. Only a moderate attendance assembled, and owing to the indisposition of the home team to play the legitimate football, a very tame game resulted. The Cliftonville included a couple of internationals, Crookston and Stansfield, and, to their credit, they may be said to have shown far better form than their companions.

Liverpool at the commencement held complete sway, and the game had not long progressed when **McQueen**, with a capital side shot, and put the homesters in front. Shortly afterwards **Miller** threaded his way through the opposing defence, and obtained a second point; and although he and the other forwards were complete masters of the game, yet, by descending to gallery play, they were not able to increase their score by half-time, although Crookston had stopped several stinging shots in praiseworthy style.

Upon turning round the visitors played somewhat better, showing much more dash and cohesion, and McQueen, in goal, on one occasion had to be remarkably smart to stave off disaster from a good attempt by Stansfield. Brilliant play by McBride then led up an attack upon the visiting goal, and **Miller** again got through in inimitable style, and added a third point for Liverpool. Then followed a period of even play, Williamson and Stansfield both having shots at McQueen; while McVean also sent in a stinger, which was nicely got away, but the left wing of the Cliftonville, getting off with a nice run, sent across to **Stansfield**, and that individual scored for his side. Liverpool then threw off their lethargy, and made matters warm for Clinton, who, playing in splendid form was only beaten once again, **Smith** being the executor in this instance, and when the whistle blew the score read:

RESULT: Liverpool 4 – Cliftonville 1

LIVERPOOL: M. McQueen (goal); McCartney and McLean (backs); Cameron, McQue and McBride (halves); Wyllie, Smith [1], Miller [2], McVean and H.McQueen [1] (forwards).
CLIFTONVILLE: Clinton (goal); Crookston and {Thompson} (backs); {Crawford}, {Brown} and {McKee} (halves); {Anderson}, {Gibson}, Stansfield [1], {Williamson} and {Small} (forwards).
Player names in braces {} are probable – **not** confirmed.

The Anfielders ventured north for a first visit to St. James Park to visit another club newly formed that season – although in Newcastle United's case as the result of a merger between the older Newcastle East End and West End clubs. Delays on the 150 mile journey meant that Liverpool arrived just in time for the kick off.

08/04/1893 OM: Newcastle U v. Liverpool
Shields Daily Gazette - Monday 10th April, 1893

A good number of spectators were attracted to the St. James's Park, Newcastle, to witness the meeting of the above teams. The visitors played their full strength, including J. Smith, who used to play with the old East End team. Played before a good company in fine weather.

In the first half the game was evenly contested, and pretty passing was shown by both sides.

In the second half playing downhill United settled down to one long attack on the Liverpool goal. The forwards played splendidly, but all their efforts could not break the defence offered by McQueen and his backs, and the game ended without a point being scored.

RESULT: Newcastle Utd 0 - Liverpool 0

LIVERPOOL: M. McQueen (goal); Hannah and McLean (backs); McCartney, McQue and McBride (halves); Wyllie, Smith, Miller, McVean and H.McQueen (forwards).
NEWCASTLE UTD: Whitton (goal); Jeffrey and Miller (backs); Creilly, Graham and McKane (halves); Reay, Crate, Thomson, Pattison and Collins (forwards).

Liverpool travelled to Newtown in Wales to play the Welshmen, who they had knocked out of the English Cup, a return fixture in an ordinary match. The previous week Newtown had been humiliated to the tune of 9-0 at Goodison by Everton reserves, but on that occasion they had been without their two regular full-backs (Taylor and Townsend) who were playing for Wales against Ireland at Belfast.

10/04/1893 OM: Newtown v. Liverpool
Montgomeryshire Echo - Saturday 15th April, 1893

The last match of the season at Newtown was played on the Comings on Monday evening last between Liverpool and at Newtown. The Liverpool team won the toss and played downhill.

All through the first half the new town men were severely pressed, but through the excellent play of their backs - Taylor and Townsend - and also the goalkeeper Edwards, they withstood it and prevented any score being effected.

On reversing position of the game became more even, Newtown having several looks in, but they were very unlucky at the goal and could not score. The game was no doubt the best played at Newtown this season, the head work and beautiful passing of the

Liverpudlians being very clever. New town were also in excellent room and no more goals were scored on either side.

RESULT: Liverpool 0 – Newtown 0

LIVERPOOL: McQueen (goal); Hannah and McLean (backs); McCartney, M. McQue and Kelso (halves); Wyllie, Cameron, Miller, Kelly and H. McQueen (forwards).
NEWTOWN: Edwards (goal); Taylor and Townsend (backs); {Tucker}, {Chapman} and {Read} (halves); {Pryce-Jones}, {Evans}, {Worthington}, {Thomas} and {Morgan} (forwards).
*Player names in braces {} are probable – **not** confirmed.*

Liverpool travelled to Southport for their final League fixture having now been reduced to the position of outsiders for the championship. Blackpool shared the same number of points as Liverpool but had two games remaining to improve upon that to Liverpool's one. With Bury also waiting in the wings to take advantage of any slip, it certainly appeared that nothing less than a win would do.

15/04/1893 LL22: Southport Central v. Liverpool
Cricket and Football Field - Monday 17th April, 1893

At Southport. Considerable delay was caused by the non-arrival of the referee, and eventually, on the agreement of both sides, a local man officiated.

Liverpool started, Miller missing a chance, whilst at the other end Hastings shot over the bar. Smart play ensued and **Hastings** scored. Liverpool took up the attack and **Miller** equalised. A fruitless corner fell to the Sandgrounders, McCabe afterwards making a big effort for goal.

RESULT: Liverpool 1 – Southport Central 1

LIVERPOOL: McOwen (goal); Hannah and McLean (backs); McCartney, McQue and M. McQueen (halves); Wyllie, McVean, Miller [1], Kelly, and H. McQueen (forwards).
SOUTHPORT: {J. Gee} (goal); {Smith} and {Fairhurst} (backs); {C. Gee}, {Muir} and {Dodd} (halves); {Halsall}, {Devonport}, McCabe, {Winstanley} and Hastings [1] (forwards).
*Player names in braces {} are probable – **not** confirmed.*

Liverpool's draw meant that Blackpool could have taken the Lancashire League title with a win at Fleetwood. Like, Liverpool, however, Blackpool only managed a draw. Worse, at the end of that match the Blackpool left winger, Parkinson, who had incurred the ire of the Fleetwood supporters was brutally assaulted by a mob of the latter before he could leave the field and was beaten unconscious! Still, with Liverpool's League programme now complete, Blackpool only needed one more point from their last remaining fixture to claim the honours – a point they would now have to win without Parkinson!

Liverpool made the short trip to Bootle again in the semi-final of the Liverpool Senior Cup. With Everton having already booked a berth in the final the week previously after crushing Aintree Church 7-1 in the other 'semi' it was a chance for a first meeting between the prior and current occupants of the Anfield ground.

17/04/1893 LiSC-SF: Bootle v. Liverpool
Liverpool Mercury - Tuesday 18th April, 1893

This cup tie roused rather more than normal interest, as in the two previous meetings each side had secured a victory.

Fully 5000 spectators assembled when Miller started on behalf of Liverpool. A foul immediately resulted in Liverpool quarters, which being well taken by Hughes was allowed to pass out by his own forwards - a grand chance lost. Playing up strongly Bootle had rather the best of it, and a little indecision between Hannah and McLean almost cost them a tangible point. A nasty foul by McEwan caught the referee's eye, and being steered straight for goal by Hannah, the home team had a good look in. Fouls then became frequent, but nothing resulted, the defence on both sides coping in an efficient manner with all assaults. Miller worked up a grand opportunity, but missed wretchedly when he had the goal at his mercy. Half-time arrived with no score, the result being indicative of the play.

Upon resuming the game remained very even, and although Liverpool had the best of the midfield manoeuvrers no side could claim any decided advantage. Eventually a change became apparent, and when Hughes had to kick out to save, then Liverpool held command for some time. After the McQueen's had exhibited capital combination **Miller** worked his way round Arridge and scored for the Anfielders, this success being greeted with wild applause. Liverpool after this tried a long shot, which of course did not come off, and then Bootle pressed severely, but found Hannah and McLean in much better mood than at the commencement. McLean, receiving from McQue, laid up a final attempt, but McQueen just missed when he had the goal at his mercy, and the whistle sounding for full-time, Liverpool retired victors.

RESULT: Liverpool 1 – Bootle 0

LIVERPOOL: McOwen (goal); Hannah and McLean (backs); McCartney, M. McQue and McBride (halves); Wyllie, M. McQueen, Miller [1], McVean, H. McQueen (forwards).
BOOTLE: Jackson (goal); Hutchinson and Arridge (backs); Grierson, Hughes and McEwan (halves); Clarkin, Gallocher, Brandon, McLafferty and Montgomery (forwards).

There was much controversy in the press ahead of Liverpool's final tie against Everton in the Liverpool Senior Cup when Everton let it be known they intended to field their Combination (reserve) side in the match. The 'Toffees' justified this on the grounds that since they had fielded their reserve side in the earlier rounds those same players who had got them to the final deserved to play in it! Liverpool, however, saw it as an insult and suggested that in that case they too would play a reserve side. In the event, Everton put out a mostly reserve side but one that was at least bolstered by four of their top men and several more with at least some first team experience – but notably not including either Geary or Latta, their two most free-scoring forwards. Liverpool, meanwhile, relented and gave up their best. It was the first ever meeting at any level between John Houlding's current and former clubs.

22/04/1893 LiSC-F: Liverpool v. Everton
at Hawthorne Road (Bootle)
Liverpool Mercury - Monday 24th April, 1893

The final stage of the local cup competition was reached on Saturday, when Everton and Liverpool, who had not hitherto met, played for possession of the trophy for the next twelve months. Great interest was centred in the event, notwithstanding threats that only second teams would be placed in the field. Better councils at the last hour prevailed, and though Everton were dependent on a mixed XI, the sides were strong.

Everton were first to appear to be followed quickly by Liverpool, and each were well received. Herbie Arthur[15] was referee. Elliott won the toss, and Liverpool kicked off, in the presence of about 10,000 people, with the wind, but had to face the sun. The Anfield men lost no time in getting down to goal, and Williams was forced to give a corner in fisting out a fine shot by H. McQueen. Pressure was great, and another corner was conceded by Williams. A third flag kick was taken - all to no purpose. A foul was given against Everton, and this led up to some more hard defence, during which Williams put behind from McCartney's heading shot. Wyllie also aimed very well, and then Liverpool had to defend briefly, but Hannah checked the left wing. McVean ran down nicely, when Gordon kicked out. Liverpool had the best of the play so far, being quicker and better combined than their opponents. A good movement by Hartly, Macmillan, and Elliott was the cleverest thing up to now for Everton, but the ball went out, and on McLean kicking up McBride shot in beautifully and Williams saved finely to the high aim. Hands against Boyle broke up a raid by Everton, and this was followed by exciting and good play near Williams. M. McQueen screwed the ball just over the bar, and then H. McQueen sent across, but the pass could not be reached. McOwen was at length called upon, running out and clearing cleverly, and Liverpool again bothered the Everton backs for some minutes, but Chadwick put in some useful kicks. McLean was also effective until Gordon beat both him and McBride, though a shot was prevented. Gordon, after further pressure by Liverpool, with Murray, worked the ball along very neatly, when Hannah rushed across and removed the danger. In reply, M. McQueen defeated Doyle, and H. McQueen made a jumping charge at Holt in such a manner as to be reprimanded by the referee. McCartney was then penalised for holding, but the free kick was adroitly turned to Liverpool's advantage, as on Miller passing to **Wyllie** the latter scored a good goal with a low shot, Liverpool thus taking the lead after 35 minutes play. M. McQueen next had a fair chance, but was unsteady, and put wildly over the line. Chadwick stopped a hard one from a tussle at the corner, and then the ball went into the net from a free kick untouched. McQue dispossessed the Everton right wing very cleanly, and shortly following he and Murray were at combat, the referee, after explanations, deciding to throw the ball up. Liverpool took up the attack, and sustained it almost up to the interval, which arrived with Everton in a minority of one goal.

---

15 Famous former Blackburn Rover and England International.

On resuming McCartney fouled Macmillan, but Elliott could not quite succeed in heading into goal from Collins's place kick, and Gordon rattled in with good shots, forcing corners. Liverpool moved down on the right without getting in a shy at goal and in reply Coyle came out well for effective play against Wyllie and McVean. The ball was again propelled on the Everton right, but it went out, and then Wyllie had an opening. He would not tackle Williams, however, and the otherwise smart play proved abortive. Everton came smartly back, when Elliot headed behind. McLean was next cheered for grand work, and Liverpool looked likely to jump further ahead, as, on clustering in front of goal, Wyllie shot in hard and straight, but Williams saved brilliantly. ~~Everton~~ {Liverpool} tried once more to get the mastery of Boyle and succeeded, but Holt went to the rescue and was bowled over by M. McQueen. Coyle gave hands, and this threw H. McQueen on the ball, he shooting very fairly. A hot tussle in front of McOwen was the next incident, and so hard put to were Liverpool that three corners were exacted. These were not any use, and danger was soon experienced at the other end. Miller, however, just failed to take a fine centre by McVean. Holt fouled M. McQueen, and, after some play, Miller made poor use of an easy chance. Amidst great excitement both teams played determinedly, Everton, if anything, were more frequently on the attack, but there was a weakness at close quarters, Hartley invariably being too slow for the active defenders. The Liverpool right wing menaced goal once or twice, but Collins made a good save, whilst on another occasion Wyllie almost grazed the post on taking a running pass from his partner. Liverpool then resorted to kicking out, as Everton woke up for a determined effort to save the match. They were very near equalising in the last few minutes. A corner was given them, and during the scrimmage Everton alleged that the ball had been fisted deliberately by one of the backs, and claimed a penalty kick. This the referee would not allow. After consulting a linesman (Messrs. Holt and Lamont), Mr. Arthur threw up the ball, and, it having been kicked clear the whistle sounded, amidst much confusion, with the result:

RESULT: Liverpool 1 – Everton 0

LIVERPOOL: McOwen (goal); Hannah and McLean (backs); McCartney, M. McQue and McBride (halves); Wyllie [1], M. McQueen, Miller, McVean, H. McQueen (forwards).
EVERTON: Williams (goal); Chadwick and Collins (backs); Boyle, Holt and Coyle (halves); Gordon, Murray, Hartley, McMillan and Elliott (forwards).
Referee: anon.

After the match the Everton committee lodged a protest with the attending Liverpool and District F.A. officials against the alleged general incompetence of the referee. As a result of this protest the Cup was not presented, being withheld until the protest was properly considered. This consideration took place in a meeting of the F.A. at the Neptune Hotel on Monday, April 24th, when, after some debate, the protest was dismissed. Liverpool actually won two trophies that day whilst playing only one match.

Elsewhere, in the Lancashire League, games were afoot that would settle the destiny of the championship. With Liverpool's campaign already over either Bury or Blackpool could still have wrested the title from them – a win for Bury at South Shore would have enabled them to claim the title by superior goal average so long as Blackpool did not win. A win for Blackpool, or a draw if Bury did not win, would have given them the title on points. Either way, Liverpool could only watch from the sidelines as events unfolded.

The final furlong – end of season results for the championship contenders (figures in bold show potential points available):

	Blackpool	Pts		Bury	Pts		Liverpool	Pts	
04/03/93		25	**39**	10-0 v HEYWOOD C.	30	**38**	3-2 v NELSON	29	**37**
15/03/93		25	**39**		30	**38**	5-0 v FAIRFIELD	31	**37**
18/03/93	5-3 v ROSSENDALE	27	**39**		30	**38**	4-1 v SOUTH SHORE	33	**37**
25/03/93	5-0 at Higher Walton	29	**39**	4-0 v SOUTH SHORE	32	**38**	2-1 v ROSSENDALE	35	**37**
01/04/93	6-2 v HEYWOOD C.	31	**39**		32	**38**		35	**37**
03/04/93	6-2 v NELSON	33	**39**	5-1 v ROSSENDALE	34	**38**		35	**37**
04/04/93		33	**39**	2-3 at Fleetwood Rgrs	34	**36**		35	**37**
08/04/93	6-1 v HIGHER W.	35	**39**		34	**36**		35	**37**
15/04/93	1-1 at Fleetwood Rgrs	36	**38**		34	**36**	1-1 at Southport	36	**36**
22/04/93	0-1 at Southport C.	36	36	1-1 at South Shore	35	35		36	36

With neither Blackpool nor Bury achieving the results they required, Liverpool were confirmed Champions on goal average over Blackpool. See records section for month by month tables.

With only a week remaining until the end of the football season (April 30th) all competitions had been played out, but there was still time for Liverpool to try their mettle against some of the best county opposition, starting with the Bolton Wanderers.

24/04/1893 OM: Liverpool v. Bolton Wanderers
Liverpool Mercury - Tuesday 25 April 1893

This attractive fixture, which took place at Anfield last evening, was not supported so well as the merits of the teams demanded. About 1500 spectators were present when the teams faced each other. Neither side was at its full strength, but Liverpool was the greater sufferers, as both McQueen and McQue were totally unfit to play, from injuries received last Saturday.

The visitors', having the assistance of a strong wind, were the first to open out, and Cassidy ran over the goal line. Liverpool replied with a grand attempt by H. McQueen, which Somerville cleared with difficulty. Returning to the attack the Wanderers pressed, and **Tannahough** opened the score with a splendidly judged high shot. In no way disheartened, Liverpool came again, and the Wanderers goal was subjected to a severe spell of pressure, a magnificent attempt by McQueen striking the upright and rebounding into play, and which Smith just failed to reach. Heavy kicking on both sides then became a prominent feature till Wilson dribbled through in style, and Cassidy grazed the upright. From a brilliant piece of work by McLean, Miller and McQueen caused Sutcliffe to handle smartly to save. Immediately following the restart McQueen put in a fast sprint, from which accrued a barren foul. Excitement then rose to a great pitch, as Smith forced his way through and shot with terrific force at short range. Unfortunately the ball struck the crossbar, and was promptly kicked away by Jones. Liverpool then showed to decided advantage, and the visitors' defence was severely taxed, but without success. Eventually the determination of the Liverpudlians was rewarded, as from good work by Wyllie the brothers McQueen {***H. McQueen***} equalised amidst great applause. Bolton wanderers now put in a heavy spell of pressure, which they maintained to the finish; but being unable to score, a fast and yet pleasant game ended in a draw of one goal each.

RESULT: Liverpool 1 – Bolton Wanderers 1

LIVERPOOL: McOwen (goal); Hannah and McLean (backs); McCartney, M. McQue and McBride (halves); Wyllie, M. McQueen, Miller, McVean, H. McQueen [1] (forwards).
BOLTON: Sutcliffe (goal); Somerville and Jones (backs); Weir, Gardiner and Turner (halves); Tannahough, Cassidy, Wilson, McNee and Dickenson (forwards).

25/04/1893 OM: Liverpool v Preston North End
Lancashire Evening Post - Wednesday 26 April 1893

The opening stages of the game were of a desultory character, and partook largely of long heavy kicking, without in the least troubling the defence on either side. After some fifteen minutes' work Wyllie instituted an attack on the North End charge, causing Trainer to handle the ball. The Liverpool men bestirred themselves, and kept play well within the Preston half, but the efforts were of a half-hearted nature, and provoked little interest. H. McQueen made several fine tricky runs, and from a subsequent corner M. McQueen all but scored. Once or twice the North men opened up an attack, and if the ball came to their feet they kicked it away; but for the most part of the first half (which finished with a clean sheet) McOwen, the Liverpool custodian, was reclining full stretch on the ground in the shade of his goal posts.

After some 25 minutes "work" in the second half, during which period neither goal had been in any danger of succumbing to any of the "shots" directed against them, Becton was responsible for two capital shots, one of which McOwen cleared, while the other fairly shook the supports of the Liverpool citadel, and subsequently McOwen and the ball were charged through, but the point was disallowed for a previous infringement of "hands" or something of the kind. Then, a minute later, M. McQueen sent in a fine shot to Trainer, who just managed to finger the leather away. This, with the exception of the referee blowing his whistle to stop hostilities (which occurred soon after) was the last "exciting" incident, and no doubt Mr. Gough's cease play signal sounded as welcome music in the years of the players.

RESULT: Liverpool 0 – Preston North End 0

LIVERPOOL: McOwen (goal); Hannah and McLean (backs); McCartney, M. McQue and McBride (halves); Wyllie, M. McQueen, Miller, McVean, H. McQueen (forwards).
PRESTON: Trainer (goal); Holmes and Greer (backs); J. Holmes, Saunders and Thornber (halves); Gordon, Barton, Drummond, Becton and Cowan (forwards).

The next match at Anfield was the annual charity match between the Lancashire League Champions (Liverpool) and a composite side representing the Rest of the League.

26/04/1893 OM: Liverpool v. Rest of Lancashire League
Liverpool Mercury - Thursday 27 April 1893

This match was played at Anfield last evening, in the presence of a very fair attendance of spectators. Smith took the place of M. McQueen in the Liverpool team.

Winning the toss the homesters took the advantage given by the sun and were not long in improving their position by scoring a fine goal, obtained by **Wyllie**. Almost immediately following Hannah put through is **own goal** from a free kick given against McLean, and this score was unaltered at half-time. The visitors who now exhibited splendid combination obtained a decided monopoly, and before long secured the lead {**Barbour**}. But this point was not to be the crucial test, as the Rest of the League, by sheer force of determination, gave the Liverpool defenders a tremendous amount of work, notwithstanding their gallant defence. Hannah again had the chagrin of presenting his opponents with another point {**own goal**}. The visitors seeing that most of them were unaccustomed to each others play, gave every satisfaction, and deserved their victory; but it was certainly evident that Liverpool, through the enormous amount of work they have gone through lately, were somewhat out of condition, and lost by three goals to one.

RESULT: Liverpool 1 – Rest of League 3

LIVERPOOL: McOwen (goal); Hannah and McLean (backs); McCartney, M. McQue and McBride (halves); Wyllie [1], Smith, Miller, McVean, H. McQueen (forwards).
REST: Not known. Scorers Barbour (Bury)[1], [2 og].

After the match the club were presented with the two trophies they had won that season, the Lancashire League Champions Cup and the Liverpool Senior Cup.

27/04/1893 OM: Liverpool v. Blackburn Rovers
Liverpool Mercury - Friday 28 April 1893

Played at Anfield last night before a poor attendance. Play ruled even, Wyllie and Miller being best for Liverpool, while Lofthouse and Hall were prominent for the Rovers. Both goalkeepers were tested, but the interval arrived with a clean sheet.

During the second half play was generally of an even character, both goalkeepers being called on frequently. **Hall** scored for the Rovers, and nothing further being done the visitors' won by a goal to nil.

RESULT: Liverpool 0 – Blackburn Rovers 1

LIVERPOOL: McOwen (goal); Hannah and McLean (backs); McCartney, M. McQue and McBride (halves); Wyllie, Smith, Miller, Cameron, H. McQueen (forwards).
BLACKBURN: Walton (goal); Smith and Forbes (backs); Dewar, Anderson and Forrest (halves); Taylor, Hall [1], Southworth, Sawers and Lofthouse (forwards).
Liverpool ended the season with another fixture against near neighbours, Bootle.

29/04/1893 OM: Bootle v. Liverpool
Liverpool Mercury - Monday 01 May 1893

These teams, at Hawthorne road, on Saturday, were engaged for the fourth time this season - a fitting termination to the game being a draw of two goals each. Previously the teams have met twice in Cup ties (Lancashire and Liverpool) and once in a "friendly," and whilst Bootle had ousted their opponents out of the Lancashire tie, and also defeated them in the friendly game, Liverpool had the advantage in the local trophy competition.

Bootle playing with the wind, scored a couple of goals during the first half, Liverpool getting through upon one occasion, **McVean**, who played centre, doing the needful, whilst **Carthy**[2] scored both points for Bootle.

The play in the after portion of the game was well contested, and, Liverpool scoring again {*Wyllie*}, a draw was the result. Thus of the season's fixtures between the clubs, Bootle have won two, drawn one, and lost one, scoring altogether five goals as against four, thus showing how evenly matched the clubs are.

RESULT: Bootle 2 – Liverpool 2

LIVERPOOL: McOwen (goal); Hannah and McLean (backs); McCartney, M. McQue and McBride (halves); Wyllie [1], M. McQueen, McVean [1], Smith, H. McQueen (forwards).
BOOTLE: Jackson (goal); {Hutchinson} and {Arridge} (backs); {Grierson}, {Hughes} and {McEwan} (halves); Carthy, {Gallocher}, Brandon, McLafferty and {Montgomery} (forwards).
Referee: anon.
*Player names in braces {} are probable – **not** confirmed.*

Although neither side knew it at the time, this would be not only the last time the clubs would meet but also Bootle's last game against any opposition. Although the club had finished above the re-election place in Division Two of the Football League, they were in dire straits financially. Three years earlier, at the club A.G.M. on 11th July, 1890, it had been revealed that, due to cavalier if not criminal mismanagement, the club had been around £800 in debt - although the actual amount was unsure, so muddled were the clubs accounts. An investigative committee subsequently found that in the previous season alone, a successful one on the field, the club had lost around £400. New officials had then been appointed, but the debt had subsequently proved too much to overcome.

Burnley later complained to the F.A. that Liverpool had reneged upon a promise to play them on this date but the complaint was not entertained.

For The Record – Season 1892/93

List of Fixtures - Results

01/09/1892	H	OM	ROTHERHAM TOWN	W	7-1
03/09/1892	H	LL:01	HIGHER WALTON	W	8-0
05/09/1892	A	OM	Middlesbrough Ironopolis	L	0-5
08/09/1892	H	OM	BARROW	W	2-0
10/09/1892	H	OM	STOCKTON	W	2-1
15/09/1892	H	OM	GRANTHAM ROVERS	W	3-1
17/09/1892	H	LSC-Q1	SOUTHPORT CENTRAL	W	2-0
22/09/1892	H	OM	MIDDLESBROUGH IRON	L	1-2
24/09/1892	H	LL:02	BURY	W	4-0
26/09/1892	A	OM	Stoke	L	1-2
29/09/1882	H	OM	QOS WANDERERS	W	1-0
01/10/1892	H	LL:03	WEST MANCHESTER	W	3-1
06/10/1892	A	OM	Glasgow Rangers	L	1-6
08/10/1892	A	LSC-Q2	West Manchester	W	3-1
15/10/1892	A	FAC-Q1	Nantwich	W	4-0
22/10/1892	A	LL:04	Higher Walton	W	5-0
29/10/1892	H	FAC-Q2	NEWTOWN	W	9-0
05/11/1892	A	LL:05	Blackpool	L	0-3
12/11/1892	A	LL:06	Fleetwood R.	W	3-1
14/11/1892	A	OM	Aston Villa	W	3-2
19/11/1892	A	FAC-Q3	Northwich Victoria	W	2-1
26/11/1892	A	LL:07	Rossendale	W	2-1
03/12/1892	H	LL:08	FLEETWOOD RANGERS	W	7-0
10/12/1892	A	OM	Heywood Central	D	1-1
17/12/1892	H	LL:09	BLACKPOOL	L	0-2
24/12/1892	A	LL:10	South Shore	W	1-0
26/12/1892	H	OM	SHEFFIELD UTD	W	1-0
27/12/1892	A	OM	Southport Central	D	2-2
31/12/1892	H	LL:11	HEYWOOD CENTRAL	W	5-1
02/01/1893	A	LL:12	Fairfield	W	4-1
07/01/1893	A	LL:13	Heywood Central	W	5-1
14/01/1893	A	LL:14	West Manchester	D	0-0
21/01/1893	A	OM	Bury	D	0-0
28/01/1893	H	LSC-R1	DARWEN	W	1-0
04/02/1893	H	OM	STOKE	L	1-2
11/02/1893	A	LL:15	Bury	L	0-3
18/02/1893	A	LL:16	Nelson	W	3-2
23/02/1893	H	OM	STOKE	D	0-0
25/02/1893	H	LL:17	SOUTHPORT CENTRAL	W	2-0
03/03/1893	H	OM	LANCASHIRE C.C.	D	2-2
04/03/1893	H	LL:18	NELSON	W	3-2
09/03/1893	H	OM	ASTON VILLA	L	1-3
11/03/1893	A	LSC-R2	Bootle	L	1-2
15/03/1893	H	LL:19	FAIRFIELD	W	5-0

18/03/1893	H	LL:20	SOUTH SHORE	W	4-1	
22/03/1893	H	LiSC-R1	CHESTER	W	4-0	
23/03/1893	H	OM	BOOTLE	W	2-1	
25/03/1893	H	LL:21	ROSSENDALE	W	2-1	
31/03/1893	H	OM	DARWEN	W	1-0	
01/04/1893	A	OM	Stockton	D	2-2	
03/04/1893	H	OM	CORINTHIANS	W	2-0	
04/04/1893	H	OM	CLIFTONVILLE	W	4-1	
08/04/1893	A	OM	Newcastle United	D	0-0	
10/04/1893	A	OM	Newtown	D	0-0	
15/04/1893	A	LL:22	Southport Central	D	1-1	
17/04/1893	A	LiSC-SF	Bootle	W	1-0	
22/04/1893	N	LiSC-F	Everton (at Bootle)	W	1-0	
24/04/1893	H	OM	BOLTON WANDERERS	D	1-1	
25/04/1893	H	OM	PRESTON NORTH END	D	0-0	
26/04/1893	H	OM	REST OF LEAGUE	D	0-0	
27/04/1893	H	OM	BLACKBURN ROVERS	L	0-1	
29/04/1893	A	OM	Bootle	D	2-2	

Table of Player Appearances (1st Team Competitive Matches)

Appearances	Pos	LL	FAC	LSC
Ross	G	17	3	3
McOwen	G	1		1
(McQueen M.)*	G	4		
Hannah	FB	22(1)	3	4
McLean	FB	22(1)	3	4
McBride	HB	20(4)	3	3
McQue	HB	18(2)	2	4
McCartney	HB	18	3(1)	2
Pearson	HB	1		
Richardson	HB	1		
Wyllie	FW	22(11)	3(4)	4(1)
Miller	FW	21(22)	3(3)	4(2)
McVean	FW	21(9)	3(2)	4(1)
McQueen H.	FW	16(3)	1(1)	2(1)
Smith	FW	10(5)	1	3(1)
Cameron	FW	8(3)	2(1)	2
Kelso	FW	4	2	2(1)
Kelly	FW	3		
Kelvin	FW	1		
McQueen M.*	UT	12(5)	1	2

* goalkeeping appearances shown separately.

LL = Lancashire League. FAC = F.A. Cup, LSC = Lancashire Senior Cup.

Lancashire League Standings – Month by Month
(Table positions after last major round of matches in each month)

26/09/1892	Pld	W	D	L	For	Agst	Pts	Avge
Fleetwood Rgrs	3	3	0	0	12	4	6	3.00
Bury	4	3	0	1	14	6	6	2.33
Liverpool	**2**	**2**	**0**	**0**	**12**	**0**	**4**	**12.00**
Blackpool	2	2	0	0	4	0	4	4.00
South Shore	2	1	1	0	10	6	3	1.67
Heywood Central	1	1	0	0	6	1	2	6.00
Liverpool Cal.	2	1	0	1	4	4	2	1.00
Nelson	3	1	0	2	7	9	2	.78
Fairfield	3	1	1	1	7	10	3	.70
Southport Central	2	0	0	2	2	4	0	.50
West Manchester	2	0	0	2	4	12	0	.33
Rossendale	2	0	0	2	1	5	0	.20
Higher Walton	4	0	0	4	3	25	0	.12

29/10/1892	Pld	W	D	L	For	Agst	Pts	Avge
Liverpool	**4**	**4**	**0**	**0**	**20**	**1**	**8**	**20.00**
Blackpool	4	4	0	0	11	3	8	3.67
Bury	6	4	0	2	21	11	8	1.91
Fleetwood Rgrs	4	3	1	0	14	6	7	2.33
Liverpool Cal.	4	2	1	1	10	7	5	1.43
South Shore	4	1	3	0	15	11	5	1.36
Fairfield	4	1	2	1	9	12	4	.75
Heywood Central	3	1	0	2	9	9	2	1.00
Rossendale	4	1	0	3	9	13	2	.69
Southport Central	4	1	0	3	6	9	2	.67
Nelson	4	1	0	3	9	14	2	.64
Higher Walton	6	0	1	5	6	33	1	.18
West Manchester	3	0	0	3	5	15	0	.33

28/11/1892	Pld	W	D	L	For	Agst	Pts	Avge
Blackpool	7	7	0	0	26	6	14	4.33
Bury	9	7	0	2	35	15	14	2.33
Liverpool	**7**	**6**	**0**	**1**	**26**	**5**	**12**	**5.20**
Liverpool Cal.	7	3	2	2	14	12	8	1.17
Fleetwood Rgrs	6	3	1	2	17	16	7	1.06
Fairfield	7	2	3	2	14	17	7	.82
Heywood Central	6	3	0	3	19	18	6	1.06
South Shore	7	1	4	2	20	22	6	.91
Rossendale	7	2	1	4	14	19	5	.74
Higher Walton	9	2	1	6	13	41	5	.32
Nelson	7	1	1	5	17	25	3	.68
West Manchester	6	1	1	4	10	22	3	.45
Southport Central	7	1	0	6	8	15	2	.53

31/12/1892	Pld	W	D	L	For	Agst	Pts	Avge
Bury	12	10	0	2	42	16	20	2.63
Liverpool	**11**	**9**	**0**	**2**	**40**	**9**	**18**	**4.44**
Blackpool	10	8	1	1	33	13	17	2.54
Rossendale	10	4	2	4	28	23	10	1.22
West Manchester	10	4	2	4	32	30	10	1.07
Heywood Central	9	5	0	4	25	25	10	1.00
Fairfield	11	2	5	4	16	22	9	.73
South Shore	9	2	4	3	25	24	8	1.04
Fleetwood Rgrs	10	4	0	6	21	32	8	.66
Higher Walton	14	3	1	10	20	66	7	.30
Southport Central	10	3	0	7	15	19	6	.79
Nelson	10	1	1	8	13	41	3	.32

*Liverpool Caledonians in liquidation – record expunged.

28/01/1893	Pld	W	D	L	For	Agst	Pts	Avge
Bury	14	12	0	2	54	16	24	3.38
Liverpool	**14**	**11**	**1**	**2**	**45**	**11**	**23**	**4.09**
Blackpool	12	9	1	2	40	17	19	2.35
Heywood Central	12	7	0	5	33	32	14	1.03
South Shore	12	4	5	3	37	30	13	1.23
West Manchester	13	5	3	5	37	37	13	1.00
Fairfield	16	4	5	7	27	35	13	.77
Fleetwood Rgrs	12	5	1	6	26	35	11	.74
Rossendale	11	3	2	6	22	24	8	.92
Higher Walton	15	3	1	11	20	75	7	.27
Southport Central	13	3	0	10	16	29	6	.55
Nelson	12	2	1	9	23	40	5	.58

25/02/1893	Pld	W	D	L	For	Agst	Pts	Avge
Liverpool	**17**	**14**	**0**	**3**	**61**	**18**	**28**	**3.39**
Bury	17	13	1	3	51	16	27	3.19
Blackpool	15	12	1	2	53	21	25	2.52
Heywood Central	16	7	4	5	50	39	18	1.28
Rossendale	16	8	2	6	42	35	18	1.20
West Manchester	15	9	0	6	43	36	18	1.19
Fleetwood Rgrs	15	6	2	7	31	42	14	.74
Fairfield	15	4	5	6	37	45	13	.82
South Shore	18	4	5	9	30	44	13	.68
Southport Central	17	4	0	13	21	37	8	.57
Nelson	17	3	1	13	47	61	7	.77
Higher Walton	18	3	1	14	25	97	7	.26

25/03/1893	Pld	W	D	L	For	Agst	Pts	Avge
Liverpool	**21**	**17**	**1**	**3**	**65**	**18**	**35**	**3.61**
Bury	19	16	0	3	75	19	32	3.95
Blackpool	17	14	1	2	63	24	29	2.63
West Manchester	20	9	4	7	63	51	22	1.24
Heywood Central	17	10	0	7	46	46	20	1.00
Rossendale	20	8	2	10	48	49	18	.98
Fleetwood Rgrs	16	6	3	7	33	44	15	.75
Fairfield	20	5	5	10	33	50	15	.66
South Shore	19	4	5	10	40	59	13	.68
Southport Central	19	6	0	13	29	41	12	.71
Nelson	20	4	1	15	53	70	9	.76
Higher Walton	20	3	2	15	27	104	8	.26

FINAL	Pld	W	D	L	For	Agst	Pts	Avge
Liverpool	**22**	**17**	**2**	**3**	**66**	**19**	**36**	**3.47**
Blackpool	22	17	2	3	82	31	36	2.65
Bury	22	17	1	4	83	24	35	3.46
Fleetwood Rgrs	22	10	5	7	47	51	25	.92
West Manchester	22	10	4	8	68	55	24	1.24
Heywood Central	22	11	1	10	54	69	23	.78
Rossendale	22	8	2	12	46	55	18	.84
Southport Central	22	7	2	13	33	44	16	.75
South Shore	22	5	6	11	46	66	16	.70
Fairfield	22	5	6	11	34	53	16	.64
Nelson	22	4	2	16	54	73	10	.74
Higher Walton	22	3	3	16	28	110	9	.25

Lancashire League Champions

Blackpool, and to a lesser extent Bury, might well have rued the fact that from their points of view they had lost the title rather than that Liverpool had won it. Blackpool in particular could have taken the title at Fleetwood had they managed more than a draw, and even after that could still have done so at Southport simply by avoiding defeat! Blackpool could also point to the fact that in both Lancashire League meetings against the Liverpudlians, they had taken the spoils.

Liverpool, however, had done all they could throughout the season, and if it took a last minute stumble on the part of their rivals in order for them to clinch the title it was because they had put themselves in the position where that might occur. They had set the bar that their rivals had to surpass and the latter had been found wanting!

In any event, despite their impressive resources, in their very first campaign the success had been a magnificent achievement – more so considering that the Lancashire League, at the time, was one of the strongest in the country with it's best clubs probably on a par with most of those making up the newly formed Second Division of the Football League!

The Lancashire League – Review of the Season
Lancashire Evening Post - Saturday 29 April 1893

The fourth annual contest for the Championship of the Lancashire league was brought to a close on Saturday. The interest was maintained right to the close, as when last Saturday's games began there was just a chance of either Liverpool or Blackpool being the champions[16]. Blackpool were, however, the favourites, as with a game in hand they had exactly the same number of points as Liverpool, who, however, had a lot better average than their opponents.

As everybody knows, Blackpool failed to beat Southport Central, or even to draw[17] with them, and hence Liverpool, a new club this season, walks off with the cup on their goal average. The contest all through has been a really close one between the first three teams, first one and then another topping the list. The attendances at the various games have all through the winter been of a highly satisfactory character, taken all round, though, of course, as Nelson and higher Walton fell irreparably behind they did not towards the close form so great an attraction. The League is one of the best managed organisations in the country. The committee has all long been composed of sound businessmen, and the clubs have one and all shown the determination to stand together, when some of them could have got into better company, which is worthy of commendation.

---

16 In fact at this point Bury also were still in the running. They were two points behind the two leaders but with Liverpool's season already concluded, and a loss accruing to Blackpool on the final day, a win for themselves would have propelled *them* to the top on goal average (which was already the best and could only have improved under those circumstances).

17 And Bury could only draw at South Shore.

Next season there will be undoubtedly be some changes, and providing the second division of the League should be dished up Accrington might do a deal worse than join the Lancashire League. Though the organisation is managed by a committee second to none, it has not had all plain and straight sailing. There has never yet been a season in which the full complement of clubs which commenced the season finished it. In the first season they started with four team clubs, and Earlestown were unable to go through with their engagements, and after a portion of matches had been played they had to be taken out of the records. In the succeeding season Burnley Union Star shared a similar fate, leaving the number of clubs in the second portion of the games 11. Then last year the Heywood club could not fulfil its engagements, and amalgamated with the Heywood Central, the latter running their second team in the concluding Heywood fixtures. This season the Liverpool Caledonian's made a great spurt, and felt confident of running the new Liverpool club off its legs. It failed, however, and after playing seven League games it was wound up in liquidation on the 10th of December.

During the four seasons in which the League has been running there have been three champions. The first season it was Higher Walton, the second and third Bury, and this season Liverpool. Higher Walton in their season secured 32 points in a 13 club league, in the second year Bury secured 33 points in an 11 club league, in the third year Bury got 40 in a 12 club lead, and this year Liverpool have 36 to their credit in a 12 club league. The following figures show the number of games which have been played, won and drawn, and the number of goals scored during the four seasons:-

Season	Played	Won	Drawn	Goals
1889/90	110	92	18	552
1890/91	156	127	29	650
1891/92	132	110	22	710
1892/93	133	114	18	641

The total number matches played has been 132, and of these 74 were won by the home teams, 18 were drawn, and 41 by the visitors, the home goals being 378 to 263 by the visitors, so that of the 264 points obtainable 166 have fallen to the home club's and 98 to the visitors. The Bury team was the only one to win all the games played on their own ground, but Blackpool and Liverpool ran them close with ten each, Blackpool made a draw in their remaining one and Liverpool a loss. West Manchester came a good fourth with eight, Fleetwood Rangers claiming seven, Heywood Central, South Shore, Rossendale and Southport Central had five each, Fairfield four, Nelson three, and higher Walton one. Higher Walton, of course, suffered the most defeats at home, eight, Nelson coming next with six.

In the away games Blackpool and Liverpool again tied in the number of wins secured with Seven each, Bury and Heywood Central each secured six, Fleetwood Rangers and Rossendale three, West Manchester, Southport Central and Higher Walton, two. Nelson, Fairfield, and South Shore alone had the honour of failing to win a match on their opponents' pitch. In the matter of goals Bury scored more goals on their opponents' fields than anybody else, 41, Blackpool coming next with 34, Liverpool having only 22 to their credit. At home Blackpool led the way with 49 goals, Liverpool having 44, and Bury 42. Fairfield scored the smallest number of goals at home, 16, but

Higher Walton has the credit of having scored the least away with 10. The accompanying table shows the doings of the various clubs at home and away:

	Matches at Home					Matches Away					Totals	
	W	D	L	For	Ag	W	D	L	For	Ag	Pts	Avg
Liverpool	10	0	1	44	7	7	2	2	22	12	36	3.47
Blackpool	10	1	0	49	12	7	1	3	34	19	36	2.68
Bury	11	0	0	42	5	6	1	4	41	19	35	3.46
Fleetwood Rangers	7	2	2	42	5	3	3	5	20	33	25	1.11
West Manchester	8	2	1	42	16	2	2	7	25	39	24	1.24
Heywood Central	5	1	5	30	30	6	0	5	24	30	23	0.90
Rossendale	5	2	4	25	20	3	0	8	21	35	18	0.82
Southport Central	5	1	5	18	15	2	1	8	15	29	16	0.75
South Shore	5	3	3	32	22	0	3	8	14	43	16	0.69
Fairfield	4	2	5	15	23	1	4	6	18	39	16	0.64
Nelson	3	2	6	35	37	1	0	10	18	38	10	0.73
Higher Walton	1	2	8	18	53	2	1	8	10	57	9	0.25

A singular feature in connection with the contest is that there is not a single instance in which clubs have made a draw in both their engagements. There are, however, 32 instances in which clubs have secured double wins. Of these the champions, Liverpool, claim seven; over Fleetwood Ranges 7-0 and 4-1, Heywood Central 6-2 and 2-1, Higher Walton 8-0 and 5-0, Nelson 3-0 and 3-2, Rossendale 2-1 and 2-0, South Shore 4-1 and 1-0, and Fairfield 5-0 and 4-1. Six such feats have been performed by Blackpool; against Heywood Central 6-2 and 3-1, Higher Walton 5-0 and 6-1, Liverpool 3-0 and 2-0, Nelson 6-2 and 5-2, Rossendale 5-3 and 1-0, South Shore 4-0 and 6-1. Bury claims a similar number thus; Heywood Central 6-1 and 10-1, Higher Walton 6-0 and 9-0, Nelson 2-0 and 5-3, Rossendale 5-1 and 6-3, West Manchester 6-2 and 3-0, and Fairfield 2-0 and 3-0. Heywood Central have beaten four opponents both at home and away, viz.; Higher Walton 6-1 and 6-2, Nelson 4-1 and 3-2, South Shore 7-0 and 2-0, and Fairfield 4-3 and 1-0. Fleetwood Rangers beat Nelson 4-2 and 5-2, Southport Central 2-1 and 1-0, and Fairfield 3-1 and 5-1. Rossendale and West Manchester each secured a couple of double barrelled wins; Rossendale 5-0 and 3-2 over Higher Walton and 3-2 and 3-2 over Southport central; and West Manchester 8-2 and 8-1 over Higher Walton and 5-2 and 5-4 over Nelson. Nelson beat Higher Walton 11-2 and 5-2, and Fairfield beat Southport Central 2-0 and 2-1. From these figures it will be seen that Higher Walton was twice defeated on seven occasions, Nelson on six occasions, Fairfield four times, Heywood Central, Rossendale and Southport Central three times, and Fleetwood Rangers, Liverpool and West Manchester once each.

The record score of this season's competition was made by Bury against higher Walton, on the Walton ground, on January 7th, when the visitors won by nine goals to nil. Liverpool runs this close with a 8-0 win against the same club at Liverpool on 3rd September. The Bury club has also another remarkably good performance to record, viz., the win over Heywood central by 10 goals to one on March 4th. The score is a much better one than the 9-0 against Higher Walton, as the Centraliens are a lot better team, and just about that time were playing well, and had for some time previous declared what they would do to Bury for a previous 6-1 defeat at Bury. The tallest score in any match was that of Nelson against Higher Walton, on the 24th of February on the ground of the winners, when in all 13 goals were scored, 11 by the winners and two by the losers. Six and seven goals to the winning side have been quite common. The 110 goals scored against higher Walton this season is the first time three figures have ever been attached to any clubs name either for or against. The Waltonians this season have had a fairly bad time of it, and the manner in which goals had been piled up against them has been calculated to gnaw the heart out of a much better team. Bury holds the record with 15 goals to nail, Liverpool following with 13 to nil. West Manchester piled up 16 to 3, Nelson 16 to 4, whilst the best score the Walltonian's could make against a club was five against Fleetwood Rangers. Nelson, who only finish up point ahead of the Waltonian's, have a heavy aggregate against them, but the highest number scored against them in one match was six by Blackpool. On no fewer than a dozen occasions the Nelsonions have finished either on level terms or only one goal behind their opponents, so that it is quite apparent they have had exceedingly hard lines.

Losing The Trophies

On Friday 1st September, 1893, the two trophies Liverpool had won that season, viz. The Liverpool and District Association Cup and the Lancashire League Cup, were left overnight in the unguarded premises of Mr. Charles Gibson, pawnbroker and furniture dealer, at 8 Derby Buildings, Wavertree Road, where they had been on display. The following morning staff arrived to find that the door had been forced open some time during the night with a jemmy, and that the two trophies were conspicuous by their absence! Nothing else in the shop had been disturbed, indicating that the thieves had gotten away with precisely what they came for.

The Liverpool Echo printed the following description of the trophies:
"The Liverpool and District Challenge Cup is a massive silver cup, and is a capital example of the silversmith's art. There is a ribbon in front of the cup, and a figure of a football player in the top of the cup, with his foot resting on a football. The Lancashire League Cup is also of silver, and very handsome. It has two plates in front of enamelled blue, and a gold line in releif on each plate. There is also engraved a view of a football field with a man in goal. On top is the figure of a football player in the act of kicking the ball."

The trophies were never recovered and Liverpool subsequently had to pay £130 for their replacement, although their value to the thieves in scrap silver, assuming they were melted down, could only have been a fraction of that.

Into the Football League

At the Annual General Meeting of the Football League in Manchester on 26th May, 1893, the question of the following year's constitution of the Second Division was one of the main items under discussion. The four outgoing clubs were Walsall Town Swifts, Burslem Port Vale, Crewe Alexandra and Lincoln City. Small Heath and Sheffield United had been promoted to the First League replacing Accrington and Notts County, both of whom had signalled intent to their exercise their options to compete in the Second League. In view of it having been decided to increase the size of the latter from twelve clubs to fourteen there were, therefore, eight vacancies to be considered.

All four retiring clubs re-applied, and additional applications had been received from Doncaster Rovers, Liverpool, Loughborough, Middlesbrough Ironopolis, Rotherham Town and Royal Arsenal. Liverpool, indeed, had applied for direct entry into the First League, but it was determined that under the two divisional system no such application could be entertained, thereby establishing the rule that the only route to Division One of the League was by graduation from Division Two.

Six of the places were settled at that meeting, with all four departing clubs being re-elected along with the Rotherham and Newcastle clubs. The remaining two vacancies were left to be determined from the applications received when the meeting re-convened in London the following day to arrange fixtures. At that time it was decided that the two vacancies should be awarded to Liverpool and Royal Arsenal.

Thus Liverpool became, after only a single year of existence, members of the footballing elite – the Football League. Although, initially at least, a step below Everton they could look forward to what were certain to be lucrative local derbies against near neighbours Bootle! Unfortunately this last was not to be. Bootle[18], at the last moment, withdrew from the League due to financial difficulties, thus reducing the planned 16 clubs that season to 15.

FOOTBALL PROSPECTS - LIVERPOOL
Athletic News - Monday 28 August 1893

It speaks well for the executive of this club that nearly all last year's players will again be seen on the Anfield Road ground. Last season the men hardly received fair treatment at the hands of those who paid occasional visits to the old quarters; indeed, at times the conduct of the spectators, to put it mildly, was very unsportsmanlike, but for all that they are here again. The team will be:- Rennie (of Everton) or McOwen, goal; Hannah and McLean, backs; McCartney, McQue, and McBride, half-backs; Gordon,

---

18 Some Liverpool club histories have stated that Liverpool took the place of Bootle in the League that season. This is arguably true, in that Liverpool took part when Bootle didn't, but is at best misleading, since it suggests, prima facie, that it was a case of either or, when in reality it should have been both. Both clubs were actually included the Second League rosta for that season, only Bootle's subsequent financial demise prevented their participation alongside Liverpool.

McVean, Henderson, Stott, and H. McQueen, forwards. Matthew McQueen will again be the general knockabout, and I should not be surprised to see him figuring often at back. The new men are Henderson, of Annbank, at centre forward, and Stott, of Middlesbrough, and both come with good reputations. Inducements have been offered the players to qualify for the First Division of the league, which will be supplemented by a further consideration should they get a place. The team is a good one, and will undoubtedly show up better in the company they are in. Last season they were disappointing at times, but it was due to other influences more than superior play of their opponents. The travelling will be exceptionally heavy, but the executive are neutralising this by limiting the number of matches, and only a few outside the league fixtures will be taken on. Popular prices of admission will be the rule - fourpence admission, whilst another fourpence will admit to any stand in the ground. This move should find favour with the working men, and I hope to see an improvement in the attendance.

The County Palatine[19] League

The original purpose behind the creation of the Football League had been to overcome the vexed annual problem faced by all of the better clubs of arranging a sufficient number of reliable fixtures against decent quality opposition. In the 1893/94 season the First Division of the Football League provided only 30 fixtures for each member club, and the Second Division, due to the late withdrawal of Bootle, only 28. With the top clubs at the time commonly playing 50 to 60 games in a season, even after the addition of cup ties this still left a significant number of dates for which attractive fixtures needed to be found.

This situation is what led Mr. A. Clayton, the President of the Everton club, to invite representatives of several of the other leading Lancashire clubs – Blackburn Rovers, Bolton Wanderers, Burnley, Bury, Darwen, Newton Heath and Preston North End – to meet with him at the Bee Hotel in Liverpool on 10th October, 1893, to discuss his proposal for the creation of a new League to run in tandem with the Football League and provide additional quality fixtures to fill more of those empty dates.

The proposal was met with much enthusiasm, and after some discussion it was decided to call the new organisation the County Palatine League. The clubs would be divided into two regional divisions, North and South, to cut down travel costs, with the clubs in each division then playing each other home and away to decide regional champions – the latter then playing off for the overall championship. The Northern division was to be made up of Blackburn, Burnley, Darwen and Preston; and the Southern of Bolton, Bury, Everton and Newton Heath.

Notable absentees from the list were Accrington, Ardwick and Liverpool – the former due to their being in financial difficulties, and the latter pair in light of the rivalries that then existed between them and Newton Heath and Everton respectively (the First Leaguers participation in the competition being more desirable than the Second Leaguers)! As regards Liverpool, the 'Cricket and Football Field' commented "Their

---

19   Lancashire was created a County Palatine (semi-autonomous region) in 1351.

exclusion from the County Palatine League will not lower the Liverpool club in the eyes of the public. They ought to have been in. Everton will not be able to chuck them out of the First League next season."

At subsequent meetings, however, the new League relented and extended their number by two to accept Accrington and Liverpool into membership. Significantly, however, Accrington, one of the most Northerly clubs, were co-opted into the southern section, and Liverpool, one of the most Southerly, into the Northern section! This avoided Liverpool operating in the same section as Everton but to some extent penalised the new members by lengthening their away journey's. For the new Liverpool, however, it did place them in exalted company, Blackburn Rovers, four times F.A. Cup winners, and Preston North End, two times League Champions, in particular being probably the two most famous clubs in the land.

A proposal for all clubs to pay their gate money's into a central pot to be shared equally was defeated but it was agreed instead that gate monies be shared equally between the home and away club in every case. Matches would be played after the new year cup ties from March to the end of the season.

As the matches would take place late in the season when clubs might have other vitally important matches to prepare for it was also agreed at a later meeting of the management committee that clubs might be permitted, if circumstances dictated, to field reserve sides in the competition. Unfortunately this one amendment would very much devalue the competition, as several clubs, including Liverpool, then habitually fielded very much reduced sides.

The Cost of Football in 1893/94

In their first season of League Football Liverpool charged 4d (four old pence – approx 1.6p) for General Admission – this was the minimum figure set by the Football League for that season. An extra charge applied for transfer to stands and/or enclosures.

In 1893, 4d would also have bought:
1lb of Bacon **or** 1qt (2 pints) Dairy Cream **or** 1doz Eggs.
(prices from period advertisements)

at modern day prices these might typically cost:
1lb of Bacon - £3.00 / 1qt Dairy Cream - £3.50 / 1doz Eggs - £2.50
(prices from online sources)
Average: £3.00

Cheapest match day ticket in the Championship (2nd tier) in 2017/18
Average (of all clubs): £20.50

Hence it can be seen that the real cost[20] of modern football could be said to have increased almost sevenfold!

---

20 In terms of what the same money might otherwise purchase.

The Clubs

Ardwick
Colours: Blue & White Stripes / White
Ground: Hyde Road, Ardwick.
Now: **Manchester City**

Burton Swifts
Colours: Blue / White
Ground: Shobnall Street, Burton.
Now: Defunct

Crewe Alexandra
Colours: White / Royal Blue
Ground: Alexandra Athletic Grounds, Nantwich Road.

Grimsby Town
Colours: Sky blue & Red halves / White
Ground: Abbey Park, Grimsby.

Lincoln City
Colours: Red & White stripes / White
Ground: John O'Gaunts Ground, Lincoln (the ground was little more than a barren field with no stands and just a changing hut for the players).

Middlesbrough Iron.
Colours: Red with White sash / White
Ground: Paradise Ground, Middlesbrough.
Now: Defunct – no connection with Middlesbrough F.C.

Newcastle United
Colours: Red / White
Ground: St. James' Park, Newcastle.

Newton Heath
Colours: Yellow and Green stripes / Royal Blue
Ground: Bank Street Ground, Clayton.
Now: **Manchester United**

Northwich Victoria
Colours: Red / Royal Blue
Ground: The Drill Field, Northwich.

Notts County
Colours: Black & White stripes / Black
Ground: Trent Bridge Cricket Ground

Burslem Port Vale
Colours: Red / Black
Ground: Athletic Ground Cobridge.
Now: Defunct 1907 – name and ground taken over by Cobridge Church F.C., now operating as **Port Vale**.

Rotherham Town
Colours: Red / Royal Blue
Ground: Clifton Grove, Rotherham.
Now: Defunct 1896. Not connected with current Rotherham United club (or the second Rotherham Town that merged with Rotherham County to form United).

Walsall Town Swifts   Colours: Red & White halves / Royal Blue
Ground: The Chuckery.
Now: **Walsall F.C.**

Small Heath   Colours: Sky Blue (Royal Blue trim) / White
Ground: Muntz Street, Small Heath
Now : **Birmingham City**

Woolwich Arsenal   Colours: Red / Royal Blue
Ground: Manor Ground, Plumstead.
Now: **Arsenal.**

Liverpool's first taste of League Football came in the guise of a trip across country to the North-East to visit the Ironopolis club from Middlesbrough, who had gained a brace of victories over Liverpool in their ordinary match encounters the previous season.

02/09/1893 FL01: Middlesbrough Ironopolis v. Liverpool
Liverpool Mercury - Monday 4th September, 1893

In pleasant weather, and under most favourable conditions, the Liverpool club travelled to Middlesbrough on Saturday to oppose their dual victors of last season in the primary match of the league. Between 3000 and 4000 spectators lined the enclosure when the teams entered the field. Hannah lost the toss, and the home team played downhill with a good wind at their backs.

The game open very spiritedly, the "'Nops" being the first to really menace danger, and, continuing in the vicinity of McOwen, caused noisy and enthusiastic demonstrations to be exhibited by the crowd. McOwen had a very difficult shot to deal with from Cooper, followed by a similar one from McKie, but steady play by Hannah and McLean eventually repulsed the attacking party. Then Gordon receiving from McQue led up an assault upon Dixon, and the siege being well sustained by Stott, McVean and McQueen, the "'Nops" supporters went through an anxious time, till Nixon, marvellously emerging from what had been an almost rugby scrimmage, threw clear, and Miller[Nops] securing, executed a fine run down the centre, only to be pulled up by McLean. Deakin and Cooper bothered Hannah and McQueen very much, and McOwen had to be exceptionally smart on one occasion to avert disaster.

Half-time gave Liverpool the advantage of wind and hill, and immediately upon resuming it was plainly evident that the pace had told its tale upon the homesters, and for fully ten minutes the Anfielders were furiously bombarding the home goal, shots by Stott, Gordon, and McLean either being successfully turned aside or partially cleared; but such persistent attempts could not always be frustrated, and at last **McVean** opened the scoring account by a low, fast shot. The play of the "'Nops" did not fall off with the reverse, but the Liverpudlians exerted themselves with greater vigour, and had they possessed a tithe of decent shooting their score must have been considerably larger. As it was, **McQue**, the centre half, added a second point for Liverpool, who were thus accorded winners by:

RESULT: Middlesbrough Ironopolis 0 – Liverpool 2

LIVERPOOL: McOwen (goal); Hannah and McLean (backs); M. McQueen, McQue [1] and McBride (halves); Gordon, McVean [1], Henderson, Stott and H. McQueen (forwards).
IRONOPOLIS: Nixon (goal); Upton and Adams (backs); McNair, McKie and Barbut (halves); Alfort, Hunter, Miller, Cooper and Deakin (forwards).

Liverpool next faced First Division opposition in the form of a visit from Newton Heath (now Manchester Utd) in an ordinary match. The Mancunians had finished bottom of the First Division table the previous season but had escaped relegation to Division Two by defeating the Second Division Champions, Small Heath, in a test match.

06/09/1893 OM: Liverpool v. Newton Heath
Liverpool Mercury - Thursday 7th September, 1893

Last evening, Liverpool occupied their own ground in the above match for the first time this season. The visitors were strongly represented, the team being almost identically the same as that which inflicted defeat upon Burnley last Saturday, Lever playing back instead of Clements.

Hannah won the toss, and Donaldson started. McQue at once became prominent for good tackling, and the ball was taken into Newton territory. A foul gave temporary relief, but Gordon and McVean sent across, and Stott initiated another attack, but failed with his final shot. Strong back play by Mitchell and Davidson prevented disaster, but a grand shot by McVean following some excellent work by Gordon, deserved a better fate than a futile corner. Donaldson next headed a forward movement, and although assisted by McNaught and Fitzsimmons the home backs proved too good, and again the Liverpool forwards were in the vicinity of Falls, where Stott spoiled a previous good effort by placing outside. Farman, for the visitors, then raced away on the right, and from his centre Peden tested McOwen with a finely judged shot. Gordon replied with a similar run, and, giving to McVey at the right time, **McQueen** finally Converted the latter's pass into a tangible point. Indifferent play by McVean and Henderson ruined a splendid opening given by Hannah, and shortly afterwards Newton Heath livened up considerably, and serious danger was threatened by a couple of well placed corners, taken by Perrins, which, however, were got away by McQue. Returning to the assault, Farman showed a clean pair of heels to McLean, but danger was averted by Hannah's judiciousness, notwithstanding that McNaught and Perrins tested McOwen with two magnificent shots.

Immediately after the interval Stott broke away in characteristic style, and finished up with an attempt that Falls cleared with great difficulty. Long kicking was then indulged in by the visitors, and Peden caused McOwen to use his hands. Still having slightly the best of the game, Gordon put on a second point, which, however, was disallowed by the referee. Both sides now put more energy into their play, and Peden executed several rapid sprints on the left, from one of which Donaldson had distinctly hard lines with a shot which struck the crossbar. The home team responding to the cries of their supporters, took up the running, and but for the weak play of their centre must have found a way into the net. Ultimately the game ended in a win for Liverpool.

RESULT: Liverpool 1 – Newton Heath 0

LIVERPOOL: McOwen (goal); Hannah and McLean (backs); M. McQueen, McQue and McBride (halves); Gordon, McVean, Henderson, Stott and H. McQueen [1] (forwards).
NEWTON: Falls (goal); Mitchell and Laver (backs); Perrins, Stewart and Davidson (halves); Farman, McNaught, Donaldson, Fitzsimmons and Peden (forwards)

Liverpool's first home match in the Football League saw the visit of Lincoln City to the Anfield ground. After his poor performance in the match against Newton Heath the committee left out Henderson, moving up the ever-versatile Matt McQueen to take over the role of centre-forward.

09/09/1893 FL02: Liverpool v. Lincoln City
Liverpool Mercury - Monday 11th September, 1893

Liverpool played their first home league engagement on Saturday, at Anfield, and despite the threatening weather fully 5000 enthusiastic spectators assembled to witness the game.

Liverpool opened in promising fashion, and had the best of the early exchanges, when McQue kicked over the line. M. McQueen then followed with a smart run down the centre, when Jones just managed to effect a clearance. Chadburn, on behalf of Lincoln, raised the siege, and pretty combination brought the leather into the vicinity of McOwen, who, however, was on the alert, and saved easily. McQue initiated an attack, and parting to Gordon, that player gave a nice chance to McVean, who almost defeated the visiting custodian. Chadburn again essayed to break through the impregnable defence of Liverpool, but generally found McBride and McLean too much for him, although on one occasion he succeeded in eluding the latter, and sprinting in grand fashion, tested McOwen with a stinger. A foul well taken by McCartney was cleverly headed out by Neill, but **McBride** met the return, and by a finely judged attempt sent the ball into the net with a fast low shot. Upon restarting Lincoln endeavoured to break through, but exceptionally fine play by McQue repelled all their efforts, and the home team were again the aggressors. But a short time had elapsed when **McBride** added to his previous success by scoring a second point, amidst tremendous cheers. The home forwards now played up with great dash, and Gordon and McQueen secured fruitless corners. Brilliant passing on the left wing threatened fresh danger, but H. McQueen's final stroke was gamely repulsed by Tice. After the "citizens" had had a momentary look in, principally through the efforts of Chadburn, Lees, and Hewitt, Stott obtained possession, and with his characteristic headlong dash brushed aside all opposition, and passing at the right time **Gordon** easily converted the attempt into another goal for Liverpool.

In the second half the visitors' livened up a little, and after a gallant piece of play by McBride, Lincoln retaliated, and obtained a foul close in the mouth of goal, which, upon being taken, passed into the net without being touched. Still maintaining the advantage, the visitors formed an exciting scrimmage in front of the Liverpool goal, which was only saved with the greatest difficulty. Liverpool again took up an offensive position, and Gordon and McVean doing a good service on the right, carried the ball into the enemy's territory, and **McVean** wound up by securing the fourth goal. The point seemed to completely demoralise the visitors, all their efforts being met with the greatest ease, and eventually the game ended in a decisive win for Liverpool.

RESULT: Liverpool 4 – Lincoln City 0

LIVERPOOL: McOwen (goal); Hannah and McLean (backs); McCartney, McQue and McBride [2] (halves); Gordon [1], McVean [1], M. McQueen, Stott and H. McQueen (forwards).
LINCOLN: Jones (goal); Neil and Simpson (backs); McMillan, Richardson and Willshire (halves); Chadburn, Irving, Lees, Flewitt and Raby (forwards).

Looking for a third successive win in League encounters, Liverpool next travelled to Manchester to face the Ardwick club (now Manchester City). The previous week the Mancunians had defeated Middlesbrough Ironopolis 6-1 after the visitors arrived short-handed - two men having cried off at the last minute, only one of whom could be hastily replaced! No such problems for Liverpool, however, who arrived with their best eleven.

16/09/1893 FL03: Ardwick v. Liverpool
Cricket and Football Field - Saturday 16th September, 1893

Last year's Lancashire League champions (whoa, Blackpool!) made their initial appearance at Hyde road, this afternoon. Since their formation consistent form has been shown, and from the way they have commenced in this competition it is quite possible that they will be found amongst the three qualifying for the First League. Under these circumstances it was not surprising to hear that a bumper gate was anticipated, though on account of the injuries the players received on Monday last, only a weak team was out. In today's eleven "Danny" appeared again much to the delight of the crowd.

It was a magnificently fine day when play commenced before an attendance of over 4000, and they still rolled in encouragingly. Carson started promptly to time and Bowman initiated a fine attack, McCartney heading over his own lines. Nothing came from the flag kick, and Robson followed with a header in exactly the same way, Reagan coming in for applause for sticking to his man. There was nothing to choose between the teams now, hard and determined work being given. A foul relieved Ardwick's quarters. Robson nearly let in Gordon but made amends by good work afterwards. Stott shot a trifle wide at short range. A beautiful attempt by Bowman deserved to score, Yates centreing well, the ball just skimming over the bar. Two goal kicks only rewarded persistent attacks by the Liverpudlians in which McQueen (M) and Gordon were very prominent. Close play came next, each set of halves doing finely. H. McQueen was then penalised, Robson again relieving with a huge kick. Liverpool kept most on the attack, but Saddington got through, and with no one to beat several of the home forwards kicked anywhere but the right place, and McOwen just scrambled the ball up. A few a rough knocks again brought the visitors' under the banner of the referee, and McQueen (M) missed a beautiful opening. Robinson forced Hannah to put outside, and Yates raced along the right and, with Bowman, kept McLean very busy. Robinson then failed to get hold of a neat pass from Carson, and a throw in looked dangerous. Both Carson and Whittle got shots clear at McOwen, who threw away, and two low grounders were put close to Douglas by Stott. The crowd had by this increased to nearly 6000, and the play was keenly watched, and loud applause greeted Yates and Carson for nearly lowering the visitors colours. Another corner was conceded Ardwick but McOwen got to it in time. A shot from Yates was appealed for as a goal, but the ball had gone through the corner.

In the second half Liverpool at once got down, but were strongly repulsed, and a free kick to Ardwick was put over the line. Reagan stuck to Gordon, and McQueen lost the ball when favourably placed, and his namesake lost a clear opening. A moment later a flag kick by H. McQueen was not converted, and Gordon received an injury to his knees. McOwen saved finely from Robinson.

*{Gordon was forced to leave the field for a lengthy period during which time **Stott** scored the only goal of the match.}*

RESULT: Ardwick 0 - Liverpool 1

LIVERPOOL: McOwen (goal); Hannah and McLean (backs); McCartney, McQue and McBride (halves); Gordon, McVean, M. McQueen, Stott [1] and H. McQueen (forwards).
ARDWICK: Douglas (goal); Steele and Robson (backs); Middleton, Whitter and Regan (halves); Yates, Bowman, Carson, Saddington and Robinson (forwards).

Liverpool made a quick return to Manchester for the reversal of the ordinary match against the Newton Heath club. The heathens were without right back Clements and centre-forward Donaldson; Liverpool were without Stott.

20/09/1893 OM: Newton Heath v. Liverpool
Manchester Courier - Thursday 21 September 1893

Played at Bank lane, Clayton, before 1000 spectators.

Liverpool started the game, and Fall had to clear a long shot from the half-back line. Perrins had a big struggle with the Liverpool left wing, but beating them he centred, Rothwell just being too late. Another raid by the visitors made things warm, Lever missing his kick, but Fall cleared a grand shot from Gordon. A free kick against the home team made things look dangerous, but Fall cleared a couple of shots in fine style. Lever got in a couple of long shots right in the goalmouth, but after a brisk struggle the ball was worked away, and the two McQueen's made things dangerous, but Fall cleared his charge once more. Stewart and Hood worked the ball down, and Rothwell just topped the bar with a grand shot. The visitors were having far the best of the play, and from a free kick **McVean** scored with a fine overhead kick, the goalkeeper having no chance.

The second half was again in favour of the visitors, and they made it warm for the home defence, but they were not to be beaten. Again McNaught and Peden and were doing some fine work on the home left, and a grand centre by the latter was only just got away by McOwen. Farman and Hood had one or two chances, but seemed rather slow. Just afterwards the visitors got away, and from a fine cross **H. McQueen** put on the second goal for them, which was shortly afterwards followed by a third, **Gordon** this time doing the needful.

RESULT: Newton Heath 0 - Liverpool 3

LIVERPOOL: McOwen (goal); Hannah and McLean (backs); McCartney, McQue and McBride (halves); Gordon [1], McVean [1], Henderson, M. McQueen and H. McQueen [1] (forwards).
NEWTON HEATH: Fall (goal); Mitchell and Lever (backs); Perrins, Stewart and Davidson (halves); Farman, Hood, Rothwell, McNaught and Peden (forwards).

From the 'Heathens' of Manchester to the 'Heathens' of Birmingham, and last season's First League wooden spoonists to Second League champions. Small Heath (now Birmingham City) had topped the Second Division league table but failed to gain promotion after being beaten by Newton Heath in a test match. After four League games in the current season, like Liverpool, Small Heath were as yet to drop a point!

23/09/1893 FL04: Liverpool v. Small Heath
Liverpool Mercury - Monday 25 September 1893

The splendid form shown this season by the Anfielders, together with the fact that their visitors were last year's champions, caused great interest to be evinced in the game on Saturday, and drew an enormous gate of about 9000. The threatened rain kept off, the sun shone brilliantly during the greater part of the match, whilst the turf, despite the recent heavy falls of rain, was in splendid condition. Hannah won the choice for ends, and decided to defend the Oakfield road goal. Barely five minutes after the advertised time the teams lined up. Henderson the new centre forward, making his debut[21] to a thoroughly sympathetic audience, and M. McQueen taking up McCartney's place at half-back.

Ixon gave the initial kick to what proved a most exciting and interesting match, and the new centre forward immediately made himself a favourite by pushing his way through the ruck, and with Stott and McVean carried the ball well into their opponents' half, while from a nice pass by McQueen Gordon put over the goal line. A couple of fouls against the "Heathens" looked none too promising, as Gordon struck the crossbar with a finely judged attempt, and Stott found employment for Hollies, but Devey at length eased the pressure by sending up the field to his forwards, who at once made tracks for McOwen's charge, but before the opposing quintet got within measurable distance Hannah and McLean had sent them rightabout, and a chance was given to Gordon, which he availed himself of to the fullest extent, executing as fine a run as he is capable of, but unfortunately his centre was not utilised as the opportunity demanded. From the kick out Hallam and Lees obtained possession, and combining effectively carried the ball past McBride and McLean, eventually forcing a corner from the former. This was so well placed that **Jenkyns** had but little difficulty in shooting into the net, thus securing for his team the honour of being the first to break through the almost impregnable defence of the Anfielders. This unlooked for reverse came as a complete surprise both to the home players and spectators, but it had the good effect of steadying them down, and it soon became apparent that Liverpool meant winning. But a short time had elapsed when **Stott** forged his way through the opposing backs, and equalised matters with a high dropping shot, which Hollies only partially cleared. Ringing cheers greeted this signal event, while it gave a fresh impetus to the home team, and it was quite evident that Small Heath would not be allowed any quarter. Brilliant play by McQueen and McQue led up another attack upon the Heathens citadel, but the defence of Smith and Pomfrey, especially the latter, was so sound that some time elapsed before one of the many splendid passes of Gordon and McVean was neatly converted by **Henderson**. This was the signal for a wild burst of cheering, the home team being now in front and going strong and well. Directly afterwards the

---

21   *Home League* debut.

whistle blew for the welcome cessation, and both sides were heartily applauded for their undoubted fine display.

Small Heath soon got to work upon restarting, and McOwen was called upon twice to repel shots from Weldon and Ixon, and a corner following, a sigh of relief was heard all round when H. McQueen came out of the scrimmage with the leather at his toe, and he and Stott raced down the left wing, the latter finishing with a shot which just only missed by a few inches. Once in the enemies quarters the Anfielders were very stubborn to remove, and if anything increasing the pace, kept up a terrific bombardment upon Hollies and his confrères, Henderson on one occasion taking the ball out of the goalkeepers hands, but failing to score. Presently the persistent and well applied energy of the Liverpool team earned its own reward, as **Stott** neatly tricking the half-backs, propelled a low fast oblique shot - the best of the day – which landed into the corner of the net, completely defeating Hollies, the Small Heath custodian. Liverpool were now on good terms with themselves, and the applause meted out to them was richly merited. From this point there was but one team possessing any chance, and but for the arduous and clever work of Smith, Pomfrey, and Jenkyns the champions of last season would have looked very small fry indeed, as the latter portion of the game was a continuous assault by Liverpool against the Heathens goal, whose custodian backed up the Herculean efforts of the backs with capital goalkeeping, and Liverpool not being able to increase their score retired winners - more decisive than the score indicates.

RESULT: Liverpool 3 – Small Heath 1

LIVERPOOL: McOwen (goal); Hannah and McLean (backs); M. McQueen, McQue and McBride (halves); Gordon, McVean, Henderson [1], Stott [2] and H. McQueen (forwards).
SMALL HEATH: Hollies (goal); Smith and Pomfrey (backs); Ollis, Jenkyns [1] and Devey (halves); Hallam, Lee, Ixon, Weldon and Hands (forwards).

Liverpool next travelled to visit Notts County, who had been relegated from the First League the previous season but were already pressing hard to make a return, and, despite their current reduced status, still boasted no fewer than five International players in their side.

30/09/1893 FL05: Notts. County v Liverpool
Nottingham Journal - Monday 2nd October, 1893

In perfectly delightful weather and before a really capital attendance the Notts. Club on Saturday resumed football on the famous Trent Bridge enclosure, scene of so many exciting encounters. The fact that across the water the rival "reds" were contesting hotly with the West Bromwich Albion men in the First League had some effect on the attendance undoubtedly, but the sixpenny side of the ground was crowded as ever in the old days. The game was of a most interesting character, but there is little doubt that Notts. ought to have won. Not that they were entirely the better team on the day, but the goal scored by Liverpool which made the game level, was one of the luckiest ever made in a big match. Some roughness or unevenness of the ground caused the ball to bound just as Hendry was taking what he no doubt thought was a very sure kick, and the ball lobbed past him very simply into the net. It was a complete "astonisher" for everybody, and was received in entire silence. It is doubtful whether spectators except in the immediate vicinity of the goal knew that a goal was scored. The value of Watson to the Notts. side during the game cannot be over-estimated. It was his day certainly. He was yards faster on the ball than either McBride, the half-back, or McLean - he of the Copper-top - and time after time relieved the Notts. side by his fast runs, when nothing else could have done. It seemed almost sure that Bruce and the half-backs were giving the young fellow too much work, but he stuck to it all through very capitally, and appeared capable even of more exertion. Hendry came out of the game with flying colours, and Harper by his very fine forward tackling gave Hendry invaluable assistance. Harper faced the heavy Liverpool forwards with the greatest pluck. Calderhead and Osborne - the latter in the second half particularly - played even better than one had a right to expect. The Notts. forward rank were not seen to their best advantage on account of the style of wing play adopted for the game, but Daft's clinking run and Bruce's volley to the right were responsible, with Watson's aid, for the only goal they scored. The Liverpool team playing a "roughing" game, and Fox had no easy time of it. The visitors were lucky to get off without defeat, but they are a capable team for all that, and the equals of more than a few of the First League clusters. It was a feather in the cap of the Notts. men that they virtually beat the Liverpool men. They didn't get the second goal given to them, but there was little doubt that the ball was over the line on an occasion in the first half when McLean or McOwen (the goalkeeper) kicked it away. It was a long rolling shot by one of the Notts. half-backs - so it seemed, and most people thought the ball through.

Just before three o'clock the ball was started in the direction of the Pavilion goal by Bruce, but the Notts. men did not get, and a sally was made straight away by McVean and Gordon on the visitors' right. There was a lively minute in the left corner of the Notts. territory, but Hendry prevailed finally, and the ball went out on the Liverpool left. Harper, whose throws-in are more powerful than the kicks of some players, gave the ball to his right wing, and Watson roused a hearty cheer by a dashing little run and a clever trick of foot which beat D. McLean, the Liverpool left back. Watson, however, kept the ball a moment too long, and McQue, the centre half-back, dispossessed him. Desultory play, principally in the Notts. half, ensued for a period following McQue's pass to his centre forward, till once more Watson removed the scene of play to the vicinity of the Liverpool goal by a fine run and centre. Hannah, however, punted back, and a foul against Hendry might have been dangerous, but wasn't. The Liverpool forwards certainly passed well, but failed to get near enough for a shot, Harper, Shelton, Calderhead, and Hendry being most persevering and dashing in their defence. Presently, amid a chorus of excited shouts, Watson once more made off with the ball, and put in the most brilliant run of the afternoon - fully half the length of the field - past four of the Liverpool men, leaving the big back, McLean, yards behind him. Watson finally sent in from some twelve yards distance a really grand shot, which, however, the goalkeeper McOwen had the luck to stop with his chest and arms. It rebounded from him, and Watson coming up after his shot with a hot rush, met the ball only to send it against the side-post. Better play and more deserving of success could not have been seen. This incident seemed to be a sort of turning point in the immediate fortunes of the game, for Notts. now took up the play with such remarkable vim and energy that Liverpool were forced well into their own half, and the strength of their defence was thoroughly tested. Daft made some quick runs, and centred several times, Kerr once putting just over. Bruce was ready to make use of a favourable opportunity, but McQue was a close attendant on the Notts. centre forward. Still the attack of the home team was so vigorous and sustained that a goal was almost certain. And this came a few minutes later, as the result of a neat kick to Daft by Osborne. Daft, well placed on the outside, ran and middled to Bruce, who, skipping by McQueen, volleyed the ball to **Watson**. The latter player, meeting the pass very cleverly, sent the ball past McOwen with a smart oblique shot, and the first goal at Trent Bridge Ground of the 1893-4 season was booked to Notts. amidst ringing and vociferous cheers. It was a brilliant success, and gained by play of the first order. The doughty opponents of Notts., however, were merely stimulated to further exertions by the fact of the score against them, and on the right Gordon and McVean made two very effective runs in quick succession. Gordon once shot very neatly across the Notts. goal mouth, but Harper came in with a cool big kick that placed the ball out on the wing. Daft got off from the throw-in, but was checked by Hannah, and once more the play was taken near the Notts. goal by the Liverpool right wing. Just at this point. Mabbott, who had been playing smartly along with Watson, was injured by a kick, and retired for some minutes. Nothing happened in the meantime, and the reappearance of the young. player was hailed with loud applause. Osborne and Harper were doing exceedingly well against their wing, and up to now the Liverpool right outside, H. McQueen, had been altogether unable to get in a single serviceable centre. It was their right wing which seemed to be doing all the work. Henderson, the visitors' centre forward, repeatedly put the ball to the left, but the defence of Harper was really excellent. So indeed was that of Harper and colleagues, seeing that at the end of half an hour Toone had hardly been tested, and there had been only two really dangerous attacks by the visiting forwards. This, however, was due as much to the energetic work of the Notts. forwards as to anything else. They were so often on the ball, and pegging away in the Liverpool half that the halves had all their work cut out to defend, and the Liverpool forwards had to fetch the ball if they wanted it. It was a very fine, fast, and good game, and with the sun casting its autumn glow over the turf the scene was picturesque as well as animated. The sixpenny stand was packed, and their good play gave the liveliest satisfaction. The Liverpool team - such a collection of "Macs" ne'er has been seen - are a heavy, sturdy body of men, undoubtedly clever at the game, skilful both in passing and tackling, but the dash of the Notts. forwards more than counterbalanced the extra weight and power of the others. The question, however, must have occurred to spectators as to whether the greater weight and size and naturally superior physical power of the others might not enable them to last the fast game longer than lads like Watson, Mabbott, and Kerr, plucky and enduring as these youngsters were. To answer this there was the second half to wait for. In the last few minutes of the first half the pace of the game perceptibly slackened, both teams evidently reserving themselves for the final stage of the struggle. Half-time: Notts., 1; Liverpool, 0.

The second half quickly produced a sensation. There was a brief space of play near the Liverpool goal; then with a very fine exhibition of passing the Liverpool forwards went towards the pavilion goal like a wall. Then Toone had the liveliest time he has known this season in an attack that lasted about three minutes. McBride, the right half-back, presented the Notts. goalkeeper with the ball first, just under the bar. He had only just punched this shot out, when Henderson fired it straight back, and McVean put in a third, all of them real scorching shots. There was a perfect storm of cheers at the successful repulse of a most determined and dangerous attack, in which Toone fairly excelled himself. Hendry, too, was specially noticeable, and a few seconds later he had a rousing cheer for beating Gordon in a fair tackle. Then running twenty yards with the ball at his toe he passed it forward to the right. Osborne and McQue had a kicking duel - the ball being the kicked party - before Watson got off at a tremendous pace, and but for McOwen's really clever goalkeeping a score was certain. A minute later another warm attack was made on the Liverpool goal, but the backs this time cleared, and when Watson made his final shot the ball went into the side net. The Liverpool men were, however, playing in such a manner that it was evident the game had yet to be won in spite of the goal advantage held by Notts. Calderhead was certainly doing his best to nullify the efforts of the visiting forwards by taking Henderson out of the centre as often as possible, but the big men wanted a great deal of stopping. On the Notts. forward side the feature was the play of Watson, who appeared to be possessed of endless energy and spirit. Bruce fed the ball to him over and over again, and four times out of the five he got past H. McQueen and McBride, and put in his centre, the efforts of the two backs being particularly directed towards stopping the youngster's attack. Daft got only occasional work, the question suggesting itself whether it would not have been advisable to give Watson a rest, and play the left a little more, particularly as Mabbott was hardly in a condition to play as he otherwise could have done. A free-kick to the Liverpool men roused some excitement, especially as the ball struck the goalpost from the "bully" which followed. Another free kick just afterwards to Liverpool, through the hot haste of Shelton in playing the ball before it had touched the ground after the referee had thrown it up in the Liverpool half. Hannah took the free-kick, but with a long shot put the ball over to the left, where, so simply and foolishly was the goal won that half the spectators possibly never realised it until the ball was thrown up the field. McQueen and Stott ran forward with it when it came on the left, and Hendry apparently missing his kick, when McQueen {***H. McQueen***} shot as Harper went forward to tackle him, the ball rolled into goal, in the simplest Manner, Toone being altogether unprepared to retrieve Hendry's mistake. Notts., l; Liverpool, 1. And twenty minutes to play. It was a saddening, dispiriting incident. But, like Jacob Faithful, spectators consoled themselves with the reflection that they might have better luck next time, and the team went at their work again with vigour in response to cries of "All together; play up Notts!" For some time the game was carried briskly on in the Liverpool half, but on the Notts. right as usual, where McLean headed away a capital shot by Watson. Half-backs and forwards, even Hendry from full back, had shots at the Liverpool goal, both McOwen and Hannah coming out to Hendry's shot. Matters were growing deeply exciting, and more and more so when from a nice pass by Calderhead to the left Daft beat Hannah and centred. McLean gave a corner, and a fierce struggle ensued from a fine place kick. Hannah, however, upset both Kerr and Daft and cleared. Then Hendry - who had mostly the best of his struggles with the Liverpool right wing during the second half beat Gordon and McVean all ends up, and the struggle still went on fiercely in the Liverpool half. It was only through Hendry slipping that the forwards of the visiting side did eventually get away. Then Toone had a shot to stop, but the man who sent it in - H. McQueen - was given off-side quite justly. Liverpool appeared pretty well contented that they were drawing the game, and just now for a spell their efforts were more confined to defence, with occasional kicking - than to getting another goal. In the last few minutes, the strains of the bugle band of the Robin Hoods echoed shrilly over the ground, as the lifeboat procession streamed its way over Trent Bridge, and there was a general exodus of people in the last two or three minutes. Even the players seemed anxious to be off, and the referee's whistle to signal the finish was a relief.

RESULT: Notts. County 1 – Liverpool 1

LIVERPOOL: McOwen (goal); McLean and Hannah (backs); McBride, McQue and M. McQueen (halves); Gordon, McVean, Henderson, Stott and H. McQueen [1] (forwards).
NOTTS: Toone (goal); Harper and Hendry (backs); Osborne, Calderhead. and Shelton (halves); Watson, Mabbott, Calderhead, Kerr and Daft (forwards).

A break from League fare brought a visit to another struggling League One club, Darwen, at Barley Bank. The Darreners played a weak team against a full strength Liverpool.

03/10/1893 OM: Darwen v Liverpool
Manchester Courier - Wednesday 04 October 1893

Played at Darwen before 1000 spectators. Hannah was away from the Liverpool team and Darwen were without Orr, Sutherland, Smith, and Dunlop.

Henderson started, and following a nice run by Stott, H. McQueen shot just above the Darwen goal. Grand passing work by the visitors forwards gave them a distinct advantage in the game, and they pressed severely, but were unfortunate in running the ball over the line. Liverpool got down, but the attack was repulsed. They were soon at it again, and Kenyon had to save a hot one from Matthew McQueen. Then Darwen had a rush up, and, passing the backs in fine style, **McKnight** and Wade ran the ball through fifteen minutes from the start. Liverpool tried hard to equalise, forcing two corners, but the Darwen goal was kept intact by fine defence, Caterall on one occasion saving with three men on him. At length, however, the visitors attacked strongly, and from a scrimmage in the home goal the ball was rushed through {***McCartney***}. A second goal soon followed by **Hugh McQueen**. No further scoring took place up to the interval when the score stood:- Liverpool, two goals; Darwen, one goal.

On re-commencing hostilities the home forwards worked down on the right, and vigorously attacked the Liverpool goal, but the determined defence baffled them, and they had to retire profitless. The visiting forwards then regained the ground, and there was a dashing assault made on the fortress, H. McQueen, Henderson, and McLean causing Kenyon to handle. Darwen escaped for a minute or so, but were not allowed to travel far, and on Liverpool's return there was a repetition of the hard battling process, a goal being obtained after some vigorous play {***H. McQueen***}.

RESULT: Darwen 1 - Liverpool 3

LIVERPOOL: McOwen (goal); McCartney [1] and McLean (backs); M. McQueen, McQue and McBride (halves); Gordon, McVean, Henderson, Stott and H. McQueen [2] (forwards).
DARWEN: Kenyon (goal); Catterall and Leach (backs); Shaw, Maxwell and Fish (halves); Wade, McKnight [1], McKennie, Owen and Hough (forwards).

The first return of the season brought the Ironopolis team from Middlesbrough to Anfield. Defeat on their own ground on the opening day of the had proven to be an ominous portent of the 'Nops season. They had managed only a single victory from five League encounters to date (the rest all being defeats), and now found themselves looking to recover from a 5-0 reverse suffered at Crewe the previous weekend.

07/10/1893 FL06: Liverpool v. Middlesbrough Ironopolis
Liverpool Mercury - Monday 9th October, 1893

Notwithstanding that the visitors to Anfield on Saturday last were figuring near the bottom of the League table, yet a large crowd assembled, numbering some 7000.

Hannah won the toss, and Mooney (late of Bootle) gave the initial kick. Liverpool immediately went to the front, and at once ran over the "Nop's" goal line. From the kick out M. McQueen returned to Henderson, whose shot almost reduced the enemies fortress ere a couple of minutes had elapsed. Keeping in their opponents' half continually Adams and Ord had a warm time of it, and relief was only obtained by McQue putting over the crossbar. A miskick by McLean let in Allport and Moonie, but Hannah came to the rescue and sent up the field, and Stott securing possession, earned a corner, which after some difficulty was cleared by Upton, but a foul against McNair threatened a new source of danger. This was attended to by Grewer, but **McLean** timely meeting the ball banged into the goalmouth, with the result that it passed into the net, and the burly back had the gratification of opening the score. Giving the opposition little or no quarter, the Liverpudlians kept the game confined to Middlesbrough territory, Gordon and McVean being most assiduous in their efforts to reduce the 'Nops citadel. A free kick taken by Hannah was but poorly manipulated, and a miskick by McLean - a very rare occurrence - let in Moonie, who with his support menaced the home goal till Hannah relieved and gave to **Stott**, who culminated a grand piece of work by scoring a second point. Neat passing by all Allport and Mackay carried the ball momentarily into the home half, but M. McQueen raised the siege, and with Gordon and McVean fairly brought down the house by a series of magnificent passes and short fast dribbles, finally ending in Gordon obtaining a fruitless corner. Immediately **Stott** headed a third point through. A slight alteration now took place in the situation of the play, but Gordon settled matters by a fast dribble on the right, which led up to a most severe attack upon Ord, out of which **Henderson** scored a fourth goal. Just previous to half-time the visitors rallied, but were easily repulsed.

Upon resuming Liverpool went at once to the front, but Gordon opened most inauspiciously, as within a couple of minutes this player landed four excellent chances high over the bar. The play of the home team from this point slackened down, and although at times responding to the calls of the onlookers to "play up." yet their whole play lacked that vim and earnestness which delights the spectators. Eventually **H. McQueen** and **Stott** added points, and the game ended in a hollow victory for Liverpool by:

RESULT: Liverpool 6 - Middlesbrough Ironopolis 0

LIVERPOOL: McOwen (goal); Hannah and McLean [1] (backs); M. McQueen, McQue and McBride (halves); Gordon, McVean, Henderson [1], Stott [3] and H. McQueen [1] (forwards).

IRONOPOLIS: Ord (goal); Upton and Adams (backs); McNair, Grewer and Bell (halves); Allport, Mackay, Moonie, Hunter and Deakin (forwards).

Having just achieved their first double League victory of the season, Liverpool had the immediate opportunity of adding another with a trip to Birmingham to visit the Small Heath club. Such was the attraction of the meeting of the previous season's Second Division and Lancashire League champions that the Brummies turned out to fill the home ground in record numbers, the reputations of the protagonists promising a fast, hard-fought game.

14/10/1893 FL07: Small Heath v. Liverpool
Liverpool Mercury - Monday 16th October, 1893

Liverpool's task on Saturday in having to face last year's champions on their own peculiarly shaped ground, was as difficult an order as they will have to complete this season. Anticipating a grand game a large and welcome crowd lined the enclosure, and who gave both teams a very hearty greeting. Liverpool were represented by their usual team, while Small Heath made four alterations to the names which did battle on their behalf four weeks ago at Anfield. No time was lost in marshalling the teams, and, with Liverpool having a slight wind at back, Mobley started the game amidst cheers and counter cheers.

The game had but just commenced when Liverpool were to the front, and **Gordon** completed a fine piece of work on the part of his comrades by shooting a capital goal from a very awkward position. This unlocked for success partially upset the intentions of the home team, while spurring on the visitors', and it was but two minutes later when Gordon slipped along the right, after good work by Henderson and McVean, and dropped the leather in front of Hollies, allowing **Stott** to score a second point. An ordinary team would have broken down under this crushing state of the game, but the Small Heathens played gamely on, and nearly sent the crowd mad by opening their scoring account within a couple of minutes of the last point obtained, a smart run by the outside right and timely centre being met by **Weldon** and headed past McOwen. Now the excitement grew intense, the spectators shouting themselves hoarse as the Liverpool underwent some near shaves, but they toned down a little when Gordon repeated his former performance and raced along the wing finishing with an accurate pass, which **Henderson**, assisted by McLean and Stott, rushed through the "Heathens" goal. Upon the ball being again kicked off, Mobley sent to Hands, on the home left, and he got the best of a tussle with Hannah, and shot in, but although the danger was temporarily removed, yet the persistency of the "Heathens" forwards would not allow the Liverpool defence to get the ball clear, and from a feeble fist out by McOwen, **Jenkyns** lowered the Liverpudlian colours for a second time. Again the spectators showed their animation in a most demonstrative manner, and it was plainly evident that their feverish state had infected the players, as at times the game became a trifle wild, but up to half-time no further damage was created, although a shot by Gordon was not allowed by the referee.

Upon getting to work again the whole pace in no way fell off, and the home forwards were seen to great advantage, many a tight scrimmage being formed in the vicinity of the Liverpool custodian. After about a quarter on an hour's play a goal {***anon***} was awarded to the "Heathens," when, the Liverpool players maintained, the ball had not been in the net, but was picked up from behind. This led up to some wrangling, the Liverpool players being very loath to line up, and when at last the game was recommenced, it was seen that it was a case of war to the knife and give no quarter. McQue was penalised for kicking Mobley, and while the ball was being placed Jenkyns rushed up to move McQue and struck him, for which offence he was ordered off the field. From this point the visitors subjected the home goal to a heavy siege, and the greatest praise must be given to Smith and his coadjutors for their sound defence under such decreasing circumstances, and allowing but one point to be scored after Jenkyns retirement {***H. McQueen***}. Right up to the finish the game could scarcely be called over, as the home forwards made one or two desperate attacks upon the Liverpool goal, but M. McQueen came splendidly to the rescue, and one of the best games that has been played this season resulted in Liverpool winning:

RESULT: Small Heath 3 – Liverpool 4

LIVERPOOL: McOwen (goal); Hannah and McLean (backs); M. McQueen, McQue and McBride (halves); Gordon [1], McVean, Henderson [1], Stott [1] and H. McQueen [1] (forwards).
SMALL HEATH: Hollies (goal); Smith and Reynolds (backs); Ollis, Jenkyns [1] and Devey (halves); Hallam, Walton, Mobley, Weldon [1] and Hands (forwards). [1 anon]

Contrary to the above report, the Anfielders complaint regarding the Heathens third goal, which had equalised the score at 3-3, was not that it had not entered the net, but rather that it had done so by passing through a gap in the side netting where a portion of the latter had become detached from the post! The dispute then caused the game to become bad tempered resulting in McQue being cautioned by the referee for an intemperate tackle on the home centre, Mobley. That was when the opposing captain, Jenkyns, had rushed at McQue and, according to 'The Athletic News,' thrown a punch "worthy of a Corbett[22]" at him, knocking him to the ground, for which conduct he was dismissed from the field. The referee's report, however, was less dramatic, mentioning no punch, and merely stating "I was cautioning McQue when Jenkyns, of Small Heath, came up and pushed him over. I thought the best course to pursue was to send  *Jenkyns off the field." He went on to say that Jenkyns had played a fair game up to that moment and had apologised to him immediately afterward. Jenkyns was subsequently suspended for four weeks over the incident.*

---

22 James J. Corbett - famous heavyweight boxer of the period.

Liverpool now travelled to Preston to battle the famous North End club, who, in five seasons since the formation of the League, had finished twice as champions and three times runners up. With Preston playing their full League team it was Liverpool's sternest test so far.

16/10/1893 OM: Preston North End v. Liverpool
Preston Herald - Wednesday 18th October, 1893

The Liverpool team paid a visit to Preston on Monday, and played Preston North End at Deepdale. There was not a large attendance. The home team were the same as Saturday, with one exception: Waring, an amateur took the place of M. Saunders, who was down with slow fever. The visitors put their strongest team in the field. The afternoon was moist and the ground was rather soft and slippery from the rains of the previous days.

The home side kicked off facing the hill. They at once made for their opponents goal, but a penalty kick relieved the pressure. Play went to and fro, but once Trainer had to handle a big shot from McLean. At the end of ten minutes play, and after a pretty bit of passing **McCann** put through from a pass by Waring. A moment later Trainer had to fist out from a shot from mid-field by McLean. North pressed, and a bombardment followed, but the ball was sent out. A corner was forced from Trainer, but the ball was sent into the next field, McLean's kicking being more vigorous than judicious. At the other end Cunningham failed to gain a footing to turn a good chance to account. Play was desultory for some time. North End got a corner, but it was non-productive. Play went to the other end, and Trainer had to run out. Liverpool pressed, but could not score. Sharp was penalised for a foul. The kick was close in the Preston goal, and looked like going through, but "hands" was given against Liverpool. A moment later McOwen had to punch over the bar, but the corner came to nothing. Half-time came with no further scoring, the home side leading by one to nothing.

After the interval North End had a good run up, but Liverpool sent the ball out. After that Trainer had to kick out. Both ends were visited, and Trainer had two or three anxious moments, but he saved cleverly. McLean's long shots from the back rather bothered him. The visitors peppered furiously for a time, but the Preston custodian saved marvellously. Preston relieved the pressure, and got through the lines of defence, but were pulled up for off side just as a goal seemed certain. A moment later McOwen was called upon to save. "Hands" were given against Preston within two yards of Trainer, who now had a long gleam of sunshine in his eyes, but the ball was got away, and **Cunningham**, taking a pass from McCann, beat McOwen, amid much cheering. North End were now playing in fine form, and McOwen was beaten a third time, the trick being done by **Waring**. McOwen was called upon several times subsequently, but there was no further scoring.

RESULT: Preston North End 3 – Liverpool 0

LIVERPOOL: McOwen (goal); Hannah and McLean (backs); M. McQueen, McQue and McBride (halves); Gordon, McVean, Henderson, Stott and H. McQueen (forwards).
NORTH END: Trainer (goal); R. Holmes and Ross (backs); Sharp, Grier and J. Holmes (halves); Cunningham [1], McCann [1], Waring [1], Becton and Cowan (forwards).

The defeat at Deepdale was Liverpool's first loss of the season at any level.

Liverpool travelled to Burton for a clash that the home team advertised as being "The Match of the Season", and Liverpool gifted their second opponents of the season with a new record home 'gate'.

21/10/1893 FL08: Burton Swifts v. Liverpool
Liverpool Mercury - Monday 23rd October, 1893

Liverpool journeyed to Burton to play the Swifts in the above competition on Saturday. The weather was very fine, and for a second time this season the home club have benefited by Liverpool's success in having a record gate. With but little delay Mr. Charlton had the teams lined up for the kick-off.

Bogie kicked off on behalf of Burton, who played with the sun in their faces. Liverpool were the first to attack, McBride sending in a fine shot, which was as finely met and punted clear by Furness. Mason, on the Burton right, made a short dribble, but McBride robbed him, and sent across to Gordon, who failed to reach the ball just as it was going over the line. Ekins secured from the kick off, and, getting nicely away, centred, but McLean sent out of danger. The Burton forwards all began to exhibit splendid dash, and a little over-weening confidence by McQueen let in the left, and the Liverpool goal was in immediate danger, Mason putting his toe to the ball when very close in, but McOwen saved. Although McLean by a tremendously hard kick sent well down the field Burton soon returned to the neighbourhood of McOwen, and Hannah and McLean were called upon to use some energetic work, which, to their credit, they did well. A long spell of midfield play followed. Stott then had a shy at Jones's charge, but missed by a foot, while Gordon and McVean imitated this non-success a little later on. A sharp dash by Burton gave Monro a very easy chance, which he made a sad mess of, much to the spectators disgust. Immediately after the slip, Liverpool wakened up a little, and Jones, Furness, and West had plenty to do to keep out their visitors', but eventually **McVean** scored, and Liverpool were leading at half-time by a goal.

Upon resuming the visitors rallied, and then the ball not being to Hannah's liking the game was delayed while another was produced. For some time Liverpool were in their opponents territory, but were not able to get a shot through. Stott, McVean, and Gordon made meritorious efforts, but a lack of combination ruined most of the opportunities. The game continued to be of a ding-dong nature, neither side claiming any advantage. Towards the end of the second half the Burton team came out strongly, and, showing more combination, made matters warm for Liverpool; and **Monro** at length beat McOwen with a fast low shot, which McOwen made a gallant effort to divert. Immediately afterwards Ekins, the outside left, put in a splendid run over half the length of the field, but McOwen took the ball away from him just when he was about to shoot. No further scoring took place, and a keenly contested game resulted in a draw of one goal each, Liverpool thus still keeping their record unsullied by a defeat, an honour not held by any other league club.

RESULT: Burton Town Swifts 1 – Liverpool 1

LIVERPOOL: McOwen (goal); Hannah and McLean (backs); M. McQueen, McQue and McBride (halves); Gordon, McVean [1], Henderson, Stott and H. McQueen (forwards).
BURTON: Jones (goal); Furness and Bury (backs); Laurence, West and Parry (halves); Mason, Birch, Bogie, Monro [1] and Ekins (forwards).

Although Liverpool only managed a draw, defeats for Notts County and Burslem Port Vale meant that the single point gained was enough to send Liverpool to the top of the Division Two standings on goal average. Notts County's defeat in particular, also left Liverpool the only club in the English League (either Division) as yet undefeated in a League fixture.

Liverpool made their first trip to the nation's capital to take on the Woolkwich Arsenal at Plumstead. Like Liverpool, Arsenal were newcomers to the Football League that season, in their case being the first Southern club to join and extend the League into new territories. McQue was unavailable due to a strained thigh muscle.

28/10/1893 FL09: Woolwich Arsenal v. Liverpool
Sporting Life - Monday 30th October, 1893

Nearly 8,000 spectators were present during the match at the New Manor Field, Plumstead, on Saturday. It, however, did not turn out so exciting or so pleasant a match to the supporters of the home team as anticipated. During the initial portion of the game half a gale of wind prevailed. The visitors having won the toss took the goal nearest the entrance with the wind at their backs. It was noticed when the homesters made their appearance on the ground that both Davis and Gemmel were still absent from the side through illness.

Heath started the ball, which at once travelled towards the visitors citadel, and was sent behind by Elliott. Following this the ball was worked down the ground by the visitors, and a corner fell to their share, as did one to the home team a few minutes later, but from neither was anything definite scored. The teams seemed now fairly settled down to their work, and some fine fast play was witnessed, each goal in turn being attacked. Another corner was secured by the visitors which proved unproductive, and the ball being sent up the ground by Powell, Booth and Elliott got possession, when the latter sent behind. Plenty of cheering went on from the spectators for various pieces of individual play on both sides. A free kick resulting from a claim for hands from the Reds was of little use to them, as the wind carried it high in the air, but just half an hour from the start Henderson[Ars] had the misfortune to touch one of his opponents, and from this claim **McCartney** sent the ball through, and registered the first goal for the visitors. Restarting the leather, the Reds made a good attack on the visitors' stronghold, but McLean cleared for his side, and almost immediately after McQueen {***M. McQueen***}, by a very long shot, secured the second goal for his side. Appeals were frequent from both sides for trifling causes, and the referee stopped the game, and threw the ball on the ground, and, the visitors gaining possession, took it down in front of the Arsenal stronghold, when, from a scrimmage, **H. McQueen** sent through, adding another notch to the visitors score, Williams at the time being on the ground. Following up their advantage, the visitors kept up the pressure, and although Powell relieved for his side, and Buist and Howat made some good attempts to score, the ball was worked back again and both **Stott** and **H. McQueen** scored again for the visitors, five goals being obtained within a trifle over ten minutes. Neither side relaxed their efforts until the whistle sounded, when they crossed over with the score:- Liverpool, 5 goals; Woolwich Arsenal, 0.

Bradshaw restarted the game, and the home team now having the wind in their favour, attacked in force, but the defence of the visitors was very stubborn, a good shot by Elliott was sent back by McOwen, and both Heath and Booth tried to score, without avail. Then followed a lot of play in mid-field. An attack on the home citadel resulted in a corner for the visitors, but nothing came of it, whilst each side had claims allowed them for infringements, with like result. The wind had now dropped considerably, and the Liverpool representatives again looked like scoring, but Williams was equal to the emergency, and nothing further being obtained up to the end, Liverpool won:

RESULT: Woolwich Arsenal 0 – Liverpool 5

LIVERPOOL: McOwen (goal); Hannah and McLean (backs), McCartney [1], M. McQueen [1], and McBride (halves), Dick, McVean, Bradshaw, Stott [1] and H. McQueen [2] (forwards).
ARSENAL: Williams (goal); Powell and Storr (backs); Crawford, Buist and Howat (halves); Shaw, Henderson, Heath, Elliott and Booth (forwards).

A bumper crowd turned out at Anfield for their heroes return after a run of four away matches which had seen them not play on their own ground in almost a month! In contrast to Liverpool, Newcastle had made an unexpectedly poor start to the season, garnering only five points from their seven opening games in the League, and leaving them languishing low in the table. On the same day Everton Combination (the name used for the reserve side that played in a Midlands league called 'The Combination') played an ordinary match against Liverpool's promotion rivals Small Heath at Goodison, but despite the counter attraction Anfield still recorded a magnificent turnout.

04/11/1893 FL10: Liverpool v. Newcastle United
Liverpool Mercury - Monday 6th November, 1893

This game was played at Anfield on Saturday, before a capital muster of spectators, numbering about 8000. For the first time in a league match this season Hannah was unfortunate in the spin of the coin, and Graham elected to defend the Oakfield road goal.

Bradshaw commenced the game by sending to Stott, who in attempting to break through the half-back line was blocked by Graham, and a foul against Liverpool following, matters did not look too bright for the homesters. However, a run by Gordon and Dick, assisted by Bradshaw, changed the scene of action, but the ball was destined not to remain long, as owing to some misunderstanding by McCartney, Gillespie and Wallace cleverly worked the leather into close proximity to McOwen, but M. McQueen punted clear. Gordon, Bradshaw, and Stott then put in some nice combination, and Lowry was lucky in saving from Bradshaw, who endeavoured to turn to account a centre from Gordon. Having now slightly the best of the play, the home team kept Jeffrey and Miller very busy, and when the former deliberately fouled a shot of **Stott's** close into the goalmouth, and the same player drew first blood a moment later, the yell of delight which came from the crowd testified that they did not approve of such tricks[23]. This good fortune seemed to nerve the players to greater efforts, and for a spell the play was quite of a brilliant order, in which both sides shone to advantage. Supplementing some very neat and effective work by Gordon, Bradshaw, and Dick, Stott and McBride endeavoured to work their way through, but being dispossessed by Graham the game reverted to the other end, Quin, Crate and Thomson being the executants in this scene changing, and the final pass of Quin's being expected to go over the line by the Liverpudlians, was smartly taken by **Thompson** and hooked into the net by an oblique daisy Cutter. This unexpected and preventable disaster had the effect of infusing more life into the play of the home team, who had to be very quick to gain any advantage. Danger to the Anfield fort was again threatened, and by the same player that had brought about it's downfall just previously, but an opportunistic clearance by McLean gave a temporary breather. Playing with exceptional gameness, it was with great difficulty that the visitors were shaken off, but not before McKain and Gillespie both had shies, which were too close to McOwen's charge to be pleasant. At length the siege was raised and away the Liverpool forwards travelled towards their enemies goal, to save which Miller had to concede a corner, and from a resulting foul, again close in, the excitement became intense as the ball bobbled about, and hustled so dangerously near the fatal line; but, mainly due to the almost superhuman efforts of Lowry the charmed space was not intruded upon, and his side could again breathe freely. Not to be staved off, Stott, McQueen and McBride placed the visitors' goal under another assault, McLean coming to the assistance of the half-backs, and shining in grand style with his final attempts, Lowry had no other alternative than to grant a corner, which, being well placed by H. McQueen was finally headed into the net by **Gordon**. Playing on in brilliant fashion, the home team, as if to make amends for the loss of the one goal, subjected the United custodian to a severe bombardment, the earnestness of the Anfield forwards delighting all, and at length some sharp play by Gordon, Dick, and **Bradshaw** culminated in the latter securing the third point for Liverpool. To this the Newcastle men, headed by Thomson, showed some excellent combination which was nipped only just in time by McBride. Half-time found Liverpool leading by three goals to one.

Upon restarting H. McQueen brought himself into unenviable notice by sending two shots in succession yards over the bar. Creilly took up the kick off, and giving his wing an opening they worked the ball nicely up, but the local pass was met by Hannah, who sent to Gordon, and that player travelled rapidly along the right wing and centred in beautifully, Stott making a gallant effort to reach the leather. A period of uninteresting play followed, till Bradshaw dribbled down the centre and passed to Gordon, who, making a fine opening for **Dick**, that player had little difficulty in scoring. The visitors at this stage showed signs of roughness, and when the referee allowed the goal by **Gordon** to count several lost complete control of themselves, and it is not to their credit that M. McQueen was not more seriously injured. As it is, he will have to lie up for a week or two, if not longer. Eventually the game ended in Liverpool scoring their eighth league victory by 5 to 1.

---

23   Presumably meaning Jeffrey's foul, not the goal.

RESULT: Liverpool 5 – Newcastle Utd 1

LIVERPOOL: McOwen (goal); Hannah and McLean (backs), McCartney, M. McQueen, and McBride (halves), Dick [1], Gordon [2], Bradshaw [1], Stott [1] and H. McQueen (forwards).
NEWCASTLE: Lowry (goal); Jeffrey and Miller (backs); Creilly, Graham and McKain (halves); Quin, Crate, Thompson [1], Gillespie and Wallace (forwards).

At Walsall, for the third time in the season, Liverpool presented their hosts with a new record 'gate'. Such was the repute of the Liverpudlian's already that Walsall had spent the preceding week in special training in the hope of putting on a "good show."

11/11/1893 FL11: Walsall Town Swifts v. Liverpool
Walsall Advertiser - Saturday 13th November, 1893

The success of the new Liverpool team in this season's Second League matches has been in every footballer's mouth, and it is not surprising there was a record gate for the new ground last Saturday, when they opposed Walsall, about 5,000 spectators being present. Liverpool came with their best team, including the two most recent acquisitions - Bradshaw and Dick - and Walsall trusted to the eleven (with one exception - Hawkins superseding Warner) which performed at Stourbridge the preceding Saturday. Walsall were first on the field, and directly afterwards Liverpool followed, their blue and white stripes contrasting nicely with the red and whites of the home eleven[24]. The referee got the men punctually to work, and Liverpool, winning the toss, naturally elected to kick downhill with the wind in their favour.

Bradshaw collared the ball from the kick-off, and Hawkins kicked away a faint attempt; the Liverpool centre a second later, when close in, sending the ball into the side of the net. Walsall raised the enthusiasm of their supporters early in the game by the determined way they went for the top end, O'Brien, Cox, and Holmes having good tries. After Liverpool had been penalised for pushing Copeland, the visitors' right wing got down, only to shoot outside twice. A corner fell also to their share, and Dick from this sent in a hot one which only just missed going into the net. The wind greatly assisted the blue and whites, and a second corner tell to them, which O'Brien secured, and went away upheld, only to put the ball over the touch line. Liverpool maintained the offensive for some time, and when Walsall managed get away Cox was pulled up for offside - a decision not relished by the spectators. Returning to the attack, a skirmish round the top goal resulted in Walsall securing their first corner. This was cleared without difficulty, and Gordon went down the right, but was stopped by Smellie. McQueen tried a flying shot, and some hot work round the Walsall fortress on two occasions saw the ball shot out. Holmes and McWhinnie raced away, but McLean knocked the former off the ball and the leather was worked down again, where Bailey was cheered for some good defensive work. The game was full of exciting moments, but a stoppage took place owing to Forsyth getting hurt. He was able to resume play after few minutes, but limped badly for a time. Cox was cheered for some tricky work, but Liverpool speedily gained possession, and after two futile attempts to score **Bradshaw** received a pass close in and beat Hawkins after thirty minutes play. Liverpool gave the home defence

---

24   Very broad stripes! Read halves for both sides.

no rest, and Hawkins caught a splendid shot and threw away. Copeland and Cox broke away and passed to Holmes, who sent across to O'Brien, the latter's attempt to score being foiled by what looked like a foul, but the referee ruled otherwise. Hawkins twice saved grandly, and then long crossing between Copeland and the two wings left the ball with Holmes, who centred beautifully, and Mc Lean missing, **Cox** dashed in sent the ball into the net, the equalising point being greeted with deafening cheers. Encouraged by this success, Walsall played up spiritedly, O'Brien and Cox being very noticeable. McLean got possession, and sticking to the ball had three of his opponents on to him, and the referee, who certainly did not look upon Walsall with a lenient eye, awarded the visitors a foul. This was taken close in, but the ball passed outside without being further touched, half-time immediately following with the score one all.

The interval over, Walsall were the first to show up, but McVean worked his way up the field very prettily, Davies relieving. A foul for hands against Liverpool was negotiated, and Forsyth shot over the bar. A corner shortly after this fell to Walsall, Holmes kicking just on to the net. Two more corners and a foul for bands followed for Walsall in quick succession without bearing fruit, but the ball was kept well in Liverpool quarters, Holmes doing most of the shooting, erratically, however. Cook was playing a sterling game at centre half, repeatedly placing the ball right into the mouth of goal. Liverpool at last broke away, but McQueen was ruled off side. The same played directly after had stiff a tussle with Davies, who lost his feet but kept the ball. The ball was returned and Smellie in saving kicked over the bar, the ensuing corner dropping into the centre and being lifted towards the clouds. Play was very open for a time; Holmes received a long pass from Cox, and dashed down, but in the act of shooting was knocked off the ball by McLean, giving a corner in saving. This proved of no advantage, and the blue and whites took up the running only to be driven back. Holmes gained a corner - again fruitless - and Cook sent in a terrific shot which McOwen saved. Both elevens worked strenuously to gain the point, but without avail, the game ending in a draw.

RESULT: Walsall Town Swifts 1 – Liverpool 1

LIVERPOOL: M. McOwen (goal); Hannah and McLean (backs), McCartney, McQue, and McBride (halves), Dick, Gordon, Bradshaw [1], McVean and H. McQueen (forwards).
WALSALL: Hawkins (goal); Baillie and Smellie (backs); Davis, Cook and Forsyth (halves); Holmes, McWhinnie, Cox [1], Copeland and O'Brien (forwards).

This was only the third League point Liverpool had dropped in eleven matches since the start of the season, and by all accounts the outcome could have been very different had the forward line been firing on all cylinders – it being only bad shooting on their part that had allowed Walsall to remain in contention.

In the away fixture at the end of September, Notts County had given Liverpool the sternest test they had so far experienced in League Two, but the Anfielders had emerged with a coveted point, having held the lace-men to a draw. Now, for the return at Anfield, the two teams were separated by only a single point at the head of the standings - could Liverpool go one better? McVean was absent for Liverpool with an injured knee, whilst Hannah failed to predict the fall of the coin for only the second time since the start of the season.

18/11/1893 FL12: Liverpool v. Notts. County
Liverpool Mercury - Monday 20th November, 1893

The real fight for the position of honour in the second division took place at Anfield on Saturday, when these clubs met each other for the second time. In the previous encounter Liverpool were fortunate enough to make a draw, which, with a fortunate collusion of circumstances, caused widespread interest to be evinced in the game. Notwithstanding the miserably cold weather, about 8000 enthusiasts braved the elements, and they were rewarded in witnessing an exciting game and a satisfactory finish. Both teams were thoroughly representative, the visitors having, however, a decided pull in the way of names of repute. Hannah having lost the choice of ends, Henderson kicked off against a strong wind.

The opening exchanges were rather in favour of Notts, Logan passing over the goal line. From the kick off **Dick** obtained possession and passed out to Gordon, who in his unique style tracked Hendry, and racing off at top speed outdistanced all his opponents, and drew first blood within a few minutes from the start. This eye opener rather surprised the visitors', and special attention was immediately given to Gordon, who almost got clear of his men a little later on, but Harper came rushing across and tumbled him over. The Notts men now got to work in earnest, and some beautiful passing was displayed, Logan, Kerr, and Watson especially being noticeable - the final shot of the latter bringing out the best efforts of McOwen, who thus early on showed himself to be in excellent form. Although gamely repelled by Hannah and McLean the county men were not to be so quickly denied, and again the ball was carried to the home half, Daft and Bruce being responsible for this manoeuvre, and it took McOwen all his time to get rid of a shot from Logan. A couple of fruitless corners fell to the visitors, and then McBride and McQueen changed the venue, Gordon endeavouring to repeat his early success without result, and then Shelton came in for notice for some grand tackling against Dick and Gordon, although he wound up with a badly placed shot. Again McOwen was subjected to a fierce fusillade, but to his credit he came out of the ordeal in brilliant fashion, and after a temporary raid in Toone's half the Notts men, led by Calderhead, came dashing down towards the Liverpool goal, and after several most exciting passages the persistency of the Notts players was at length rewarded in **Bruce** eventually doing the needful with a terrific shot, which was made all the more difficult by the high wind.

The interval having arrived, both teams were heartily cheered, and, after the usual rest, the players got to work again, Notts being the first to show up. Capital forward play by Logan, Kerr, and Watson, assisted by Calderhead and Osborne, menaced danger, which was ultimately cleared by Hannah, and Gordon treated the onlookers to another piece of brilliant work by dashing down the right wing in splendid style, from which a sustained attack was put upon the County goal. Although lacking the finish of the Notts forwards, the Liverpool vanguard were certainly more effective, as after several tries **Henderson** beat Toone after about 20 minutes play in the second half, and Liverpool were then ahead. Now the tug of war began, and although the visitors made strenuous attempts to regain their lost ground the powerful defence of Liverpool repulsed all attacks. To the finish the game was well fought out, and great was the delight when the whistle blew, and Liverpool were recorded victors by:

RESULT: Liverpool 2 – Notts County 1

LIVERPOOL: McOwen (goal); Hannah and McLean (backs), M. McQueen, McQue and McBride (halves), Dick [1], Gordon, Henderson [1], Stott and H. McQueen (forwards).
COUNTY: Toone (goal); Harper and Hendry (backs); Osborne, Calderhead and Shelton (halves); Watson, Kerr, Logan, Bruce [1] and Daft (forwards).

In the evening after the match several of the players got together to celebrate their latest success. The players were strolling around the town when they came upon Wombwell's Royal Menagerie, a travelling animal circus that was then exhibiting at Walton Breck Road, near the Anfield ground. Messrs. Wombwell, owners of the menagerie, were in the habit of offering a gold medal, worth £5, to any member of the audience that would enter the lions cage and remain there, among the wild-bred lions and lionesses, for one full minute. The players then challenged their captain, Andrew Hannah, to take up this challenge. Adventurous to a fault, Hannah rose to the occasion and, amid great excitement in the crowded tent, strode purposefully into the cage behind the lion tamer, and took up his place where directed in the middle of the cage, completely surrounded by the large carnivores. There he remained, seemingly unperturbed, for the required period, exiting only when he had secured his prize and the approbation of the spectators.

Liverpool's trip to Newcastle posed an unusual risk to the players - much of the North East then being subject to a smallpox epidemic. The hotbed of the outbreak was a little further south around Durham, however, with Newcastle, as yet, being relatively unaffected! Liverpool travelled sans McOwen and McVean, both of whom were ill with the flu.

25/11/1893 FL13: Newcastle United v. Liverpool
Liverpool Mercury - Monday 27th November, 1893

This return fixture took place at Newcastle on Saturday, before about 2500 spectators, the weather being cold and miserable. Both teams were minus some of their players, Liverpool being the greatest sufferers in this respect, as Newcastle were only short of Miller (fullback); whilst Liverpool had to fill three vacancies.

Henderson opened the game by kicking off against the wind and incline, but Newcastle were the first to be *en evidence*. Hands gave relief to the Liverpool side, and McQueen and Bradshaw removed the scene of operations, and but for an opportune clearance by Jeffrey might have succeeded in lowering the home team's colours. Led on by Graham the visitors were subjected to another brief siege, till Crate sent over the bar. Henderson obtained from the kick off, and with Dick and Gordon made considerable headway, but Roger's intervened. McCartney had to work desperately hard to drive back Wallace and Gillespie, who throughout the first half were a constant source of danger. Again Henderson and Dick worked the ball up, and Dick breaking clean through the defence had terribly hard lines with his shot, which grazed the bar. Gordon immediately afterwards gave Henderson an opening, but the latter dallied with the ball and thus lost the chance. The game continued to be desperately fought, no quarter being given or asked by either side, and when the whistle blew the required rest was indeed welcome to both teams.

Liverpool had done well to keep the home team from scoring, and it was anticipated that another victory would be recorded, seeing that everything was in their favour. When the players had got to work again it seemed as though the visitors were going to have matters all their own way, Lowry being kept pretty busy for a matter of ten minutes or so. Then Quinn was given a chance, and slipping past McLean he brought the game into the Liverpool 25, where, owing to some slackness by the forwards, who would not take up the passes, the ball remained for some time, till at length a long cross punt by McBride was taken up by Gordon and Dick, and Lowry had to run out to save. Liverpool then assumed the aggressive once more, but there being little vitality or sting in the play the homesters came up the hill in dashing style, several corners falling to their share. The light then began to fail, and it behoved had each side to be particularly on the alert, as a stray shot might find a billet, but the defence on both sides was excellent. The game resulted in a draw, no goal being scored, Liverpool thus remaining undefeated although three months of the season have elapsed.

This match was to prove a turning point for Newcastle. After gaining only 6 points in their opening 10 League matches, they then went on to accumulate a further 30 in the remaining 18 - a points per game average second only to Liverpool!

RESULT: Newcastle Utd 0 – Liverpool 0

LIVERPOOL: M. McQueen (goal); Hannah and McLean (backs), McCartney, McQue, and McBride (halves), Gordon, Dick, Henderson, Bradshaw and H. McQueen (forwards).
NEWCASTLE: Lowry (goal); Jeffrey and Rodgers (backs); Creilly, Graham and McKain (halves); Quin, Crate, Thompson, Gillespie and Wallace (forwards).

Liverpool's next opponent's Ardwick, had run into financial difficulties which had forced them to part with some of their best players. Indeed, only the previous day their clever and speedy right wing pairing of Yates and Morris had been transferred to the Sheffield United club.

02/12/1893 FL14: Liverpool v. Ardwick
Liverpool Mercury - Monday 04 December 1893

The return league match between these clubs took place at Anfield on Saturday. About 6000 spectators witnessed the game, which was played in very foggy weather. Both teams were short of their full complement, McOwen and McVean still being on the sick list, whilst Ardwick have dispensed with their right wing, Yates and Morris, who have gone to Sheffield united.

Henderson kicked off, and after Stott had been rocked by Middleton McBride secured possession, and a very pretty sequence of passes took place between Stott, McQueen, and Henderson, the left winger eventually obtaining a foul off McVicar's close in, from which a fierce attack was put upon the visitors' goal, McBride being greatly to the fore, ultimately causing Douglas to throw away. A forward movement by the Ardwick forwards was checked by McQue, who gave Stott a chance, but again the ever alert Douglas intervened, and no tangible result accrued. Middleton obtained the kick off a little later on, and worked the ball down the right with Saddington and Pickford, but

McLean was too good, and sent them to the rightabout. From a pass by Henderson Dick was then given an opening, but he made a bad miss of it. Immediately afterwards the same player made amends with a splendid shot, which Douglas just cleared. Several corners then fell to Liverpool, all of which proved useless, and then Egan burst away past McLean, but his final shot was wide of the mark. Again the Ardwick forwards brought the ball into the Liverpool quarters, Milarvie shooting in strongly, but with poor direction. After Henderson had essayed an individual effort, in which he was defeated, Saddington and his partner tricked McLean and crossed over to their left wing, from whose return Saddington made a sad mull of the most easy chance. Play once more ranged in the vicinity of Douglas, and at length **Stott** sent the ball into the net with terrific force.

The second half had barely commenced when Gordon caused all eyes to be directed upon him, as he sprinted past all opposition and appeared to repeat his Notts County feat, but McVicars got up to him just in time, and Gordon's shot was badly directed. From this time the Liverpool team had a decided advantage, and with the exception of an occasional burst away by the Ardwick forwards, the home team were continuous aggressors, Gordon being the cause of Douglas being defeated by {H.} **McQueen**, and again later on, when **Henderson** headed a third point for Liverpool. Towards the end of the game the fog became very dense, and the movements of the players were but partially discernible, although it was seen that Liverpool still maintained a persistent attack upon their enemies stronghold. At length the whistle blew, leaving Liverpool victors.

RESULT: Liverpool 3 – Ardwick 0

LIVERPOOL: M. McQueen (goal); Hannah and McLean (backs), McCartney, McQue, and McBride (halves), Gordon, Dick, Henderson [1], Stott [1] and H. McQueen [1] (forwards).

ARDWICK: Douglas (goal); McVicars and Robson (backs); Middleton, White and Regan (halves); Saddington, Pickford, Egan, Davis and Milarvie (forwards).

For the return visit of Walsall, McOwen was sufficiently recovered from his illness to retake his place between the posts. McVean was likewise recovered from his knee injury only to be replaced on the sick-list by Stott with a similar problem. With Henderson also unavailable, Gordon went centre whilst McVean returned on the left and Bradshaw stepped in on the right.

09/12/1893 FL15: Liverpool v. Walsall Town Swifts
Liverpool Mercury - Monday 11th December, 1893

Ideal weather favoured the second meeting of these clubs, at Anfield, on Saturday, when between 5000 and 6000 spectators were present. Hannah's previous good fortune with the coin seems to have deserted him, as he has now failed to secure the choice of goals in four successive games.

The teams lined up promptly, when Gordon started the game. Play opened in a most spirited fashion, the home club having the best of the argument, and, the ball being brought down by the left wing, McBride sent across to the right, and **McVean** drew first blood within three minutes of the start. This happy augury infused more dash than ever into the play of the Liverpudlian's, and a sharp rush by **Gordon** and McVean ended in the former securing a second point when the game was not quite ten minutes old. This second reverse did not at all dishearten the visitors', as after Bradshaw had missed a nice chance, Dunn and Leatherbarrow changed the scene of operations, and slipping past Hannah the former had a glorious chance of distinguishing himself, but sent the leather sky high, to the chagrin of his fellow club mates. Returning to the attack the visitors, by the agency of Lofthouse and McWhinnie, maintained a lengthy stay in the Liverpool quarters, but so good was the display of Hannah that the visiting forwards were rarely allowed to get within decent shooting distance. Responding to the call of the onlookers the Liverpool forwards smartened up, and being well fed by McQue, McBride, and McQueen, laid siege to Warner's charge, Gordon leading the way in splendid style with a rasping shot, which all but scored. Although repelled time after time, the home team stuck to their work with grim earnestness, Bradshaw and McQueen earning merited applause for some excellent shooting, but they could not defeat the agile custodian Warner. A spell of ragged play followed, both sets of forwards playing very indifferently. Close upon half-time Liverpool came again with a grand rush, McQue, McVean, and Dick causing the opposing side many anxious moments, but strong and sure play by Smellie and Baillie eventually gave relief, and the whistle blew for the interval with Liverpool leading by two goals.

The Anfield team now had the assistance of a slight wind, yet their opponents were the first to show up, a grand shot by Dunn bringing out McOwen's best abilities, and it was not until Hannah and McLean had put forth their finest efforts that the threatened danger was removed. Then the home forwards put in some telling work, McVean who had gone outside, tricking Smellie and shooting into Warner's hands. Copeland, McWhinnie, and Lofthouse attempted a forward movement, and, although McLean

was left behind, the ever alert McBride stepped in with a capital lunge, and a foul occurring in the visitors' half, McLean, who was entrusted with the kick, so well placed the sphere that **McVean** put on a third point, and Liverpool having much the best of the remaining play won rather easily:

RESULT: Liverpool 3 - Walsall Town Swifts 1

LIVERPOOL: M. McOwen (goal); Hannah and McLean (backs), M. McQueen, McQue, and McBride (halves), Dick, McVean [2], Gordon [1], Bradshaw and H. McQueen (forwards).
WALSALL: Warner (goal); Baillie and Smellie (backs); Holmes, Cook and Forsyth (halves); Lofthouse, McWhinnie, Copeland, Dean and Leatherbarrow (forwards).

Yet to be truly stretched on their own ground, Liverpool next received another opportunity to exert themselves against a First Division side with a visit from Nottingham Forest who brought their full League side. With Henderson available again Gordon reverted to his preferred slot on the extreme left.

16/12/1893 OM: Liverpool v. Nottingham Forest
Nottingham Journal - Monday 18th December, 1893

This match was played at Anfield on Saturday in fine weather, only a moderate attendance of spectators turning out, however.

This was the first occasion on which Brodie has made his appearance for the Foresters away from home. In the opening play Liverpool had rather the best, and Gordon shot into the hands of Brown, who removed well. Higgins and Pike tried hard to get forward, but they were nicely held in by the half-backs, and no advantage was gained. A pretty advance was made on the Forest left, as a result of which Collins sent in a fine shot which missed only by an inch or two. For a while the visitors' held the advantage, and Shaw was offered a very nice chance, but he was weak with his shot, and a very favourable opening was thus lost. The home team now asserted their form, and Scott was severely taxed. McVean had a good offer made to him, but he failed to use it. and as a consequence Brown had a somewhat lucky escape. Pike and Collins flitted away, and when they were pulled up a pass to the home forwards brought about a brilliant run by Bradshaw, who passed to **Gordon** in front of goal, and the ball was then rushed through without the goalkeeper having any chance of saving. The Forest attack was of a more consistent nature than that of the home team, but the defence was impassable, and all good forward play was therefore discounted. The Liverpool men played a surprisingly good game when they got an opening, and they ought to have scored again had it not been for the weakness of McVean. Forest were very unfortunate when in shooting range, and they had to retire over and over again. A fine combined run by the Liverpool forwards was speedily nullified by Ritchie, who certainly saved a very likely-looking goal. A pretty flash by Pike and Collins gave Macpherson a good look in, and he cracked two shots in at a hard pace, McLean saving the first, and the second going outside. Liverpool were attacking at half-time, when the score stood:- Liverpool, 1; Forest, 0.

On resuming, the Liverpool men were the first to show up, and the goal was twice in danger, but nothing more as it happened. On Forest running in on the right, Shaw smashed in a grand shot which McOwen rendered useless by the aid of his foot. Scott then sent wide, and in the ensuing play the home team held a distinct lead. A short but fierce attack was unfruitful, owing to stern defensive play. Pike did a lot of play, and enabled Forest to make themselves troublesome, but again the shooting was at fault, and Brodie, who was playing a good game in the open field, made a mull of a choice chance. The home team now made it hot for the Forest players and a fierce attack was only rendered ineffective by the most determined resistance on the part of Scott and Ritchie, who saved the goalkeeper all trouble. The Foresters, however, at last, raced off, and rattling shots were propelled by Higgins, Collins and Connor. The defence on this occasion was equal to that which the visitors had displayed, and there was no impression made. Eventually Bradshaw effected an escape, and running the whole length of the field, he passed to **Gordon**, who had no difficulty in notching the second point. The home players were now showing much improved form, and the bulk of the play went hard for the Forest defence. In fact the game resolved itself into a continual bombardment of the visitors goal, and it was merely by the smartness of the backs and the goalkeeper that the record still remained unbroken. At one time Brown fell on the ground to a shot, with the whole of the home forwards on him, but he emerged triumphant, amid loud applause. The Notts. men at this point seemed to have accepted defeat as a foregone conclusion, and did not trouble themselves particularly about attempting to break the ice. It was now a case of Liverpool doing all the pressing, and they made no mistake about their shooting, Brown having a very lively time of it. How he succeeded in saving many of the shots which were banged at him was a perfect mystery to the majority of the spectators, but he continued cool and collected, and kept the goal intact until a minute from the conclusion of play, and then he had to succumb to an attempt by **McVean**, which was afforded him by Bradshaw, the match thus ending in a victory for Liverpool:

RESULT: Liverpool 3 – Nottingham Forest 0

LIVERPOOL: M. McOwen (goal); Hannah and McLean (backs), M. McQueen, McQue, and McBride (halves), Gordon [2], McVean [1], Henderson, Bradshaw and H. McQueen (forwards).
FOREST: Brown (goal); Scott and Ritchie (backs); Connor, McPherson and McCracken (halves); Shaw, Higgins, Brodie, Pike and Collins (forwards).

Without a League fixture on the last Saturday before Christmas Liverpool accepted an invitation to make the short trip to Manchester and a third encounter with Ardwick.

23/12/1893 OM: Ardwick v. Liverpool
Liverpool Mercury - Monday 25th December, 1893

These clubs having no league match to engage their attention, amicably decided to fight a third battle, and for that purpose the Anfield club turned out at Ardwick on Saturday, before 3000 spectators.

Almost at the outset the visitors exhibited a much greater knowledge of the technicalities of the game than the homesters, and were very aggressive. The Liverpool half-backs and forwards almost reduced the home fortress with an incisive onslaught immediately following the kick off. Egan and Milarvie availing themselves of every opportunity, at length got the best of the visitors' defence, and a shot by the former was converted by **Bennett**. The home team were destined not to possess the advantage of the league long, as in less than 3 minutes **Stott** equalised, and by half-time the visitors had increase their lead by two other goals, obtained by **McVean** and **McBride**.

On reversing sides Liverpool continued to have all the play, occasional bursts away by the home left being the only work of any interest performed by the Ardwick club. Before long **McVean** found an opening with a finely propelled shot. **Stott** headed through a little later, and it was left to **McVean** to complete the half dozen. Both sides now eased up, but **White** obtained possession in midfield, and being chased by McQue sent in a finely judged shot, which McOwen caught, but owing to an injury received earlier in the game he was compelled to let the ball goal, and to the surprise of everyone it rolled into the goal space, and thus made the game read six goals to two for Liverpool, at which result the game eventually ended, Liverpool winning in ridiculously easy fashion.

RESULT: Liverpool 6 – Ardwick 2

LIVERPOOL: M. McOwen (goal); Hannah and McCartney (backs), M. McQueen, McQue, and McBride [1] (halves), Dick, McVean [3], Stott [2], Bradshaw and H. McQueen (forwards).
ARDWICK: Douglas (goal); McVicars and Dyer (backs); Middleton, White [1] and Regan (halves); Bennet [1], Pickford, Willey, Egan, and Milarvie (forwards).

Liverpool travelled to Accrington for an Ordinary Match against Accrington at their Thorneyholme Road ground. The Accrington club had started the current season in much reduced circumstances. Former founder members of the Football League, they had, until the end of the previous season, played in the First League until they lost that berth in a promotion/relegation play-off with Second League Sheffield United. Although the club at first intended to carry on in the Second League, to which they had been relegated, and went ahead and arranged fixtures, it soon became apparent that, due to travelling costs, the club's finances would not permit such a course of action. Consequently, at the end of July, tentative enquiries to the Lancashire League having met with approval, they regretfully tendered their resignation from the English League and joined the former.

25/12/1893 OM: Accrington v. Liverpool
Liverpool Mercury - Tuesday 26th December, 1893

The Anfield club having arranged fixtures with the late first league club, the initial meeting took place at Accrington ground yesterday under most miserable climatic conditions. The morning had been exceptionally fine, but just prior to the game the weather took a complete change, and a worse day it would almost be impossible to conceive. Rain fell in torrents and a Gale of wind blew from goal to goal. The home team won the toss, and of course chose the undoubted assistance of the elements.

Liverpool started in my style, and for the first few minutes had all the best of the game; but eventually the home team bore down upon McOwen's citadel, and Hannah, McLean, and McBride had an exceedingly hot time of it; but so satisfactory was their work that a long time elapsed before a breach was effected, **Brown** being the lucky individual.

This was the only score obtained up to half-time, and when the game reopened the home team exhibited an aggressive front, but were sent to the rightabout by Hannah and McLean, and then Liverpool had a lengthened innings, in which Bradshaw ought to have equalised when but two yards from the goal, but instead of which he put the ball high over the bar. After this the visitors were given two fruitless corners, but Hannah, who was playing a great game, defended splendidly, and put his side on the attack again, which they maintained with great vigour till the referee ordered the game to be abandoned, owing to the terrible weather.

ABANDONED (60 mins): Accrington 1 - Liverpool 0

LIVERPOOL: M. McOwen (goal); Hannah and McLean (backs), McCartney, McQue, and McBride (halves), Gordon, Dick, Henderson, Bradshaw and H. McQueen (forwards).
ACCRINGTON: Horne (goal); Hodge and Ditchfield (backs); Shuttleworth, McConvey and Frame (halves); Laurie, Grey, Brown [1], Matthews and Gillespie (forwards).

The ground Liverpool had yet to make up on their city rivals was illustrated when, on Boxing Day, just 6000 turned out at Anfield to witness Liverpool take on a Corinthians team mustering several amateur Internationals, whilst just across Stanley Park fully 25,000 crammed in to Goodison to see a depleted Everton play an ordinary match against Sunderland!

26/12/1893 OM: Liverpool v. Corinthians
Liverpool Mercury - Wednesday 27th December, 1893

About 6000 people collected in the Anfield enclosure yesterday to witness the contest between the famous Corinthians and the Liverpool club. The Corinthians mustered strongly, while the homesters were all in their places.

The lucky Hannah won the toss, and after the opening exchanges McQue's clever tackling gave the ball to Gordon, who got down into the enemies quarters, but was robbed when getting well in. Henfrey, in imitation, broke right through, and racing McLean in long run had an open course before him, but, unfortunately, kicked out. The Corinthian forwards were passing well, and obtained a corner and a foul, in the goalmouth. Liverpool now brightened up, but a fine centre from Gordon was allowed to go to waste, and Fryer getting the ball made a magnificent run, McLean just pulling him up in time. Gordon presently ran up and centred. H. McQueen received the pass, but failed to utilise it. In a minute Gordon raced up again, and this time McQueen put the ball in beautifully, and after one or two returns **Henderson** scored. From the kick-off Liverpool had a long spell of attack, and Moon was called upon three times to save. The visiting forwards were now making determined efforts, but although their combination at times was excellent they were unable to do anything serious, owing to the splendid defence of Hannah and McLean. Hands relieved the pressure for a while. In shooting, at least, the visitors could give the homesters a lesson. Play was now fast and exciting, both sets of forwards working hard to gain an advantage, and attacks were repelled in quick succession. From one of their rushes the home forwards were swarming round Moon, when the latter caught hold of Gordon by the arm and swung him off the ball. The ensuing free kick ended in a corner, which proved of no advantage. The ball was about to be sent into play again when the referee sounded the whistle for half-time.

On the resumption of play the Liverpool forwards made a brief incursion into the enemy's territory. The Corinthians at this stage showing their intention of settling down in the home half of the field. Two corners quickly fell to their lot, but both were useless. The kicks of Harrison and Pelly were clean and decisive and their forwards took every advantage of the position. At last Henderson led the van, and with the greatest difficulty Moon managed to clear a slow, though extremely awkward, shot. The Corinthians were soon again to the fore, McLean this time being conspicuous. At the other end Moon again saved a fine attempts from McVean. Liverpool kept up the pressure for some time, though unfortunately all the final shies were rather high, and they seemed unable to get dangerously near. The Corinthians came on again with a determined rush, and McBride was just in the nick of time to save a goal, at the expense of a corner, which was cleared easily. Pouncing on the ball from the kick off Gordon passed to McVean, who shot over, but when play was resumed **Henderson** ran right through the goal with the ball at his toe, thus registering a second point for Liverpool, amidst loud cheers. Both teams now exerted themselves to the utmost, and Moon and McOwen received attentions within the space of a few seconds. At the visitors' end Moon defended his charge admirably, and but for his wonderful display the score would have increased to a greater extent. The Corinthians are a well built set of men. In running they were superior to their opponents. They are good tacklers, and remarkably quick on the ball. Their gentlemanly conduct led to a very fine game, seldom marred by any unpleasantness. The spectators followed the plate with great interest, and every piece of good work on both sides was applauded with enthusiasm.

RESULT: Liverpool 2 – Corinthians 0

LIVERPOOL: McOwen (goal); Hannah and McLean (backs); M. McQueen, McQue and McBride (halves); Gordon, McVean, Henderson [2], Stott and H.McQueen (forwards).
CORINTHIANS: Moon (goal); Harrison and Pelly (backs); Topham, Winkworth and Bliss (halves); Fryer, Dewhurst, Henfrey, Veitch and Sandilands (forwards).

Liverpool returned to League fare with a trip to Crewe Alexandra, who the previous day had fought out a stubborn 1-1 draw with Newcastle United on the same ground. Liverpool started the day equal on points (26) with Small Heath at the head of the Divisional standings though having played three games less. With Small Heath not playing on the day it was a chance for Liverpool to break clear.

28/12/1893 FL16: Crewe Alexandra v. Liverpool
Liverpool Mercury - Friday 29th December, 1893

The Anfield club played their 16th League game yesterday at Crewe, before from 4000 to 5000 onlookers. Beautiful weather prevailed, and everything promised a fast and exciting game. Promptly to time Mr. Brodie lined out the teams.

Sandham opened the game, but McQue intervened, and gave to McVean and Gordon, who at once made tracks for their opponents' goal. Burnett nipped in with a neat kick, and at once Liverpool were put on the defensive. In this manner the game continued for a time, neither side obtaining any material advantage, till a chance was given to the homesters by a foul from McQueen, which might, with little trouble, have been better utilised. At length H. McQueen raced away, and, centring at the right moment, **Gordon** rushed the ball through, thus opening the score within ten minutes of the start. From this point, Liverpool held their opponents well in hand, but could not break the sturdy defence of Cope and Stafford. A rapid dash by the home forwards relieved the pressure for a short time, but so poor was the direction of the shooting by the Alexandrian's that McOwen was not seriously troubled. The Liverpool forwards then indulged in some very pretty and effective passing, but Henderson failed on one or two occasions to finish up well. Their persistence ultimately claimed its reward, and it came in the shade of a second goal by **Bradshaw**, from a capital screw by Gordon. Just upon half-time a well earned corner, taken by Gordon, was grandly turned to account by **H. McQueen**, Liverpool thus leading by three goals.

When the game was restarted Liverpool were at once to the fore, and almost "did the needful." Generally the play was in Liverpool's favour, Hickson having much more work to do than his business. **McVean** at length got an opportunity, and defeated the Crewe defence for a fourth time, which was succeeded by another from **Henderson** a little later on. After this the Crewe team played up with great vigour, and for the first time a shot by Bennett menaced the Liverpool goal, but McOwen was thoroughly prepared and cleared grandly. An interesting and pleasant game resulted in a decisive victory for Liverpool.

RESULT: Crewe Alexandra 5 - Liverpool 0

LIVERPOOL: McOwen (goal); Hannah and McLean (backs); M. McQueen, McQue and McBride (halves); Gordon [1], McVean [1], Henderson [1], Bradshaw [1] and H.McQueen [1] (forwards).
CREWE: Hickton (goal); Stafford and Cope (backs); Crawford, Cartwright and Barnett (halves); Burrows, Hall, Sandham, Peake and Roberts (forwards).

In a rare new record, this was the first occasion o/n which the entire five man front line scored a goal in the same game.

Having established a two point lead in the Second Division rankings Liverpool looked to maintain that with another win against Grimsby Town at Anfield.

30/12/1893 FL17: Liverpool v. Grimsby Town
Liverpool Mercury - Monday 1st January, 1894

The first visit of the fishermen's team to Liverpool did not rouse even an ordinary amount of enthusiasm, consequently the gate did not reach beyond 3000 to 4000 spectators. McLean is on the sick list, whilst Dick and Stott were given a further rest. Promptly to time the teams lined up.

Henderson gave the initial kick, and immediately operations were transferred into Grimsby quarters where McVean ruined a nice series of movements by punching over the bar. From the kick out, Ackroyd and Riddock obtained possession, and made a brief incursion into the home country, but M. McQueen sent them to the rightabout in magnificent fashion. A lengthy punt by Graham put Jones in position, and nothing but real downright hard work by Hannah remove the danger. Gordon and then cantered down the wing, but the ball was centred into touch. McCarthy took the throw, and so accurately did he perform his work but Henderson was enabled to head while in the goalmouth, and **Bradshaw**, seizing the chance, splendidly rushed the ball into the net, and scored the first point. Grimsby then worked the ball into their opponents' half, and from a grand pass by Jones (who two seasons ago played with Bootle), the Liverpool goal had a very fortunate escape, as McCairns, with an open course before him, missed the ball completely. McBride immediately removing the danger by lifting the leather into midfield, and Henderson receiving headed a rapid dash for the Grimsby goal, and sending out to Gordon at the right time the latter made further ground, and finished by returning the ball to the centre {***Henderson***}, who culminated a most brilliant piece of work by securing a second point for his side. After this success the play became more open, and by half-time no further damage had been brought about.

In the second half the Grimsby team showed more dash than hitherto, while the complacency of the home team was amply justified by the result, as it would have been the height of folly to have forced the game when the visitors were guilty of tricks - to use the mildest term - which will not add to their reputation, on or off the football field. The only item of interest in the second half was a fine sprint by a Bradshaw, who secured the ball from a corner taken by an antagonist. Eventually the game ended, leaving Liverpool victors:

RESULT: Liverpool 2 - Grimsby Town 0

LIVERPOOL: McOwen (goal); Hannah and McLean (backs); McCartney, McQue and McBride (halves); Gordon, McVean, Henderson [1], Bradshaw [1] and H. McQueen (forwards).
GRIMSBY: Whitehouse (goal); Lundie and Frith (backs); Higgins, Graham and Russell (halves); Ackroyd, Riddock, McCairns, Fletcher and Jones. (forwards).

Liverpool started the New Year with their third League Fixture in five days. Having beaten Woolwich Arsenal 5-0 at Plumstead in October, they had every prospect of continuing to improve their points tally.

01/01/1894 FL18: Liverpool v. Woolwich Arsenal
Liverpool Mercury - Tuesday 2nd January, 1894

This match took place at Anfield yesterday, being the return league fixture between the teams. Fully 5000 spectators assembled, and the weather and ground were most favourable to the game. Liverpool turned out their full team, while the visitors were also fully represented.

Henderson kicked off against the Anfield goal, and the play was of a give and take nature for some little time, till the visitors opened out somewhat, and Hannah was called upon to defend. The Liverpool forwards responded, and Gordon and McVean changed the venue, Henderson almost completing some excellent work by his supports, and Liverpool then held command for a time, and corners fell freely to the home team, who, however, were unable to find the right spot. After a spell of really fine play by the "Reds" the ball was again brought to the immediate vicinity of the visitors' goal, and from the resulting corner **McBride** open the score with a fast low shot. Immediately succeeding this play took place in the Arsenal's quarters, a pretty bit of combination bringing about a futile corner for Liverpool. Midfield play then became general till Liverpool again took up the running, and smart work by McQueen and Stott gave **McVean** an opportunity, which he promptly accepted, and added a second point to Liverpool score. The Arsenal were now put entirely on the defensive, shots coming in from all quarters, but their defenders repulsed all the attempts, and half-time arrived with Liverpool in the ascendancy by two goals to nil.

Upon resuming the game was mostly played in the visitors' half, till a sudden rush by the Arsenal forwards made matters look none two rosy for the Liverpudlian's. McLean, however, with a heavy punt removed imminent danger. After this the visitors had somewhat the best of the game, but the home team held them well in hand, and, although not exerting themselves as they might have done, kept the Southerners from scoring, and the game ultimately resulted in another win for Liverpool.

RESULT: Liverpool 2 – Woolwich Arsenal 0

LIVERPOOL: McOwen (goal); Hannah and McLean (backs), McCartney [1], M. McQueen [1], and McBride (halves), Dick, McVean, Bradshaw, Stott [1] and H. McQueen [1] (forwards).
ARSENAL: Williams (goal); Powell and Storr (backs); Crawford, Buist and Howat (halves); Shaw, Henderson, Heath, Elliott and Booth (forwards).

In was customary in those days, due to the rigours and costs of travelling on the railways, for teams to travel with just the requisite number of men; or in the case of a more cautious few with one man extra - 'just in case[25].' On the occasion of their trip to Rotherham it seems that Liverpool chose to take with them their entire first team playing staff (except Bradshaw, who was lame) – despite serious doubts as to whether the match would go ahead. Heavy snow had fallen overnight whilst a heavy fog hung over Rotherham right up to the time of the visitors arrival. The fog, however, then promptly dispersed and despite two inches of snow still laying upon the ground the referee ruled that conditions were adequate to proceed with the game as a League match. The severe conditions did, however, mitigate against the expected bumper 'gate'. Kick-off was delayed 20 minutes, however, due to the non-appearance of the home side's centre forward, Rodgers forcing a reshuffling of their team – centre-half (Longden) to centre-forward, full-back (hobson) to centre-half, and reserve player (Simmonite) to full back. Town's keeper, Arthur Wharton was something of a novelty, born on the Gold Coast (now Ghana) and being now generally regarded as the World's first black professional footballer!

06/01/1894 FL19: Rotherham Town v. Liverpool
Sheffield Daily Telegraph - Monday 8th January, 1894

The ground being covered with snow did not prevent this fixture being brought to issue at Clifton Grove, Rotherham. Mr. Gilbert, of Notts, referee, inspected the playing arena, and declared it fit for the game. Liverpool had left nothing to chance, bringing along all their first top men, something like sixteen in number, being thus prepared for any

---

25 There were innumerable instances of away teams that didn't take this precaution arriving a man short because a player missed the train or was taken ill *en route*.

emergency. Hannah and Bradshaw stood down, the latter being lame. Considerable disappointment was occasioned by Rodgers not turning out for Rotherham and a delay was occasioned in finding a substitute, Simmonite at last filling the vacancy.

Rotherham started in the direction of the Park, close on twenty minutes after the advertised time. Liverpool's lines were at once entered, but the stay there was brief, a visit to the opposite end seeing McQueen shoot wide, M. McQueen failing similarly. McBride forced Wharton to give a corner. It was unavailing and the Townsmen then forced play out to the centre. Rae then sent out to the right, Turner jun. and Longden responding with a spirited attack, McBride only foiling them close on the line. The game being carried across, Gordon gave Wharton a scorcher to negotiate. He was equal to it, a raid at once following in the Liverpool goal. Barr, however, shot wide. Warm and even exchanges succeeded, Rotherham giving quite as much as they had to take. One grand run from Turner, jun., as nearly as possible leading to the downfall of the Liverpool goal. Superb defence, however, saved it, but it underwent more of the same thing. A capital passing run by McCormick and Fairburn failing to bear fruit, the Liverpudlians forced their way up, and after the forwards had failed, hit the bar. A further attack by the visitors yielded them a corner, but this being abortive the Townsmen had another go; Longden's miss, however, went harmlessly over the line, and the visitors rushing straight up from the goal kick **Stott** served a grand goal, this coming just half an hour from the start. With the renewal Rotherham forced the play, but being driven back a corner fell to Liverpool. It was profitless, as was a free kick to the same side shortly afterwards, Rotherham then going down by their right and centre. The ball going out, Liverpool again took up the running, Henderson hitting the upright. A kick against Turner, sen., looked bad for Rotherham, but the ball was got away, the Townsmen in turn having a determined go for goal. Nothing came of it, the Liverpool defence being too good to be pierced. The visitors retaliating, H. McQueen sent in a beauty, which **Henderson** just caught and converted into a goal, an appeal for offside not being entertained. With the ball again set in motion, the Townsmen forced the game. Turner, sen., was pulled up when off-side in a fine single-handed run. The crowd lustily hooted the referee's ruling, and while this was at its height the half-time whistle sounded, change of ends being taken with the score:- Liverpool, 2 goals; Rotherham, none.

Liverpool entered Rotherham's half when the ball was again set rolling, but being driven back, Fairburn sent in a grand shot that McOwen only just cleared. The Townsmen coming again, a free kick was given against Liverpool for tripping, and Turner taking this, McOwen only saved his goal by pulling the bar down. Other attacks on the Liverpool goal succeeded quickly, but, being in the main not over well organised, nothing came of them. Gordon at length transferred. With his first attempt he ran the ball out, but getting a further opportunity he gave McVean a rare chance. That player troubled Wharton greatly with a rare shot, but the home custodian getting the ball away, Liverpool's end became the scene of operations. A free fell to the Townsmen, but though nothing came of this, the home front rank kept the game going, and **Turner, jun.**, getting the ball nicely away, that player finished up with a grand goal. Liverpool forced matters strongly when the game was again set going, and but for stout defence, coupled with faulty shooting, the Rotherham goal might easily have been lowered. A corner at last rewarded them, but failing with it, Rotherham broke loose. Turner, jun., however, took poor advantage of a good opportunity; but the Townsmen returned to the attack. McCartney having twice all he could to dispose of the attacks of the Rotherham right. A change coming over the scene, Wharton twice saved well, McQueen's shot for goal being especially fine. Keeping up the pressure, Liverpool at last got a corner, and this being nicely dropped was converted into a goal, **Stott** putting the finishing touch. The front rank playing up strongly, Wharton again was beaten, **H. McQueen** shooting a beauty off a pass from Gordon. Nothing further followed. The game ending:

RESULT: Rotherham Town 1 – Liverpool 4

LIVERPOOL: McOwen (goal); McCartney and McLean (backs), M. McQueen, McQue and McBride (halves), Gordon, McVean, Henderson [1], Stott [2] and H. McQueen [1] (forwards).
ROTHERHAM: Wharton (goal); Simmonite and Turner sen. (backs); Barr, Hobson and Bartlett (halves); Turner jun. [1], Longden, Rae, Fairbairn and McCormick (forwards).

On January 8th, Liverpool entertained an almost full strength First Division Burnley in a benefit match in favour of the "McGregor Fund." William McGregor, the founder and former chairman of the Football League had been forced to give up that office during the previous summer due to ill health. In recognition of all he done for the sport the Football League had subsequently initiated the McGregor Fund in his benefit to aid him in his time of need, and had let it be known at the general meeting in December 1893 that they expected all clubs to actively participate in contributing to the fund. Several, like Liverpool and Burnley, did so by participating in benefit matches. Unfortunately, the severe cold on the day limited the crowd at Anfield.

08/01/1894 BM: Liverpool v. Burnley
Liverpool Mercury - Tuesday 9th January, 1894

Owing to the arctic-like conditions under which this game was played the spectators did not reach anything like a respectable number. Hannah again stood out of the Liverpool team, whilst Bowes was the only absentee on the Burnley side. McLean was fortunate enough to win the toss, and elected to play with a slight wind in his team's favour.

Espie started on behalf of the visitors, but the ball was pounced upon by Stott, who forced his way through the ruck and gave to the right wing, they running down towards Hillman, but their final aim was misdirected, a goal kick only resulting. McQue met the kick out, and, nicely placing in, a rush by Dick and Henderson caused Hillman to use his fists to clear. Burnley then replied with some excellent combination, and carried the game into Liverpool Territory, but owing to want of nerve and determination lost many a good opportunity. Midfield play next ensued, Liverpool having slightly the better of the argument, but it was not till Dick broke away that a real change came about, Henderson, although given a splendid opening by the right winger, failing to utilise the chance, fumbling rather awkwardly till Nicol removed the danger with a huge kick. Liverpool, however, came again, and, the left wing giving to Henderson, that player shot in, Dick rushing up and completing the effort, but the referee gave the point off-side. A heavy lunge by Crabtree at length let Burnley in, and Hill and Place worked the ball nicely up to the Liverpool goal, but failed in a miserable manner at the final pinch. Again the home team rushed the ball to the visitors end, and from a cross pass by

McQueen, **Gordon** obtained possession and scored a grand goal. Stott immediately headed over the bar, and then Turnbull missed a golden opportunity given by his partner. Burnley then held command of the game for a spell, but as all their attacks lacked sting they met with the usual result, failure. A splendid dash by Henderson at the last moment earned a well merited corner, which, however, was neatly closed by Hill, this bringing about half-time.

Upon resuming, the Burnley team commenced in an earnest manner, but so good was the half-back play of the Liverpool team that the visitors were sent to the rightabout, and a sprint by Gordon caused Hillman to handle. Espie, Place, and Hill replied with a speedy concerted movement, in which McCartney showed to advantage in defeating the intentions of the Burnley men. McBride was then fouled, but nothing came of it till the Burnley left wing came cantering down the left wing, and from their pass Turnbull brought out McOwen with a spanking shot, but the Liverpool man was not to be caught napping, and removed the danger magnificently. Liverpool then endeavoured to break through the Burnley defence, but were only partially successful, Crabtree being a great stumbling block. Before long the home side got well into the Burnley quarters, and **Henderson**, taking full advantage of an accurate pass, put on a second point for Liverpool. After this both sides warmed to their work, Burnley striving to score, while the homesters were content to keep the visitors at bay. As time drew near Liverpool came with a great rush, and it looked as though they would increase their score, but the game finished as above, Liverpool being returned winners:

RESULT: Liverpool 2 – Burnley 0

LIVERPOOL: McOwen (goal); McCartney and McLean (backs), McCartney [1], M. McQueen [1], and McBride (halves), Dick, McVean, Bradshaw, Stott [1] and H. McQueen [1] (forwards).
BURNLEY: Burnley (goal); Nicol and Lang (backs); King, Crabtree and Livingston (halves); Brady, Turnbull, Espie, Place and Hill (forwards).

Only a week after severe winter weather had spoiled the gate for the benefit match with Burnley, conditions, considering the time of year, could hardly have been more different for the return visit of Rotherham, which took place on the mildest of spring-like days.

13/01/1894 FL20: Liverpool v. Rotherham Town
Liverpool Mercury - Monday 15th January, 1894

The return engagement between these clubs took place at Anfield on Saturday, in ideal football weather, and before a large audience, there being fully 5000 people present. Liverpool were still without Hannah, McVean, and Stott, while the visitors required the services of Bartlett and Pickering sen. to complete their team.

Rae, having started on behalf of the visitors', the game was immediately located in the Rotherham half, McQue sending over the bar after pretty work by Dick and Gordon. Sustaining the attack Bradshaw was unfortunate to put on the net, and a foul given against Turner was so well manipulated by M. McQueen that **Henderson** had little difficulty in opening the score. Still maintaining full possession of the game the Anfield team made strenuous endeavours to again pierce Wharton's defence, but that wily and self possessed individual was in magnificent form, and although fairly peppered with shots by Henderson, Bradshaw, and McQue, he still remained the victor. Turner, the left back, was compelled to grant several corners, all of which proved useless owing to the famous sprinters clever display. At length some timely following up by Rae and Pickering gave Cutts a chance, and he, tricking M. McQueen, had a clear field, but McCartney came to his comrade's assistance, and the threatened danger was for a time evaded. Strong half-back play on the part of the visitors confined the game in the vicinity of the home 25 flag, but the failure of Turner to take advantage of a chance enabled McLean to lunge out and placed his side in possession of the attack, but the final attempts of the right wing met with but little success. Rae who throughout was ever on the alert for the slightest chance, again got away with a nice dribble, but "hands" ruined what appeared to be a splendid opportunity. Being well supported by McQue, M. McQueen, and McBride, the Liverpool forwards put in some really clever passes, Henderson in particular playing the passing game with rare judgment. A sudden break away by **Bradshaw** and McQue carried the leather into the neighbourhood of the visitors' goal, the former winding up with a terrific shot, which Wharton could not reach. Shortly after this Gordon put another past the visiting custodian, but was chagrined to find the point disallowed on an appeal for offside. The Rotherham forwards then had a spell, and Rae, Cutts, and Turner jun., initiated a rather mild attack upon McOwen, who, however, had to use his hands to clear. To this futile effort the home forwards replied with grand dash, Turner, sen., kicking past the post to save what would have been an almost certain goal.

Half-time arrived with the home team leading, and barely had the game been resumed when, from a combined run by Dick, **Gordon**, and Henderson, the Liverpool left winger met the pass and beat Wharton with a good shot. Playing with great skill and ingenuity, the home team bore down again upon Wharton's charge, Dick working the ball into the goalmouth, and crossing to Bradshaw, whose shot was grandly nonplussed by Wharton, but **Henderson** lying handy added a fourth point. In no way disheartened the visitors resumed work with greater vigour and skill and were rewarded by notching a unit against the champions {*Turner*}. This warmed up both sides, and the game was more keenly fought than ever, Dick shooting several capital Rugby goals, whilst Rae headed out a fine attempt by Turner. Hands against Rotherham resulted in a free kick being awarded, which being again beautifully planted by M. McQueen, allowed the irresistible **Bradshaw** to head into the net giving Watson no chance and interesting game concluded in another win for Liverpool:

RESULT: Liverpool 5 - Rotherham Town 1

LIVERPOOL: McOwen (goal); McCartney and McLean (backs), M. McQueen, M. McQue, and McBride (halves), Gordon [1], Dick, Henderson [2], Bradshaw [2], H. McQueen (forwards).
ROTHERHAM: Wharton (goal); Broadhead and Turner sen. (backs); Longden, Hobson and Barr (halves); Turner jun. [1], Cutts, Rae, Pickering and Fairbairn (forwards).

For the Lancashire Senior Cup tie at Blackburn, no fewer than four of the team were carrying injuries or suffering from some other indisposition. Consequently, Liverpool travelled with the full squad, and the team to face the Rovers was only selected in the dressing room immediately before the match.

20/01/1894 LSC-R1: Blackburn Rovers v. Liverpool
Liverpool Mercury - Monday 22 January 1894

These clubs antagonised each other for the first time at Ewood Park on Saturday. The weather was not of the pleasantest description, rain falling at frequent intervals, yet fully 8000 spectators witnessed the game. The Rovers, with the exception of Whitehead, turned out their usual team, while Liverpool at the last moment relied upon what may now be styled their representative team. Murray, the Rovers captain, having won the toss, a feat which the spectators cheered heartily, set Hannah and his team to face an oblique wind.

Mr. T. Helme having given the signal for the commencement of hostilities, Henderson kicked off, but the Rovers forwards broke through with the ball, and Calvey completed the incipient piece of work by shooting wide of the desired mark. The Rovers left next introduced the play into Liverpool quarters, and after Hall had beaten Hannah, McLean came to his comrade's assistance, but was compelled to grant a corner. Gordon then obtained possession, and with McVean made considerable headway, but Brandon eventually sent them to the rightabout by transferring the leather to the centre of the field, where Haydock and **Calvey** fastened on to it, and dribbling sharply down towards the Liverpool fortress, the latter shot past McOwen from about 20 yards range, with a fast low shot after 6 minutes play. Upon restarting, Gordon and McVean made play for the visitors', ultimately sending over to Bradshaw and H. McQueen, and the latter shot very poorly when in a fairly good position. The Rovers during the early stages had all the best of the argument, their forwards and half backs combining beautifully. From a high dropping shot of Forrest's, the Liverpool custodian had to fully exert himself to evade disaster, and cheers arose when he finally emerged victorious. Very persistently did the Rovers maintain the pressure, and the defence of Hannah and McLean were sorely taxed. A beautiful centre of Chippendale's was only dealt with at the expense of a corner, which, being grandly placed, was headed by Calvey to **Chippendale**, who wound up by directing a straight, high shot, McOwen making but a feeble effort to clear, this goal coming after 20 minutes play. In spite of these disasters, Liverpool kept pegging away, and Henderson, by many timely passes, opened the game somewhat, a run by Gordon earning a futile corner. Hardly had this taken place when Hannah was deservedly cheered for a magnificent save from "Chip," the game being of a fast and furious nature. A promising run by Gordon, McVean, and Henderson was nipped in the bud by Marshall, who gave to Hall, and he and Haydock carried the sphere in close proximity to McOwen's charge, but without any tangible result. A new ball being requisitioned McQue led up an attack led up an attack upon Murray, but the final efforts of Liverpool were weak in the extreme.

After the usual interval the Rovers were the first to show up, but a huge lift by McLean opened up a furious attack upon Ogilvie, and from a weak return by Murray Bradshaw sent forward to Henderson, who, defeating Brandon, dribbled close in upon the Rovers' goal, and, giving to **Bradshaw**, the latter promptly sent into the net. The play of the visitors was unquestionably improving, their forwards and half backs commendably imitating their opponents mode of procedure with success, and as a result the play chiefly ranged in the Rovers' half. A beautiful opening was given to H. McQueen by Henderson, but he dallied too long, and Murray interposed with effect. Still sustaining the improvement in their play, Gordon, McVean, and Henderson were responsible for some telling shots. Campbell and "Chip" then removed the venue, but found a stumbling block in Hannah. However, the Rovers attacked strongly, and from a bully in front of goal **Chippendale** increased his team's lead. Showing great determination, the Liverpool team again for a time overplayed the Rovers, and Gordon, after being heavily grassed by Brandon, got the best of the famous back and crossed to **H. McQueen**, who safely planted inside the charmed space. The game now became more exciting than ever, both sides using vigorous means to obtain their ends. A sudden rush by Hall and Haydock changed the scene of action, and McBride, in attempting to head the leather out of his goal, accidentally handled the ball, and from the doubtfully awarded penalty kick, **Forrest** added another point for the Rovers. Not in any way disheartened, the Anfield players showed splendid grit, and were at length rewarded by again piercing the Rovers' defence, **Henderson** being the operator, and a highly interesting and well fought game resulted in a victory for the Rovers.

RESULT: Blackburn Rovers 4 - Liverpool 3

LIVERPOOL: McOwen (goal); Hannah and McLean (backs), M. McQueen, M. McQue, and McBride (halves), Gordon, McVean, Henderson [1], Bradshaw [1], H. McQueen [1] (forwards).
BLACKBURN: Ogilvie (goal); Murray and Brandon (backs); Forrest [1p], Anderson and Marshall (halves); Chippendale [2], Campbell, Calvey [1], Haydock and Hall (forwards).

After the match the Athletic News noted that "although beaten, Liverpool were not disgraced at Blackburn. To run the Rovers to a goal in a Cup tie is a feat which clubs with far greater pretensions than Liverpool cannot accomplish." *Indeed to score three goals against the famous cup fighters on their own ground was in itself a signal achievement. Moreover, with just a little bit more luck they could easily have won. Not only did the Liverpool players feel the penalty awarded against them was unjust, they were also adamant that when Ogilvie stopped a shot by McVean just before the final whistle it was already considerably over the line.*

In the First Round of the F.A. cup Liverpool were drawn against Grimsby Town, the fishermen drawing the right for choice of ground. Thanks to what the Liverpool Mercury described as "the disbursement of a fairly large monetary solatium," however, the Liverpool committee were able to induce their North Lincolnshire counterparts to make Anfield the choice of venue.

27/01/1894 FAC-R1: Liverpool v. Grimsby Town
Liverpool Mercury - Monday 29th January, 1894

This tie, originally to have been played at Grimsby, took place at Anfield on Saturday, before about 8000 spectators. A high wind sadly interfered with the game, while later on rain added to the discomfiture of both players and spectators. Each side had a representative eleven.

Liverpool having won the toss, McCairns set the ball rolling towards the Oakfield Road goal, but Stott was given possession, and from his centre a fruitless corner resulted. Henderson next had an opening, but met with a resolute opposition from Graham. Assisted by the wind, the home side were continually on the aggressive, but could not make much impression upon the visitors' rearguard. From a foul against Grimsby McLean nearly headed through, this being Liverpool's best effort up to that stage of the game. Grimsby then made an incursion into the Liverpool half, Jones and Riddock working the ball up nicely against McQueen and Hannah. McLean came to his confrere's assistance, after which McQueen was penalised for a foul throw in. The referee's decisions had the effect of rousing both teams, and, as a consequence, fouls became more frequent than the game warranted. Liverpool still continued to have the better of the argument, on one occasion the ball being almost rushed into the net from a rugby like scrimmage in goal. After McQue had sent forwards, Bradshaw topped the crossbar, McVean imitating his club mate immediately afterwards. Rough play then characterised the game, in which Grimsby were awarded several free kicks, from one of which Jones outpaced Hannah, and sprinted towards the Liverpool goal, crossing to McCairns at the right moment, who transferred to Rose, the latter player thoroughly testing McOwen with a fast daisy Cutter. After this Liverpool again returned to the attack, and laid siege to Whitehouse, but no vulnerable spot could be discovered, although the assault was maintained with great resolution. Another break away by Riddock, Jones and McCairns ended in the latter bringing the home custodian to his knees with a stinging shot. Liverpool now improved, and after 35 minutes play **Bradshaw** scored for the home team, while a little later on **McQue**, with a grandly judged shot, defeated Whitehouse for a second time.

While the teams were away during the customary interval rain began to fall heavily, making the conditions as miserable as can be imagined. Liverpool, by good forward play, reopened in promising fashion, but Frith nipped in and returned the leather to his forwards, Jones again treating McOwen to a most difficult shot. A rapid dash by Stott removed the danger temporarily; but the Grimsby team bore down upon the Liverpool defenders with a characteristic a rush, almost doing the trick. Hannah and McLean were, however, fully prepared for their opponents, and no tangible result accrued, Grimsby were not making so much use of the assistance of the elements as was expected, while the Liverpool half-back line were settling down into some beautiful work and fed their forward rank in much better style than hitherto. Henderson, Stott, and Bradshaw got clean away, but a deliberate trip by Higgins grassed Stott just when danger was imminent. Hannah and McQueen then became prominent in pulling up Jones and Riddock. From a throw in by McQueen Gordon was given possession, and after making some little headway sent to Henderson whose meritorious effort just failed to score. The Liverpool forwards and half-backs were now virtually becoming masters of the situation, and had more of the play than their opponents. At length a splendid piece of combination between McVean and Gordon resulted in the latter moving up to the corner, and centring accurately, **Bradshaw** rushed up and scored the third goal for the home team. Eventually the game ended in a decided win for the Liverpool team by three goals to nil.

After the game it was understood that, owing to the generous support given to the Anfield road club, they will not be out of pocket after paying the Grimsby claims.

RESULT: Liverpool 3 - Grimsby Town 0

LIVERPOOL: McOwen (goal); Hannah and McLean (backs); M. McQueen, McQue [1] and McBride (halves); Gordon, McVean, Henderson, Bradshaw [2] and Stott (forwards).
GRIMSBY: Whitehouse (goal); Lundie and Frith (backs); Higgins, Graham and Russell (halves); Ackroyd, Rose, McCairns, Jones and Riddock. (forwards).

The big talking point ahead of Liverpool's Division Two fixture with Northwich Victoria was the draw for the second round of the F.A. Cup in which Liverpool had been awarded a home tie against Preston North End. Preston were no longer the side that a few season's earlier had earned the appellation of 'The Invincibles,' but they were still a considerable force to be reckoned with, and one of only two teams, Blackburn Rovers being the other, to have defeated Liverpool in any kind of match that season. As for the current match, Liverpool were without some key men, but as the runaway leaders in the division pitted against the hindmost stragglers an easy victory was expected.

03/02/1894 FL21: Liverpool v. Northwich Victoria
Liverpool Mercury - Monday 5th February, 1894

The first meeting between these clubs, who occupy rather unique positions in the league table, took place at Anfield, on Saturday, before nearly 4000 spectators. Both teams were without some of their regular players, but Liverpool were the greatest sufferers in this respect.

Liverpool having won the choice of ends, Eyres kicked off against a strong wind, but at once McQue intervened, and gave to Henderson, who in turn put over to McVean, the latter spoiling the effort by sending high over the bar. Hughes met the kick off, and returned into Hornby's hands, who at once demonstrated his utility as a custodian. Never allowing the opposing forwards any chance, the home half-backs completely confined the game in the "Vics" quarters, but brilliant goalkeeping on the part of Hornby, and sturdy defence by Scanlon, Postles, and Guest, kept the intruders at bay, although some good work by McQueen, Dick, and McVean was almost turned to account by Henderson. Shortly afterwards one of the visitors palpably fouled the ball within the dreaded twelve yards limit, and **McLean** taking the kick safely piloted into the net. Directly afterwards another foul took place in the Northwich goalmouth, and the little custodian brought about a marvellous save from Bradshaw. Continuing the bombardment, McQueen raised a laugh by the crowd against himself by endeavouring to lift the leather into Anfield road, when a nice opening showed itself in the visitors' well packed goal. Hutton and Gallimore once got past McCartney but McLean returned, and corner succeeded corner; but at length **Stott** converted one, and just before half-time arrived the same player {**Stott**} put the finishing touch to some capital work by Hughes and Dick, Liverpool thus leading by three goals.

Upon resuming, the home team held their opponents well in hand, McQue and Hughes repeatedly repelling rushed by Finnehan, Eyres, and Drinkwater, and the play after some little time settled down in the immediate vicinity of Hornby, who was seldom allowed a rest. Shots assailed him from all directions, Dick, McVean, and Henderson each suffering hard luck, but eventually **Henderson** by a single-handed effort added a fourth point to Liverpool's credit, who thus won a rather quiet and uninteresting game.

RESULT: Liverpool 4 – Northwich Victoria 0

LIVERPOOL: McOwen (goal); McCartney and McLean [1p] (backs); M. McQueen, McQue and Hughes (halves); Dick, McVean, Henderson [1], Bradshaw and Stott [2] (forwards).
NORTHWICH: Hornby (goal); Postles and Scanlon (backs); Clarke, Guest and Barlow (halves); Drinkwater, Finnehan, Eyres, Gallimore and Hatton (forwards).

This was not in fact the first meeting of these clubs as the reporter states. They had actually met for the first time in an F.A. Cup tie at Northwich the previous season. It was, however, the first at Anfield and the first in a League fixture.

The arrival of the Cup tie against Preston being eagerly anticipated excitement was high on the day of it's arrival. The day had initially been scheduled for Liverpool's return trip to Northwich in a Division Two fixture against the Vics, the latter having had to be re-arranged. As for the Cup tie, not only had Preston beaten the Anfielders in an ordinary match earlier that season, but extra spice was added to the tie by the fact that it had taken three epic battles for Liverpool's illustrious neighbours, Everton, to edge past them the season before! Indeed such was the turnout that many had to be sent away disappointed, the gates being closed early on a full house.

10/02/1894 FAC-R2: Liverpool v. Preston North End
Liverpool Mercury - Monday 12th February, 1894

When it was found that Liverpool were drawn against the famous North Enders in the second round a great tie was anticipated, and in this respect no one was disappointed. Fortunately, the weather held up; and although a high wind prevailed, blowing from end to end, the ground was in capital condition. Liverpool turned out with a fully representative team, although Stott, fit and well, is an improvement to the left wing. North End's persistent ill-luck still clung to them in this match, and they had to face one of the stiffest conflicts of the year without the redoubtable N.J. Ross. Owing to the insufficiency of accommodation, a large number were unable to witness the game, the gates being closed some time before the teams turned out. Hannah led the way with the home team, and he received an enthusiastic reception; but the warmer greeting was accorded to Trainor and his men. Mr. Lewis, the referee, soon called the respective captains together, and the fall of the coin was most anxiously awaited by the crowd, who, when it was found that the Liverpool captain had secured the choice of ends, gave vent to their pleasure in an unmistakable manner.

Promptly the teams lined up, and upon the signal to commence hostilities being sounded, Ross gave the initial kick to what proved a most exciting and highly interesting day. The ever ready McQue pounced upon the leather and sent out to Gordon, who found Drummond too good, but McQue again obtained possession and sent over the bar from a lengthy range. By a series of throw-ins on their left wing, the North End team removed the play, and a foul occurring within the Liverpool quarters, a sigh of relief was heard when Ewart missed by the upright. From the kick off the home team went right away, and Gordon dropped into the goalmouth in nice fashion, and after bobbing about in a dangerous manner, in which several of the players endeavoured to get at the ball, Holmes in driving hard out had the misfortune to see the leather cannon off **Henderson**'s legs into the net, Trainor having not the slightest chance of saving the shot. This unexpected success imbued the Liverpool team with great confidence, and a well sustained attack was levelled at Trainor's charge, Henderson eventually sending outside. Led by Ross, the North End team laid siege to the home goal, and a heavy scrimmage took place in the immediate neighbourhood of McOwen, who, however, was not personally called upon. Beckton then fouled McVean, but the resulting free kick involved no tangible point. Fine play by Grier against the Liverpool left was nullified by McBride, who gave to Henderson, but that player rather wildly sent too high. Although having by far the most of the game, several dangerous excursions were made into the home half, Gordon, Cunningham, and Ross generally being to the fore, but the exceptional judgment of McBride, who twice robbed Ross when in possession of a clear field, defeated the aims of the invaders. Some good work by Gordon and McVean, assisted by M. McQueen, gave Drummond and Holmes some anxious moments, but Sharpe came to the rescue and passed to his wing forwards, who, in conjunction with Ross, initiated a sharp attack upon the home goal, Grier giving relief by skimming the crossbar. Returning to the attack, Gordon and Henderson did some pretty work, the former repelling a fine cross shot, which McQueen just missed - a near thing for Preston. Even exchanges prevailed for some time, both sets of half-backs doing magnificent work, and breaking up all attempts by the opposing forwards. A fine punt by McLean was secured by McQueen, who wound up with striking the upright. Both sides exhibited a splendid game, and Liverpool had rather the best of matters. With a splendid cross shot **McVean** added a second point to the team's score. Hardly had the game been restarted when Gordon and Cunningham took the ball into the corner, and after some little finessing it was centred into a favourable position, and **Ross** rushed up and crashed the leather through, without giving McOwen a possible chance. Up to half-time Liverpool were mostly on the aggressive, Henderson getting a beautiful shot at Trainor which almost defeated him.

On resuming, with but such a slight lead it was anticipated that North End would run out rather easy winners, but after a few minutes play it was found that the Liverpool halves were playing in such a fearless manner that it would require a special effort on the part of North End to get through. Sharp lifted much too high when in a good position, and a heavy goal kick by McLean sent the leather well up the field, and McVean fastening on the ball put in some clever work. North End came again, and from some good forward play **Beckton** equalised. The fight now began if possible even more earnestly, each side striving every nerve to gain a leading point, but Liverpool staying the better outplayed the Preston team, and succeeding a nice run by Gordon, **Henderson** converted the pass of the former in a most finished manner into a third goal. From now to the finish the game was most keenly contested, both goals undergoing sharp attacks, and a welcome cheer was raised when the whistle blew, leaving Liverpool winners of a most sensational game.

RESULT: Liverpool 3 – Preston North End 2

LIVERPOOL: McOwen (goal); Hannah and McLean (backs); M. McQueen, McQue and McBride (halves); Gordon, McVean [1], Henderson [2], Bradshaw and H. McQueen (forwards).
PRESTON: Trainor (goal); Holmes and Drummond (backs); Grier, Sanders and Sharp (halves); Gordon, Cunningham, J. Ross [1], Beckton [1] and Cowan (forwards).

The crowd that packed into Anfield on that day was estimated at around 18,000 with gate receipts amounting to around £460. For those unable to gain admission there was at least an easy, if not so attractive, alternative, just a short walk away across Stanley Park Everton compensating for their own earlier exit from the Cup competition by entertaining Sheffield United in an ordinary match.

After Northwich complained to the Football League over the non-fulfilment of their League fixture Liverpool were ordered to pay them £25 in compensation! This seems to have been based on the premise that the fixture would have to be rearranged for midweek when Northwich could not expect as large a 'gate.' Even so, it seems a little harsh on Liverpool who were not responsible for the fixture clash other than by their success in the cup competition!

In the third round of the F.A. Cup, Liverpool's tremendous drawing power was felt even at Bolton's Pike Lane, accustomed as it was to hosting top First Division matches as well as exalted Cup ties. Despite the normal admission price being doubled on the day (from 6d to 1s.) the 16,000 that turned out was the largest crowd seen on the ground in ten years. In League terms, Bolton were having a poor season, lying low in the table, giving the Liverpudlians real hope for a victory, especially if conditions suited them and their fast attacking style of play. Indeed, a journalist of the 'The Athletic News' noted that a few days before the match Mr. Barclay, the Liverpool secretary, had said "If the ground is dry we will win; it it is not we shall lose." Either way, they would have to do it without two key men, McBride and Henderson being on the sick list.

24/02/1894 FAC-R3: Bolton Wanderers v. Liverpool
Liverpool Mercury - Monday 26 February

When it was found that these two clubs were drawn together, at Bolton, it was generally admitted by those who knew anything about football that the Wanderers would prove just a trifle too good for their more younger opponents, and the result more than confirmed this opinion. Unfortunately our local club, through the indisposition of some of the players, were unable to place anything like a representative team upon the field, and this, coupled with the sticky and heavy going nature of the ground, combined to bring about the defeat of Liverpool. Long before the teams appeared the ground and stands were fairly packed, and by the time of the kick off every coign of vantage was occupied by enthusiastic followers of the great winter game. According to the computation of accredited individuals and officials the gate fully reached 20,000 so that Liverpool, if at length defeated, have greatly increased their bank account. The ground had undergone special preparation, and to all appearances looked firm and easygoing, but it's deceptive nature was soon found out when the game had been in progress but a short time. Hannah having won the toss elected to play with a fierce wind at his back.

Promptly to time Cassidy set the ball rolling, and he and his flanks were at once off towards the Liverpool goal, but a foul occurring caused the game to be transferred to close proximity with Sutcliffe, where, however, a free kick given against McQueen for offside play gave relief. Mainly due to excellent offensive play by McQue and M. McQueen the play was mostly confined in the Wanderers quarters, but a huge kick by Jones temporarily eased the pressure, and after McQueen had caused Sutcliffe to handle Bradshaw suffered very hard lines with a headed ball just grazing the bar. A strong rush by Willocks carried the ball to the other end of the field. M. McQueen failing to follow up, and a misunderstanding occurring between the backs, the Bolton forwards promptly seized the chance and rushed the ball through ere the game was seven minutes old {**Dickenson**}. Liverpool showed up better after this, and monopolised the game, forwards and halves all shaping well; but what with weak centre play and the magnificent work of Somerville, Jones and Sutcliffe the visitors could not find a vulnerable point. A fine opening was given to Liverpool, the result of a foul; but although well placed in by McLean was badly finessed, as was the succeeding corner. Just as half an hour had elapsed another dash by the Wanderers' forwards culminated in **Bentley** converting a lofted pass by Willocks. Try as they would, the Liverpool men could not break the defence of the trio mentioned above, but the Wanderers goal underwent two narrow squeaks - one from Bradshaw, and also from a bully formed right in the mouth of goal.

Ultimately half-time arrived with Liverpool claiming no advantage after having the assistance of the wind, but upon restarting showed more nerve and skill than hitherto, and several times looked like scoring, but when the Wanderers had put on a third goal {**anon**} the game was irredeemable, but it was not till McVean was hurt that the home team asserted superiority, and the last part of the game was entirely in favour of the Wanderers, and it is a rather remarkable feature of the match that neither side made that use of the semi-gale, when having it's great assistance, as was expected. Eventually the Wanderers retired victors.

RESULT: Bolton Wanderers 3 - Liverpool 0

LIVERPOOL: McOwen (goal); Hannah and McLean (backs); McCartney, McQue and M. McQueen (halves); Gordon, McVean, Stott, Bradshaw and H. McQueen (forwards).
BOLTON: Sutcliffe (goal); Somerville and Jones (backs); Paton, Hughes and Turner (halves); Tannahill, Willocks, Cassidy, Bentley [1] and Dickinson (forwards).

At half-time the Liverpool captain had made a formal complaint to the referee over the state of the pitch. After the match, however, the Liverpool committee chose not to proceed with this and in the true spirit of sportsmanship sent a letter to Bolton informing them of that decision and tendering heartiest congratulations upon their victory!

For their second annual charity festival, rather than emulating the established annual Everton event, as they had the previous season, Liverpool now chose to go their own way, leaving the thespians to Everton and instead celebrating the two rival codes of football – but still all in favour of the same needy causes, the Liverpool hospitals. Centrepiece was a second friendly encounter with the Newton Heath club, a match which was given especial significance by a glance at the respective League tables.

With Newton Heath points adrift at the foot of the higher League and Liverpool points clear at the head of the lower it was looking odds-on the pair would face each other in the first of the end of season promotion/relegation test matches. In the event, however, the match was hardly a true test, as, due to many of their first team players being caught up in a court case[26], Newton Heath were unable to raise even a full side, let alone a representative one.

01/03/1893 CH: Grand Charity Festival
Liverpool v. Newton Heath
and Liverpool Old Boys v. Birkenhead Park and New Brighton (Rugby)
Liverpool Mercury - Friday 2nd March, 1894

The second annual football festival, inaugurated by the committee of the Liverpool F.C. in sole aid of that most deserving, yet inadequately supported, institution, the Stanley Hospital, took place yesterday at the Anfield ground. Catering for followers of both codes, an Association and a really excellent Rugby game was provided, and, without doubt, the latter created more interest than the former. The dismal meteorological conditions under which the festival commenced completely nullified the arduous efforts of the special committee, as when the game Liverpool v. Newton Heath commenced there were but about 2000 spectators. Owing to almost the whole of the Newton Heath team being in requisition at the law courts in Birmingham as witnesses in the unique libel suit, "Newton Heath football club v. Birmingham Evening News," the visitors were but poorly represented, and, to make matters worse, played throughout with but ten men.

In the first half Liverpool had much the best of matters, and held complete sway, the monotony being only relieved by occasional bursts away by Clerkin and Farman, who frequently showed a clean pair of heels to McLean; but by half-time the home players were leading by two goals. The remainder of the play was of an uninteresting character although the visitors had the assistance of the wind, and Liverpool adding a third point won somewhat rather easily by three goals to nil.

Shortly after the close of the Association game the local rugby teams - Liverpool and Old Boys v. Birkenhead park and new Brighton - turned out. The game opened evenly, but eventually Liverpool took the lead and Wilson placed a goal from a fair catch. On restarting the Cestrians put in some neat work, principally forwards. Eventually Nicholson sprinted beautifully down the left, and scored. But the goal kick was a failure. Scoring was now fairly brisk, for the Cheshire men secured a penalty goal, following which Allen ran in a try. Nothing further was scored up to half-time, when the Liverpool team was leading by seven points to six.

---

26 The Newton Heath club had brought a libel action against the "Birmingham Daily Gazette" over comments in it's report of their home match against West Bromwich Albion in which the newspaper had characterised the Heathens players as being brutal, cowardly, cheats! After a lengthy court hearing the Mancunians were vindicated in winning the action, but the jury showed their contempt for the case in awarding damages in the amount of one farthing (¼ of a penny!) - both sides to pay their own costs.

After the change of ends the Liverpool contingent attacked strongly, but owing to the sloppy nature of the ground there were many mistakes made. Bell twice essayed at goal, but the ball glided harmlessly over the line, and only minors accrued. Fenton and Nicholson at length brought the play to midfield, where Melly saved nicely, when Henshaw started a capital dribble, which resulted in Goold scoring near the corner. Wilson took the place kick, but failed at goal. After the dropout Bell sprinted nicely down the left, but when a try seemed certain Nicholson stepped in the breach and punted nicely into touch. A moment later Bell was off again, and after a clever dodgy run scored near the corner flag, Wilson again failing at goal. Loose forward play was of rare service to the Liverpudlians, and for a lengthy period packs were contested near the Cheshire line. At length Fenton got off with a capital run, and Bleasedale being in attendance the ball was carried to the Liverpool half. Goold recovered to midfield, and this brought about time, with the Liverpool contingent leading by one goal and three tries (13 points) to one goal (penalty) and one try (6 points).

A more detailed account of the Newton Heath game:

Manchester Courier - Friday 2nd March, 1894

The first item on the programme was the game between Liverpool and Newton Heath, but unfortunately neither team was represented at anything like its full strength.

The opening stages of the game were entirely in favour of Liverpool and the play had not long been in progress before Dick and Stott both struck the crossbar. Some splendid hard work was shown by both teams, the only difference being that the visitors used their heads for purposes of defence whilst Liverpool were almost uninterruptedly on the attack. Newton Heath at length made an incursion into their opponents territory but were not allowed to get within shooting distance of McOwen. Liverpool soon returned, and Bradshaw missed the upright with a stinging shot, Worgan immediately afterwards heading into Douglas's hands. Again the visitors attacked strongly, and by means of pretty passing placed the Liverpool goal in serious jeopardy. Once the crossbar was struck with a lightning shot, and the visitors were also granted a free kick near the goalmouth, which was however unsuccessfully negotiated. Liverpool were not long before they retaliated, and a brilliant shot by Dick was grandly saved by Douglas. The latter was severely tested during the next few minutes, one save from H. McQueen being a real beauty. It was evident that this pressure could not long be maintained without breaking through the visitors' defence, and **Dick** at length scored with a swift high shot. The game was conducted in rather a listless fashion, with the advantage all in Liverpool's favour, and after several hot shots **Worgan** scored a second goal, which the visitors vainly appealed against on the ground of offside. Half-time result: Liverpool, two goals; at Newton Heath, nil.

Upon resuming rain was falling heavily. Liverpool immediately commenced to press, and McQue and McLean both had shots at goal. Eventually **Bradshaw** scored from Stott's centre, and the same player afterwards put the ball through again, but was ruled offside. Both ends were afterwards rapidly visited in turn, and McOwen and Douglas both had ticklish handfuls to negotiate. Liverpool continued to attack strongly, but the defence from this time forwards proved impenetrable.

RESULT: Liverpool 3 - Newton Heath 0

LIVERPOOL: McOwen (goal); McCartney and McLean (backs); M. McQueen, McQue and Hughes (halves); Stott [1], Worgan [1], Dick, Bradshaw [1] and H. McQueen (forwards).
NEWTON HEATH: Douglas (goal); Felton and Lever (backs); Hood, Stone and J. Mathieson (halves); Farman, Clarkin, Rothwell, Parker and W. Mathieson (forwards).

The Mercury gave no teams but asserted that Newton Heath played with ten men. The Manchester Courier, however, enumerated eleven (as above). It is likely that the eleven named by the latter were those selected to play before the event, one of whom was subsequently unable to do so.

Liverpool's injury and sickness problems continued with now four regular first team members, Stott, McBride, Gordon and McVean unavailable for selection – the latter three suffering from bad colds. As well as regular replacements McCartney, Bradshaw and Dick this left an opening also for Albert Worgan, a young amateur player (and therefore technically a free agent) from Aigburth Vale who had been playing with the reserves. Worgan had been tested in the festival match against Newton Heath and scored one of the three goals. Stott, meanwhile, would never regain regular his berth in the Liverpool side, losing his place to new signing Givens, and then transferring to Grimsby at the end of the season.

03/03/1894 FL22: Liverpool v. Burton Swifts
Liverpool Mercury - Monday 5th March, 1894

The return engagement between these teams in the League tourney took place at Anfield on Saturday in bright and ideal football weather, and before about 8000 people. Despite the recent heavy rains the turf was in capital order. The visitors turned out as advertised, while Liverpool were compelled to take the field with what was generally remarked to be an "experimental team."

Having won the toss the Swifts captain set the Anfielders to face a strong breeze, and Henderson started the game by sending to Bradshaw, who, however, lost possession and the game was early on located in the home quarters, but no real danger became apparent. Good half-back play on both sides was the most prominent feature till a capital dribble by M. McQueen carried the play into the neighbourhood of Jones's charge. However, a dashing run by Ekins, who received from Bury, menaced the home goal, but the visitors right failed to take a grand opening which presented itself. McCartney, who throughout played strongly, at length gave the ball to Dick, who went away at top speed, but Worgan failed to utilise the final pass. Liverpool now began to have a look in, and Henderson, being given possession by McQue, headed an onslaught upon the visitors' defence, but Dick was rather wild when the finishing touches were required. Some erratic kicking by McLean allowed the visitors to make progress, Hannah eventually coming to his confrère's assistance by giving a corner. Henderson was noticeable when the kick was taken by fastening on the ball and getting nicely away, Dick winding up with a grand centre, which brought Jones to his knees. The Burtonians replied with some clever combination, and the Liverpool halves had to bestir themselves to put off the strong attack initiated by their *vis-a-vis*; but after M. McQueen had brought off a great coup, **Ekins** at a second venture safely landed the leather in the net, after half an hour's play. This reverse rather nettled the home players, and as a consequence Jones became very busy being lucky with a shot from Dick. Grand back play by Furniss neutralised several good attempts by H. McQueen and Bradshaw, but a nice cross pass by the former suffered extremely hard lines in not been turned to account. Still maintaining the pressure the Liverpool attack could bring about nothing tangible, owing to being met with a finished defence, although numerous shots just skimmed the bar and passed near the uprights.

Half-time arrived with Liverpool in a minority, but the game was barely five minutes older when **McLean** equalised from a foul in goal. From that moment the Liverpudlians persistently attacked Jones's citadel and corners fell frequently to the share of the home team. From a throw in by McQueen the ball bobbled about in front of Jones in a most dangerous fashion, and after Henderson, Bradshaw, and McQue had attempted to score **Worgan** neatly placed the leather past Jones, the same player {*Worgan*} adding a third point after Jones had partially cleared a splendid shot by Henderson. Several times Burton made tracks for the Liverpool goal but were generally dispossessed before getting within range of McOwen and Liverpool ultimately ran out winners.

RESULT: Liverpool 3 - Burton Town Swifts 1

LIVERPOOL: McOwen (goal); Hannah and McLean [1p] (backs); McCartney, McQue and M. McQueen (halves); Dick, Worgan [2], Henderson, Bradshaw and H. McQueen (forwards).
BURTON: Jones (goal); Furness and Bury (backs); Perry, West and Birch (halves); Dewey, Rowan, Bogie, Monro and Ekins [1] (forwards).

Liverpool started off their campaign in the new County Palatine League with a home fixture against Preston North End. The committee of the new league had passed a resolution that reserve teams may be fielded in Palatine League matches subject to the discretion of the clubs involved, and on this occasion Preston fielded a decidedly mixed side against a virtually full strength Liverpool – the latter including new signing John Givens (inevitably another Scot, signed from Paisley Abercorn!).

10/03/1894 PL01: Liverpool v. Preston North End
Liverpool Mercury - Monday 12th March, 1894

This match, the first of the Palatine League fixtures, took place at Anfield, on Saturday, before 12000 spectators. The weather was very fine, although a strong wind rather marred the game. Owing to the late appearance of the visiting team the start was delayed fully a quarter of an hour. Both sides were fairly representative, but Liverpool were the better off in this respect.

Hannah having won the toss elected to play with the wind. Operations at once were transferred to the Anfield goal, Henderson receiving from McBride and compelling Trainor to save a straight but rather slow shot. From the kick out Liverpool again worked the ball down, but a foul against Givens gave relief, and Ross, Cowan, and Roy obtaining possession from Grier immediately changed the venue, the ball being run over the Liverpool goal line. Even exchanges followed till McVean skimmed the bar with a fast attempt. A poor kick by Dunn was carried into touch by the wind, and from McCartney's throw a scrimmage was formed in front of Trainor, out of which **Givens** safely steered the leather into the net, thus opening the score for Liverpool. Led on by Ross the North End forwards essayed a forward movement, and being well backed up by Grier and Sharpe ultimately secured a barren corner. To this the Liverpool right replied with a dashing run, Nidd having to concede a corner to Henderson. Some clever work now took place round Trainor, but that custodian was in brilliant form, and saved repeatedly. At length a fine individual effort by Gordon carried the ball into the North End territory, and placing to **McVean** at an opportune moment that player scored with a magnificent shot, which roused the enthusiasm of the crowd to its highest pitch. Up to half-time Liverpool maintained a heavy attack, but did not increase their score, while the Prestonians almost brought about the downfall of the Liverpool colours by an excellent shot of Roy's.

Upon resuming Liverpool were at once to the front, Trainor barely saving from Henderson. Then the visitors' Vanguard got to work in downright earnest, and only good defence on the part of Liverpool saved McOwen's charge. As the result of some pretty work by Ross, Cowan, and Roy, the ball was taken in front of the home goal, but Henderson (Preston) removed the danger by sending over the bar. Both goals then went underwent narrow shaves. North End rather had the best of matters, but could affect no breach in the solid opposition of Liverpool, and for the second time the North End had to retire defeated.

RESULT: Liverpool 2 – Preston North End 0

LIVERPOOL: McOwen (goal); Hannah and McLean (backs); McCartney, McQue and McBride (halves); Gordon, McVean [1], Henderson, Givens [1] and H. McQueen (forwards).
PRESTON: Trainor (goal); Dunn and Nidd (backs); Grier, Orr and Sharp (halves); Henderson, Cunningham, Roy, J. Ross, and Cowan (forwards).

Despite the below strength nature of the Preston side, Liverpool's victory imbued the team with confidence ahead of the trip to face another First Division side, Burnley, three days later in another Palatine fixture.

12/03/1894 PL02: Burnley v. Liverpool
Liverpool Mercury - Tuesday 13th March, 1894

Liverpool paid their first visit to Turf Moor yesterday to meet the Burnley team in this league match. Neither team was at its full strength.

Burnley won the toss and took advantage of the wind and incline. After a period of even play Burnley took command of the game and pressed the visitors, **Turnbull** sending in a fast low shot. To this Liverpool replied in a most spirited fashion, and **Bradshaw** headed the best goal of the match, thus equalising within 10 minutes of the start.

Burnley came again, and had rather the best of matters, and owing to a mistake on the part of Hannah **Espie** scored a second, adding a third goal {*Espie*} before half-time.

Upon restarting Liverpool broke away, but were repulsed by McCall and McLintock, and a foul being given against a Liverpool forward Nicol so well placed a free kick that the ball was landed into the goalmouth and rushed through {*anon*}, making a fourth point against Liverpool. After this the visitors had more of the game than hitherto, and after **McQueen** had sent into the net from Bradshaw, they should have scored again, but Henderson kicked over the ball when within two yards of the goal line. A period of even play followed, both sides pressing in turn, but nothing further was scored, and an interesting game resulted in Liverpool meeting their fourth reverse:

RESULT: Burnley 4 - Liverpool 2

LIVERPOOL: McOwen (goal); Hannah and McLean (backs); McCartney, McQue and McBride (halves); Gordon, Bradshaw [1], Henderson, Givens and H. McQueen [1] (forwards).
BURNLEY: Place (goal); Nicol and McLintock (backs); King, Lang and Livingston (halves); Morrison, Turnbull [1], Espie [2], Egan and Hill (forwards) [1 anon].

City travelled to Lincoln confident of gaining what would have been their tenth successive League victory in consequence of the poor showing the Imps had made at Anfield in the reverse fixture. The team arrived in the Lincolnshire City with time enough in hand to visit the historic Cathedral where several of the team ventured to ascend the 338 steps to the top of the main tower to enjoy the magnificent view it afforded of the surrounding countryside – a strenuous adventure, however, perhaps not recommended to be undertaken immediately before an arduous football match!

17/03/1894 FL23: Lincoln City v. Liverpool
Liverpool Mercury - Monday 19th March, 1894

Liverpool played their return engagement with the Lincoln City at Lincoln on Saturday, before 4000 spectators, and in magnificent weather. The visitors were fully represented, M. McQueen reappearing, but Lincoln were without Richardson, their centre half.

Hannah having won the toss elected to play with the sun and incline in his favour, and after Lees had started the game Liverpool took up the running, and by the assistance of McQue and McVean carried the ball into dangerous proximity to the city goal. Neil however, removed the danger, and gave his left wing possession, Hannah finely robbing Flewitt at a critical moment. A foul then fell to Liverpool and was cleverly put in by McLean, and after the leather had been punted out by Gresham, McQue gave relief to the home side by shooting wide. The Lincoln team now had a look in, Chadburn having a clear field, running up the right and centring, but his companions were unable to find an opening. Two shots by McLean caused the home custodian to handle, following which Neil, after missing the ball, deliberately struck it out of danger, and although well within the 12 yards limit the referee, for some inexplicable reason, refused to allow a penalty kick, a decision not at all to liking of the visiting contingent.

Lincoln then pressed rather severely, the home left, Graham and Hewitt, bringing the ball along, the former sending across to the goalmouth, which, however, was improperly cleared by Hannah, and afterwards by McOwen, the result being that **Chadburn** had no difficulty in scoring. Brisk work by the Liverpool team then put the City goal under a severe attack, but so good was the combined defence of Stoddart and Neil that no opening could be found.

After the interval Gordon fell and hurt his ankle, and with but ten men against the incline matters did not look too rosy for Liverpool, but by putting in all they were worth, they began to assume the command, and Gordon improving, shots were levelled at Gresham in a promising manner. At length the Lincoln defence proved too strong, and the visitors were compelled to retire, McOwen saving cleverly from Lees in the meantime. But another spell of pressure was put upon the home goal, and **Givens** with an oblique shot equalised after 25 minutes play. This rather took some of the play out of the Lincoln men, who fell off slightly, and after several sharp attacks had been staved off by both sides the match was brought to a satisfactory conclusion to both sides, with a draw of one goal each - Liverpool at escaping defeat, and Lincoln in having taken a point out of the champions.

RESULT: Lincoln City 1 - Liverpool 1

LIVERPOOL: McOwen (goal); Hannah and McLean (backs); M. McQueen, McQue and McBride (halves); Gordon, McVean, Henderson, Givens [1] and H. McQueen (forwards).
LINCOLN: Gresham (goal); Stoddart and Neil (backs); Raby, Mettam and Wiltshire (halves); Chadburn [1], Irving, Lees, Graham and Flewitt (forwards).

In the first round of the Liverpool Senior Cup the Anfielders were antagonised by the Bootle Athletic, the latter gaining an opportunity to compete in that competition by the demise of their former illustrious neighbours Bootle[27].

20/03/1894 LiSC-R1: Liverpool v. Bootle Athletic
Liverpool Mercury - Wednesday 21st March, 1894

These clubs having been drawn together in the above competition, played off their tie at Anfield last evening, before a moderate attendance. Liverpool were poorly represented, whilst Bootle Athletic started with only ten men.

The Athletic having started, the game soon became located in the visitors' quarters, but owing to the unmethodical style adopted by the Liverpool forwards, their attempts at scoring were easily nonplussed by the solid, yet not brilliant, defence of Owens, Magher, and Pollock. After a long spell of insipid pressure, **Bradshaw** headed the first point from a well placed corner by McQueen. Following this some poor kicking by the Liverpool backs let in the Athletic forwards, who dashed along in promising style, and Rennie's charge underwent a narrow escape from a capital shot by Gibson. To this effort Liverpool replied strongly, McVean propelling vigorously, and **Henderson** completing the attempt by scoring the second point.

---

27   The eight leading clubs affiliated to the L.F.A. contested the competition.

Half-time arrived with the score two goals to nil in favour of Liverpool, and after the restart the home team attacked fiercely, but without result, McQueen spoiling a nice opening by lifting too high, but making amends later by testing Owens to the utmost with a rasping shot. The visitors then wakened up, and, from a fine dash by **Hunt**, scored a well deserved point. After this Liverpool held the upper hand, and **Dick** and **McVean**, by individual efforts, each added points, the game ultimately ending in a win for Liverpool.

RESULT: Liverpool 4 – Bootle Athletic 1

LIVERPOOL: Rennie (goal); McCartney and McLean (backs); Hughes, McQue and Stott (halves); Dick [1], McVean [1], Henderson [1], Bradshaw [1] and H. McQueen (forwards).
BOOTLE ATH.: Owens (goal); Magher and Pollock (backs); Caldwell, Marshall and McFarlane (halves); Gibson, Gill, Tag Hay, Higgins and Hunt (forwards).

In the County Palatine League Liverpool faced further higher League opposition in the form of Darwen who fielded a largely representative side against a home side which, unusually in recent weeks, was at full strength.

23/03/1894 PL03: Liverpool v. Darwen
Liverpool Mercury - Saturday 24th March, 1894

This match took place at Anfield yesterday, before 10,000 spectators, and in splendid weather. Hannah won the toss, and elected to play with the sun at his back, but against a slight wind.

Maxwell kicked off, and play was at once transferred to Liverpool quarters. A capital shot by Shaw appeared very dangerous to the home team, but relief was eventually brought about by M. McQueen, Gordon supplementing by cantering up the right wing and sending across in neat style, only to find his attempt foiled by the absence of his confrère's. Maxwell and Wade next broke away for a moment, but were repulsed by Hannah, and Briggs charge was again subjected to a fusillade, a shot by McBride testing the Darwen goalkeeper to the utmost. Excellent half-back play by Liverpool spoilt several good breaks away by the Darwen forwards, but at length Marr and McKennie beat McLean and McOwen was called upon to fist out. A foul by Maxwell gave a chance to the home team, but the exceptionally strong defence of Leach and Orr kept the attack at bay. A combined run by Givens and H. McQueen carried the game into close quarters, and Briggs had to fist out thrice in quick succession. To this Darwen replied with splendid dash, Maxwell, Wade, and Marr each doing grand work, and Hannah, McLean, and McOwen were severely tested, but were found to be equal to all demands. Fouls just now were frequently given against the visitors', and not without cause, as their general play was far from being clean. Some really fine work by McVean and Gordon placed the ball in a convenient position for Henderson, but his attempt lacked force, and a glorious chance was lost. Afterwards Liverpool played with commendable dash and vigour, and from a well earned corner by the home right H. McQueen planted into the net, but to the disgust of the crowd the referee disallowed the point. This roused the Liverpool team to greater efforts, and Briggs, with Orr and

Leach, were given a lot of work, and on one occasion it seemed remarkable how the visitors' goal escaped. Just as half-time drew near, Darwen paid a sharp visit to McOwen but without result.

Upon resuming, Liverpool at once were the aggressors, but owing to a display of overconfidence by McLean the home defence was defeated, the resulting corner menacing serious danger until Hannah intervened, and kicked clear. Another foul fell to Liverpool, and after Briggs had saved twice a goal kick was awarded amid cries of "corner." Maintaining the pressure in magnificent style Liverpool at length scored from another foul close in, {H.} **McQueen** shooting hard, and the ball rebounding through off one of the players. Gordon then got away with a splendid dribble, and wound up with a straight shot, which Briggs finely saved. A pretty piece of work by Maxwell, Marr, and McKinnie changed the scene of operations, the latter winding up with a good shot which McOwen deftly saved, although surrounded by his opponents. Darwen now played with more effect, and Shaw suffered hard lines with a grand shot which grazed the crossbar. Liverpool again made tracks for their opponents' goal, and Givens, McVean, and Henderson each had shots, but a grand clearance by Leach transferred the leather to midfield, where **Maxwell** obtained possession, tricking McQue, and upon being faced by McBride, let fly for goal, and had the gratification of seeing McOwen first hold the ball, and then drop it, allowing the visitors to score a most ridiculously easy point, which certainly ought to have been saved. Resolute defence by Darwen again saved the visitors when danger seemed imminent, and a very even game resulted in a draw of one goal each.

RESULT: Darwen 1 - Liverpool 1

LIVERPOOL: McOwen (goal); Hannah and McLean (backs); M. McQueen, McQue and McBride (halves); Gordon, McVean, Henderson, Givens and H. McQueen [1] (forwards).
DARWEN: Briggs (goal); Leach and Orr (backs); Shaw, Haddon and Lee (halves); Wade, Sutherland, Maxwell [1], Marr and McKennie (forwards).

For the home League match against Crewe Alexandra Liverpool fielded the celebrated amateur Gerald Powys Dewhurst. Based at Lymm in Cheshire, Dewhurst played football with both the Liverpool Ramblers and the famous London based Corinthians, having turned out for the latter against Liverpool earlier in the season. He had subsequently promised to aid the Anfielders as an amateur during the vital run in to the end of the season. Liverpool went into the game with a four point lead at the head of the table and the certain knowledge that another victory would make that lead unassailable to the pursuing clubs (Notts. County and Small Heath) with the matches remaining.

24/03/1894 FL24: Liverpool v. Crewe Alexandra
Liverpool Mercury - Monday 26 March 1894

This match took place at Anfield on Saturday, but as the champions had so decisively defeated the railwaymen at home some little time ago by five goals to nil, little interest was aroused, and the attendance did not exceed 3000. Hannah having won the toss took advantage of a slight wind and set his opponents to face a glaring sun.

Sandham commenced hostilities, and for a few minutes the visitors had rather the best of the argument, but being repulsed by the home captain, were immediately put upon the defensive by some clever combination between McVean and Dick, the latter causing Dixon to save. The Alexandrians then dashed away splendidly, and M. McQueen was challenged by Hall, but proved to be very safe. Liverpool, although not playing with the cohesion expected and looked for, laid heavy siege to their opponents fortress. But the resolute defence of Stafford and MacDonald kept the home team from piercing their goal space, and when half-time had arrived the score sheet remained untouched.

Dewhurst, upon resuming, was found to be busy, and with Dick and McVean threatened Hickton's charge in a far more menacing fashion than hitherto, and the home half-backs splendidly backing them up, the game became rather one sided. At length, from a nice opening given by H. McQueen, **Dick** open the score. This roused the home team to better combination and dash, and shortly afterwards Dewhurst was noticeable for a tricky run, which brought about a corner, following which the ball was finally headed in by the amateur, and a second point was snatched by **H. McQueen**. From this period to the end the home team monopolised the play, but no further scoring took place, and the game ended in a win for Liverpool by two goals to nil. Liverpool are now indisputable champions of the Second League.

RESULT: Liverpool 2 - Crewe Alexandra 0

LIVERPOOL: M. McQueen (goal); Hannah and McLean (backs); McCartney, McQue and McBride (halves); Dick [1], McVean, Givens, H.McQueen [1], G.P. Dewhurst (forwards).
CREWE: Hickton (goal); Stafford and McDonald (backs); Crawford, Bayman and Sproston (halves); Woolfe, Hall, Sandham, Jones and Barrett (forwards).

The win confirmed Liverpool as undisputed, and so far undefeated, champions of the Second League with four Second League fixtures yet to play!

Liverpool designated the return ordinary match against Accrington at Anfield a benefit for Hannah in recognition of that player's sterling service during the short life of the club. Accrington had to start with ten men after arriving without Ditchfield who had missed the train, the latter making his own way and joining the fray midway through the first half.

26/03/1894 OM: Liverpool v. Accrington
Manchester Courier - Tuesday 27 March 1894

This game was played at Anfield, the visitors making a very poor show.

A couple of corners fell to the home players, and then McVean had a nice bit of tricky play all to himself, and finished up with a correct centre. McBride got hold and passed to **H. McQueen**, who scored with his head. Two minutes later **Givens** when in goal received from a free kick, and experienced no difficulty in putting on the second point. A splendid run was made by the visiting forwards, and Gray tried at long range but the ball went over the bar. McVean and Bradshaw took part in a grand run and transferred play to the other end, where the outside right man forwarded a rattling shot which Shaw neatly fisted out, and he was likewise successful against a consignment immediately afterwards from Henderson. The game continued to be of a more open order, Liverpool being rather more accurate in the vicinity of goal, but still not more successful than their antagonists. A clever dash was then taken up by Broadley and Gillespie. McBride stopped Brown when he was about to take a shy. The "Reds" returned to the attack, and McLean headed out two shots, while M. McQueen fisted out a scorcher from Laurie. A corner was afterwards taken and rendered null, and on the home right wing getting hold, the ball was run clean down the field. McQue tried a dropping shot, which Shaw fisted out. **Bradshaw** headed high into goal, and following the ball up jumped a couple of feet and receiving with his head, again cleverly scored the third point. The home men were now going strongly, and a neat drop by McBride almost took the goal down again, Shaw just getting the ball away before Givens charged him down. After a turn of midfield play McBride again tried a shot, and Shaw had to give a corner from it. This brought about a tussle in the goal mouth, and Shaw distinguished himself with another smart save. The Reds were now put almost completely to rout, and could not break away. From a long kick by Hannah, the ball was received by **Givens** who scored the fourth goal. Half time score:- Liverpool, 4 goals; Accrington, nil.

The second stage was equally disastrous to the visitors, who were beaten at every point. Four goals were added in the second half {***own goal*** (Matthews), **Bradshaw**, ***anon***, ***anon***}, Liverpool winning a poor game.

RESULT: Liverpool 8 - Accrington 0

LIVERPOOL: M. McQueen (goal); Hannah and {McLean} (backs), McCartney, McQue, and McBride (halves), McVean, Bradshaw [2], Henderson, Givens [2] and H. McQueen [1] (forwards). [1 og] [2 anon]
ACCRINGTON: Shaw (goal); {anon} and Ditchfield (backs); Pendergast, Broadley, and {anon} (halves); Laurie, Gray, Brown, Matthews and Gillespie (forwards).

Just as Liverpool were already confirmed Champions of the Second Division with several games yet to play, so were their next opponents, Northwich, already confirmed as the wooden spoonists!

28/03/1894 FL25: Northwich Victoria v. Liverpool
Liverpool Mercury - Thursday 29 March 1894

This match in the Second Division of the League was played at Northwich yesterday, in fine weather, before 1000 spectators.

Liverpool won the toss and played with a slight wind in their favour. The first half of the game was entirely in the hands of Liverpool, who scored from a scrimmage soon after starting {***Givens***}. Hornby the Northwich goalkeeper, played a splendid game.

In the second half Northwich had rather the best of the play, but were unable to score until nearly time, when **Drinkwater** and **Finnehan** scored. Shortly afterwards Liverpool scored twice from scrimmages {***McQueen***, ***H. McLean***}.

RESULT: Liverpool 3 – Northwich Victoria 2

LIVERPOOL: M. McQueen (goal); Hannah and McLean [1] (backs); McCartney, McQue and McBride (halves); McVean, Bradshaw, Henderson, Givens [1] and H. McQueen [1] (forwards).
NORTHWICH: Not available – Scorers: Drinkwater [1], Finnehan [1].

As had so often been the case that season, the visit of the now confirmed Champions to Grimsby's Abbey Park ground established a new record 'gate' for the homesters. Whilst the championship was already sewn up the Anfielders signalised their determination to maintain their unbeaten record by travelling to East coast the day before so as to be be absolutely fresh for the start of the match.

31/03/1894 FL26: Grimsby Town v. Liverpool
Hull Daily Mail - Monday 02 April 1894

The visit of the Invincibles or, in other words, Liverpool, with its unbeaten league record, has caused an unparalleled excitement in the fishing metropolis. The mariners record is pretty well known to the reader, they having defeated such teams as Notts County, Small Heath, &c., and now stand fifth in the League table. Today they have one of the finest chances of distinguishing themselves which has ever fallen to the lot of any team, and they are determined, to a man, to leave no stone unturned with a view of achieving this. Everybody is waiting for the knockout, and from what I know of the home men I am prepared to believe they can just about win, although the vast majority of the Town supporters hold the opposite opinion. Liverpool, with its 25 unbeaten matches, have established a record, and that they mean to maintain the supremacy is evinced by their arrival last night. Making the Ship hotel their headquarters, they make no attempt to conceal their ability to knock spots off the Mariners. At the time of writing the weather is most unsettled, rain having fallen at intervals, but wet or shine the attendance will certainly create a record.

At 3.15 the players lined out. Grimsby won the toss, and Henderson kicked off before 5000 spectators, and both teams worked earnestly. Liverpool ran no risk, as, if at all dangerous, they kicked out of play. Equalised play continued for several minutes, Rose making brilliant attempts at goal. Both teams showed excellent form, Grimsby having the best of the game, with Higgins very conspicuous. After a magnificent and exciting tussle the whistle announced half-time with no score.

Resuming, Grimsby showed the best performance seen this season, for several minutes pressing furiously. Both defences were kept constantly at it, Whitehouse playing superbly. Every point was keenly fought, Grimsby having hard luck on several occasions in the mouth of the goal. It was one of the best games ever witnessed on the Abbey Park ground, and when nearing the conclusion **Givens** scored first for the Liverpudlians.

RESULT: Grimsby Town 0 - Liverpool 1

LIVERPOOL: M. McQueen (goal); Hannah and McLean (backs); McCartney, McQue and McBride (halves); McVean, Bradshaw, Henderson, Givens [1] and H. McQueen (forwards).
GRIMSBY: Whitehouse (goal); Lundie and Frith (backs); Higgins, Graham and Russell (halves); Rose, Riddock, McCairns, Fletcher and Jones. (forwards).

Despite their careful preparations, Liverpool were pressed hard from the first moment to the last and it was only due to the heroics of Matt McQueen, preferred to the off form McOwen in goal, that the Liverpool sanctum was maintained intact. In fact, according to other reports, McQueen at one point threw himself after a lost cause and swiped the ball out when it was palpably a yard over the line – the referee denying Grimsby's confident claims for a goal.

With no fewer than 14 matches to play in the month of April the Liverpool committee felt compelled to send what amounted to a relatively young and inexperienced side to contest Newton Heath at Clayton in a benefit for the "Heathens" veteran centre-half Willie Stewart – the Anfield eleven containing only two regular first team men in Givens and Matt McQueen. Newton Heath on the other hand, apart from Hood filling the forward line in place of McNaught who had dropped back to the centre line filling in for benefit man Stewart (who on the day was unable to play), were at full strength.

02/04/1894 OM: Newton Heath v. Liverpool
Liverpool Mercury - Tuesday 3rd April, 1894

This return match took place at Clayton yesterday, in the presence of about 2000 spectators. In view of the heavy nature of the work before the team the Liverpool Committee sent a very weak combination.

Liverpool played against a slight wind, and were immediately on the aggressive, Hughes striking the bar, while the ball was almost rushed through the Heathens' goal a little later on. After this the visitors were put on the defensive, but, partly owing to the good work of M. McQueen and Hughes, combined with erratic shooting by the Newton forwards, the score at half-time was only a goal {*anon*} to nil in favour of the home team.

On resuming, Givens got early to work, but a foul falling to his share, the free kick was placed into the net without being touched in its journey. Newton replied with rare dash, Clarkin rushing up and centring, and **Donaldson** completing the effort by heading past Rennie, 3 minutes after the start. The game then became more open, both sides in turn trying to break through the opposing defence, and great credit is due to the young inexperienced players for the very creditable show they made. Ultimately the game ended in a win for Newton Heath.

RESULT: Newton Heath 2 - Liverpool 0

LIVERPOOL: Rennie (goal); Millett and M. McQueen (backs); Kendrick, Hughes and Stott (halves); Gordon, Worgan, Dick, Givens and Travis (forwards).

NEWTON HEATH: Douglas (goal); Mitchell and Errents (backs); Perrins, McNaught and Davidson (halves); Farman, Clarkin, Donaldson [1], Parker and Hood (forwards). [1 anon].

Again, the Liverpool committee selected an essentially reserve side for a further visit of Darwen in an ordinary match at Anfield.

04/04/1894 OM: Liverpool v. Darwen
Liverpool Mercury - Thursday 5th April 1894

Played at Anfield last evening.

Darwen kicked off at 6.00. Liverpool had the best of the opening play, and attacked strongly at the outset. **Stott** scored in 8 minutes, and **Gordon** followed. Then, before half-time **Worgan** got through again, and at the interval Liverpool were leading by three goals to nil.

Upon resuming, **Worgan** put Liverpool further ahead, and McQue put through his **own goal**. **McKnight** scored again for Darwen.

RESULT: Liverpool 4 – Darwen 2

LIVERPOOL: M.McQueen (goal); Hannah and Hughes (backs); McCartney, McQue, McBride (halves); Gordon, Worgan, Dick, Stott and H. McQueen (forwards).
DARWEN: Not available – Scorers: [1 og] and McNight [1].

Hannah, one of the few first team players having played in the match against Darwen had had to retire early from that match with an injury, the effects of which rendered him unavailable for the trip to Stoke to face Burslem Port Vale. With McQueen being called upon to take his place, McOwen was recalled in goal.

07/04/1894 FL27: Burslem Port Vale v. Liverpool
Liverpool Mercury - Monday 9th April, 1894

This first meeting between these clubs took place at Burslem on Saturday, in magnificent weather and before a large and enthusiastic audience. Hannah was a notable absentee on the Liverpool side. McLean having won the choice of ends, set his opponents to face a rather bright sun, but having the assistance of a slight wind.

The home team were the first to show, as by some long kicking by Beats, Scarrett, and Dean, they crossed the Liverpool goal line early on. Following the kick off by McOwen, Henderson obtained possession, and executed a smart dash down the centre, sending out to McVean at a favourable moment, but Givens stumbled over when endeavouring to send the latter's pass into the net. A foul to the Valeites was badly worked by Edwards, and in a moment McVean was off at top speed, eluding Elston, and Mackay was called upon to negotiate an attempt by Givens, which he turned aside. Liverpool, mainly through some capital work by McBride, were again aggressive, but owing to poor forward play the ball was harmlessly sent over the goal line. Some good combination by Beats, Dean, and Scarrett then menaced McOwen's charge, but Dean eased the pressure by heading over the bar. The same player a little later on showed a clean pair of heels to his rivals, but shot very poorly at long range. The game continued of a very ding-dong character, first one side and then the other predominating in turn, till at length a series of passes by Beats, Wood, and Campbell culminated in **Dean** heading past McOwen, amidst great cheering. Both sides again fought the game out with great spirit, and on one occasion given against McCartney, was a real source of danger to Liverpool. However, McQueen headed out of the goalmouth, and the Liverpool forwards rushed away to the other end, when a fine attempt by McBride should have been better utilised. Scarrett then made off, and upon being tackled by McLean, crossed over to **Campbell**, who shot into the net. This point was strongly protested against by the visitors, as Campbell was standing behind the backs when he received the ball. The play after this became rather rough, and fouls were of frequent occurrence; and when half-time arrived the score remained unaltered.

Liverpool now had the assistance of the wind, and the opening stages were much in their favour, McQueen lifting over the bar followed by Mackay clearing smartly from McVean and McHugh. A rapid spin by Campbell altered the face of the game, McOwen being called upon to divert a shot by Beats. Several throw ins then fell to the share of McCartney, and he made best use of them. The game was then carried on around Mackay, and from a well judged return by Mr. McQueen, the ball was ultimately rushed past the home custodian into the net {***McVean***}. From a foul the ball was again placed into the net, but was disallowed. As time drew on the visitors' worked exceedingly hard, and were at length rewarded by a goal from **M. McQueen**, who drove a free kick past Mackay after touching several players on its journey just within a minute of the whistle sounding for a cessation of hostilities, and thus a highly exciting match ended with a draw.

RESULT: Burslem Port Vale 2 - Liverpool 2

LIVERPOOL: McOwen (goal); M. McQueen and McLean (backs); McCartney, McQue and McBride (halves); McVean [1], Bradshaw, Henderson, Givens and H. McQueen [1] (forwards).
PORT VALE: Mackay (goal); Eccles and Ramsay (backs); Edwards, McCrindle and Elston (halves); Scarrett, Dean, Beats, Wood and Campbell (forwards).

In the semi-final of the Liverpool Senior Cup the Anfielders were pitted against the White Star Wanderers, the match being played on the Bootle Athletic's Seaview ground.

09/04/1894 LiSC-SF: White Star Wanderers v. Liverpool
(at Bootle Athletic)
Liverpool Mercury - Tuesday 10 April 1894

This tie was played last evening at the Seaview ground, Bootle, before nearly 2000 spectators. Liverpool played mostly a reserve team, McLean, McCartney and Gordon, being the only first team men.

Liverpool were the first to show up, but the "Stars" early on obtained the first corner off McLean. Liverpool came again, and the resulting corner was almost converted by Givens. A spell of even play followed, the Anfield team being terribly cramped by the narrowness of the ground. May then became prominent for a long shot, Jones immediately testing Rennie with a fast grounder. However, Liverpool by some telling combination worked the ball up, and **Gordon** defeated Kay with a grand shot, after half an hour's play, but just as half-time approached the Wanderers with a rush, equalised from a good shot by **McCarthy**.

Having the wind, Liverpool now pressed continuously, and **Stott** early on added a second point. Although holding command throughout, Liverpool were unfortunate in not increasing their score, owing chiefly to weak shooting, and the game eventually resulted in a win for Liverpool by 2 goals to 1.

RESULT: White Star Wanderers 1 – Liverpool 2

LIVERPOOL: Not available (not representative) – Scorers: Gordon [1], Stott [1].
WANDERERS: not available – Scorers: McCarthy [1].

Although the reporter rightly asserts that McLean, McCartney and Gordon were the only first team men in the team, Stott, who scored the winning goal, had been a first team regular for most of the season, only recently being supplanted by Givens. The name of this club seems to suggest some possible connection with the Liverpool based Oceanic Steam Navigation Company, more commonly known as the White Star Line (although the author has been unable to confirm this).

Both teams fielded largely representative sides for the visit of Burnley to Turf Moor in the Palatine League return encounter.

11/04/1894 PL04: Liverpool v. Burnley
Lancashire Evening Post - Thursday 12 April 1894

At Liverpool. Liverpool have the best of the opening play, but missed two good chances. Burnley replied, and after McOwen had partially cleared, **Turnbull** scored with a fast low shot. Burnley had slightly the best of matters for a spell and then Hillman had his work cut out to save. The game was of an even character up to the interval, But Burnley gained a second goal from a scrimmage {**anon**}.

Liverpool opened the second half well, but Hillman saved three shots splendidly. A couple of corners to the home team availed nothing, and then Espie and Turnbull were prominent for Burnley. Bradshaw struck the visitors upright, and then Liverpool had to concede a corner, which proved fruitless. Liverpool had slightly the best of matters, but the Burnley defence was to good, and the First Leaguers eventually won by two goals to Liverpool's love.

RESULT: Liverpool 0 – Burnley 2

LIVERPOOL: McOwen (goal); M. McQueen and Hughes (backs); Stott, McQue and McBride (halves); Gordon, McVean, Henderson, Bradshaw and H. McQueen (forwards).
BURNLEY: Hillman (goal); Nicol and McLintock (backs); Place snr., Lang and King (halves); Buchanan, Turnbull, Espie, Egan and Place jnr. (forwards).
*Player names in braces {} are probable – **not** confirmed.*

This was Liverpool's first home defeat of the season and only the defeat at Anfield in a match in which they fielded a representative side!

Only 24 hours later, Liverpool sent an almost entirely reserve team to contest their next Palatine League fixture at Blackburn – the Rovers fielding a mixed team in response.

12/04/1894 PL05: Blackburn Rovers v. Liverpool
Lancashire Evening Post - Friday 13 April 1894

At Ewood park. The Rovers won the toss, and elected to play with the wind behind them. For the first 20 minutes nothing important occurred. The Rovers appeared to have the upper hand, and were frequently offside. Eventually Mr. Ormrod (the referee) awarded Liverpool a goal kick through the Rovers misconduct. Barry Campbell ran down the right and a well judged kick alighted on McQueen's foot, the pressure being temporarily relieved. A splendid sprint up the wing by Gordon was checked by Walmsley. On the restart the homesters rushed up the field and **Haydock** scored, the same player {**Haydock**} added another point a few minutes later. McOwen ran out to save, and **Campbell** from a pass by Calvey, notched a third goal. The Rovers pressed hard, and narrowly escaped scoring on several occasions. Hughes' was injured, and left the field for a short time. Ten minutes from the restart **Haydock** put on the fourth point. Dickens made a good shy at goal, but his attempt was futile. The ball visited each end of the field periodically. A scrimmage ensued in the visitors' goal, but the ball was put well away. From now the Rovers maintained the pressure, and **Haydock** notched the fifth goal on the call of time.

RESULT: Blackburn Rovers 5 - Liverpool 0

LIVERPOOL: McOwen (goal); Mullett and Hughes (backs); Trevis, Stott and Crawford (halves); Gordon, Worgan, Dies, Givens and Duckers (forwards).
BLACKBURN: Watts (goal); McFarlane and Forrest (backs); Dewer, Walmsley and Marshall (halves); Hargreaves, Campbell, Calvey, Haydock and Townley (forwards).

Liverpool entertained Burslem Port Vale for their last Division Two fixture looking to recover form after a couple of poor results in Palatine League fixtures - albeit that the latter had been the result of fielding very indifferent teams – to protect their unbeaten record in the primary competition.

14/04/1894 FL28: Liverpool v. Burslem Port Vale
Liverpool Mercury - Monday 16 April 1894

This League match, the last for both clubs, took place at Anfield on Saturday. The weather was very fine prior to the match commencing, but turned out wet afterwards. McBride was an absentee from Liverpool, M. McQueen taking his position at left half.

Hannah having lost the choice of ends, Henderson started against a stiff breeze and immediately Liverpool were on the attack, McQue sending into the net within the first five minutes, but without result. Henderson next had a shy, but found Mackay well prepared, and for a spell play was confined to neutral territory. A dash by Bradshaw and McQueen again laid the Burslem goal under assault, but Eccles and Ramsay, playing with great determination, repulsed the aggressors, and with the assistance of the wind removed the scene of operations to the other end, when Hannah and McLean were kept busy, McOwen handling several times from Scarrett, Beats, and Wood. Bradshaw then made but poor use of a free kick, sending wide, while M. McQueen repeated the performance a little later on by a free kick awarded to Liverpool. The game was evenly fought out, there being little to choose between either team up to half-time, Wood almost defeating McOwen with a fast, high shot, but which the nimble Liverpudlian adroitly put over the bar. Led up by McQue and McQueen the home team placed the visitors entirely on the defensive for some time, but so excellent was the defence of Elston, Ramsay, and Eccles that nothing tangible accrued. Henderson and Gordon then became prominent by clever combination, but McVean failed at the finish, and half-time arrived without either side scoring.

The home team now had the assistance of the wind, yet the Burslem players were the first to open out, a foul off Hannah being headed just to a trifle too high by Wood. McCartney relieved when matters were looking black for Liverpool, and Gordon, McVean, and Henderson carried the ball to the other end, but were not allowed to get a shot in, Elston and Eccles being responsible for this. At length **Edwards** opened the score by defeating McOwen with a terrific shot, which he was unable to hold, the ball glancing off the custodian's hands just under the bar. This altogether unlooked-for disaster rather unnerved the home team for a spell, and Burslem had rather the best of the midfield exchanges; but from a corner grandly earned by Gordon, and equally well placed, a terrible struggle took place in the goalmouth, and so serious did the pack threaten injury to some of the players that the referee stopped the game, and threw the ball up, and Liverpool promptly rushed it into the net {***Hannah***}. To this success the home team responded with much greater dash, and before full time arrived had secured a second point {***McQue***}, and were frequently threatening again to increase their score. Ultimately the game wound up with another victory for Liverpool.

RESULT: Liverpool 2 - Burslem Port Vale 1

LIVERPOOL: McOwen (goal); Hannah [1] and McLean (backs); McCartney, McQue [1] and M. McQueen (halves); Gordon, McVean, Henderson, Bradshaw and H. McQueen (forwards).
PORT VALE: Mackay (goal); Eccles and Ramsay (backs); Edwards [1], {McCrindle} and Elston (halves); Scarrett, {Dean}, Beats, Wood and {Campbell} (forwards).
*Player names in braces {} are probable – **not** confirmed.*

At Deepdale, but sides put out largely representative teams in the next Palatine League match. The exception for Liverpool was an experimental back division which saw Killip and Hughes of the reserves replacing Hannah and McLean at full-back, and Stott being tried at centre-half.

16/04/1894 PL06: Preston North End v. Liverpool
Lancashire Evening Post - Tuesday 17 April 1894

At Preston, before a gate of about 2000. The North End at once attacked, and McOwen, Killip and Hughes were kept busy. When Ross was in the act of shooting, Stott tripped him. Dunn took the free kick, and **Henderson**[PNE] headed a goal. Trainor saved finely from Henderson for Liverpool, and then Drummond enabled **Cowan** to score again. Miller had a couple of chances, and the home defence was several times called upon, but at half-time the score stood at two goals to nil. In the second half the Liverpudlians attacked at the commencement, and then North End time after time by neat passing got dangerous, but the only goal scored was one by **Miller** from a grand pass by Stormont. The Liverpudlians were overmatched, but the game was brimful of good football.

RESULT: Preston North End 3 - Liverpool 0

LIVERPOOL: McOwen (goal); Killip and Hughes (backs); McCartney, Stott and McBride (halves); Gordon, McVean, Henderson, Givens and H. McQueen (forwards).
PRESTON: Trainor (goal); Dunn and Nidd (backs); Stormont, Grier and Sanders (halves); Henderson [1], Drummond, Miller [1], J. Ross, and Cowan [1] (forwards).

The only man with significant first team experience sent to represent Liverpool at Barley Bank, Darwen, was the displaced Stott. The homesters, on the other hand fielded a largely representative side, including the return of Wardrop after a long absence through injury.

21/04/1894 PL07: Darwen v. Liverpool
Lancashire Evening Post - Saturday 21st April, 1894

At Barley Bank, in glorious weather, and before 1000 spectators. Darwen were without Betts, Orr, and McKnight, but they were able to play Wardrop and McNicholl. The match was not started until nearly three quarters of an hour after the advertised time, owing to the late arrival of the visitors.

Liverpool won the toss, and Darwen started. The visitors were the first to attack, but Nelson made poor use of a good opening. Darwen then got down. **Maxwell** scored when close in. From the centre kick Darwen again attacked, and **Wade** scored again from a centre by McNicholl. Play continued in Darwen's favour for a while, but eventually Liverpool got down and called upon the home backs. Darwen returned, and Rennie saved shots from Maxwell, Sutherland, and Shaw. Sutherland forced a corner and from the kick **Maxwell** headed over the bar and the next minute the home centre capped some tricky work by planting the ball into the net. Darwen, who were playing strongly, were frequently dangerous, and eventually **Marr** scored the fourth goal after some good work by the whole of the forwards. Shaw sent in a grand shot from the line, and Rennie just disposed of the ball when Sutherland rushed up. Liverpool had a short spell of attacking, but they were repulsed, and at the other end Rennie was kept very busy. Darwen slowed down somewhat, and Liverpool got down, but they could not penetrate the defence. Shortly before the interval Darwen again scored, **Marr** doing the needful.

On the game being resumed Liverpool at once attacked, and Kenyon was called upon for the first time in the game. Darwen worked their way down the field, and after Marr had shot wide, McKennie put in a grand centre, of which bad use was made. Liverpool were playing an improved game, and upon one occasion the home goal had a narrow escape. Wardrop and McNicholl exchanged places, and the change proved a wise one. Darwen attacked, and from an opening obtained by Sutherland **Maxwell** scored again. Stringer followed with a grand run, but no one was up to take his pass. The remaining play was greatly in favour of Darwen, and **Sutherland** scored their seventh goal. **Worgan** followed with a goal for Liverpool. **Marr** scored for Darwin.

RESULT: Darwen 8 - Liverpool 1

LIVERPOOL: Rennie (goal); Mellett and Kellett (backs); Hendrick, Preston and Newall (halves); Nelson, Worgan [1], Travis, Stott and Stringer (forwards).
DARWEN: Kenyon (goal); Wardrop and Leach (backs); Shaw, McNicholl and Lee (halves); McKennie, Marr [3], Maxwell [3], Sutherland [1] and Wade [1] (forwards).

A nearly full strength Darwen against a weak Liverpool had made the game, as the scoreline suggests, a very one-sided affair. The Lancashire Evening Post commented that Kenyon, the Darwen keeper was never called into play once in the first half.

Liverpool next crossed the Pennines again to take on The Wednesday (Sheffield) at Olive Grove in a benefit match for Billy Bett. Betts was a locally born player whose association with the club extended back over 12 years (but included a four year break whilst serving other clubs).

23/04/1894 OM: The Wednesday v. Liverpool
Sheffield Evening Telegraph - Monday 23rd April, 1894

If the estimation in which the beneficiaire is held in his native town is to be gauged by the attendance at Olive Grove this afternoon it is evident that appreciation of good and faithful services have ceased to be. For instead of a great crowd of ten or twelve thousand which Betts surely deserved to see crowding round the ropes, there not more than three thousand witnessed the game. Another matter for regret was the fact that in view of the coming League test match on Saturday against Newton Heath the Liverpool executive, much to their own regret, felt compelled to keep their first eleven in training, sending the reserve team to do duty in the game under notice. On the contrary, the Sheffield Club was represented by it's first team, with the single exception of Spikesly who, owing to injury received at Everton in the Inter-League match last Saturday, was compelled to stand down.

There was but little wind, and the ground was in excellent condition when, having lost the toss, Wednesday started the game in the direction of Heeley, the game at once being carried on in the visitors quarters. Once Petrie, playing at left half-back for a change, had to stop Crawford smartly, and Langley also had occasion to beat the same wing back, but for the most part it was the Liverpool lines which were most pressed, Brady ending a pretty piece of passing by shooting wide of the mark. On the other wing, Smith was within an ace of scoring with a fine shot, Stott relieving in clever manner up the centre. But the Sheffielders were in earnest, and again their right threatened danger, Davis giving Rennie a hot one to stop, which he did well. But a second put in the next moment from the same player {**Davis**} beat him, and Wednesday chalked up their first goal nine minutes from the start. One minute later, and from a long screw by Davis, Stephens shot the ball into his own net {**own goal**}, to the utter amazement of Rennie. A grand long shy by Webster was well taken care of by Rennie, though he was kept hard at work by both the Wednesday wings. A break-away by Duckers and Givens came to nothing, the former shooting over the bar, and then for a time play was decidedly slow, neither side troubling much. Then Dick got well off, easily beating Langley for speed, but Allan came out of his goal and cleared. Clever work by Petrie followed, Stott also, on the other side, doing similarly good service, but for a long time the play was only of a poor quality and uninteresting. Then Davis forced a corner from Kendrick, and from this, with Stott fouling the ball close in, danger was threatened, the ball, however, being put outside. A bit of an attack at the other end followed this, but Stott, trying a long shot, was wide. Twice after this had Rennie to handle smartly from Davis, and again from Brady, but the interval arrived with no further points, and the score:- Wednesday, 2; Liverpool, nil.

Very early in the second half Liverpool earned a corner off Brandon, but Givens headed over, and the same result attended a long shot from Davis at the other end. Subsequent work in front of Rennie, however, saw a corner forced by Smith, and after another bout of hot work close in goal Brandon missed the mark by a matter of inches only. Twice after this did Webster get in fine centres, and the latter saw a corner forced by Smith, from which Brandon was again just wide. The task of the home backs was by no means of an arduous nature, but once Langley earned a cheer for a splendid long return from Stott. But the Liverpool men came again to the attack, getting a couple of corners, for each of which the goal escaped however, and Davis dashed across, missing a goal by a mere shave. Givens, who was certainly the smartest of the Liverpool forwards, again relieved by a dashing run, and from this Allan saved his charge wonderfully, catching the ball and throwing clear with a crowd of the opposing side upon him. A corner to the home side followed soon after this, and Rennie in saving his charge had to give yet another, from which he made a wonderful save from Davis. The game wakened a little towards the finish, both sets of backs having to defend in turn, though the pressure on the Liverpool goal was by far the heavier. Davis was very wide with a fair opening, and at this point Stott, who had done good work, retired evidently lame. Another big attack on the visitors lines followed, shot after shot being poured in and kept out in splendid fashion, till **Brady** with a low cross shot beat Rennie, who fell full length in attempting to save. Still the same team attacked, the Liverpool defence being taxed. A fourth goal came soon afterwards, **Brown** beating Rennie after the last-named had saved well from the centre, and before he had had time to recover himself. Webster missed a fine opening after shooting wildly, and Givens here came off the field also apparently lame, and of course with but nine men on the field the chances of the Liverpudlians were down to zero. All the game went on at their end, but the home forwards were not in a very earnest mood.

RESULT: The Wednesday 4 - Liverpool 0

LIVERPOOL: Rennie (goal); Millett and Hughes (backs); Kendrick, Stott and Stevens (halves); Dick, Crawford, Travis, Givens and Duckers (forwards).
WEDNESDAY: Allan (goal); Earp and Langley (backs); Brandon, Betts and Petrie (halves); Webster, Smith, Davis [1], Brady [1] and Brown [1] (forwards). [1og]

Again Liverpool excused their first team men duty for the last of the Palatine League fixtures against Blackburn at Anfield – even to the point, apparently, of starting the match two men short, only one of which was subsequently made up!

24/04/1894 PL08: Liverpool v. Blackburn Rovers
Lancashire Evening Post - Wednesday 25 April 1894

At Anfield. Liverpool started with nine men, and Blackburn had the best of the opening exchanges, play being confined to the Liverpool quarters for a good spell, Rennie responding well on two occasions. Dick and Crawford made a good run down, and Brandon kicked out to save. A couple of fouls close to Rennie availed the Rovers nothing. After a long bombardment of Rennie's charge, and in half an hour from the start, **Sorley** notched the first goal for the Rovers. For some little time after the restart Liverpool had the best of the play, and narrowly missed scoring on two occasions. The Rovers got away, and **Holt** notched a second goal for them. Each side had a turn at pressing, and **Sorley** notched a third goal for Blackburn. **Clarke** followed with a point for Liverpool.

RESULT: Liverpool 1 - Blackburn Rovers 3

LIVERPOOL: Rennie (goal); Mellett and Newall (backs); Duckers, Stevens and Travis (halves); Dick, Crawford, Clarke [1] and Braniff (forwards);
BLACKBURN: not available (not representative) – Scorers: Sorley [2], Holt [1].

The return friendly against Preston North End at Anfield that had been arranged for April 25th was postponed until the following season to allow Liverpool to better prepare for the upcoming test match.

For the vital test match against Newton Heath, which would decide which of the two teams would play in the higher League the following season, the omens were much in favour of Liverpool. In four previous meetings of the clubs that season Liverpool had won three to the Heathens one. Only in the first two of these encounters, both won by

Liverpool, had both sides fielded anything like representative sides, however, whilst the Heathens only victory had been at full strength against a team made up almost entirely of Liverpool reserves!

28/04/1894 FL-TM: Newton Heath v. Liverpool (at Blackburn)
Athletic News - Monday 30th April, 1894
The Favourites Win at Blackburn.

The positions of Newton Heath and Liverpool in the tables for some time past pointed to their meeting in the test match, so that they have had plenty of time to study each other's form. Blackburn was set down as the best place for the match to be decided, as it was within easy reach of both Liverpool and Manchester, and the partisans of the two teams availed themselves of the excursions, so that neither team was in want of shouters. Indeed, there were very few Blackburnians present, for the gate could not have numbered more than 5000. Both teams had their full strength out, with the exception that Hood took Parker's place in the Newton Heath ranks, while Matthew McQueen, the all round man, displaced McOwen in the Liverpool goal, the latter, I understand, not having been up to form lately. I ought to say that Liverpool had been training at Hightown, near Formby, and Newton Heath at Lytham.

Both teams were out early, and shortly before 4.00 the ball was set going. For the first five minutes all the play was in the Liverpool half, Peden and Davidson both shooting wide, but the ball then travelled to the other end, where McQueen struck the posts. The "Heathens" had the best of matters for the first quarter of an hour, after which Liverpool put more life in their play, and after another five minutes **Gordon** smartly headed through from a free kick, which was well placed by McLean. Liverpool now played more like themselves, and in the very next minute had another very close shave, and though Fall saved grandly twice, he could not prevent another point being registered against him, this being the outcome of a centre by Gordon, to which the finishing touch was put by **Bradshaw**, who had just given some good individual work. Just on half-time Hannah and Donaldson appeared to go for each other in a manner that was not justified right in the goalmouth, and as a consequence Mr. Lewis ordered the ball to be thrown up, but amidst the cheering of the Liverpool portion of the crowd the lines were cleared, so that the Second Division men turned round with a lead of two goals.

It should be stated that Farman was off the field during the last 5 minutes, and on resuming it was seen that he had exchanged places with Clarkin[28]. Liverpool went at it with very great determination on restarting, and in the very first minute almost scored, while just after McLean put the ball through from a free kick, but no other player had touched it in transit. McVean was tripped by Donaldson, and appeared to fall with his face on the latter's foot. At any rate, he was stunned, the game having to be stopped while he was examined by a Doctor. Fall had often to show his capabilities in the second half, though the "Heathens" frequently gave trouble, but the backs were playing so well that McQueen was not often called upon. The game at no time had been above the ordinary, but with the issue apparently settled it went worse, and was not at all

---

28 In the absence of substitutes injured players often played on, but were commonly placed in either of the extreme wing positions where their disability least affected play whilst they could still contribute by supplying the occasional cross when the ball was sent out to them.

interesting in the last half hour, the only notable feature being a marked difference with which each set of forwards shot at goal, the Newton quintet shaping very slowly. Donaldson made individual efforts to reach McQueen, but McLean and Hannah gave him no chance to shoot through, and in the last minute a run by Peden looked dangerous, but all was over, and the First Division club had to acknowledge defeat to a superior team by two goals to none.

I say superior, because the best team on the day's play won. Yet, had Newton Heath been able to score in the first fifteen minutes when they were pressing I shouldn't have been surprised had they won, but after Liverpool had obtained their first goal Newton did not play at all as they had done, and never afterwards looked like winners. It is generally the case that in matches where there is so much at stake there is very little good play shown, and Saturday's match was no exception, the game being a very poor one for such an important event, and too often the players went for each other when there was no necessity. To come to the players, McQueen in goal for the winners had very little to do owing to the fine defence of the backs, McLean being much better than on the two other occasions that I've seen him this season. The half backs were strong, McBride being by far the pick of the three, but the marked superiority was in the forward division, the winners quintet being sharper and shooting far better than those of the other side. Bradshaw was the best of the whole set, followed by McVean, McQueen also doing better than I have previously seen him. The losers five did not seem to get along at all, and had they done as well as those behind them then a closer game would have been the result, but when they had chances they could not make proper use of them. Donaldson was about the best of the lot, and even he was no great shakes, for he lost his temper and at times tried to run through himself, to which the Liverpool backs greatly objected, and in which there were too many hard rubs. Peden did not exert himself, and Farman was limping all the second half, and this, of course, affected his play. The half backs were very fair, Perrins sticking to his men, while McNaught was exceedingly smart, and little fault could be found with the backs, though they were not equal to the other pair. Mitchell's kicking surprised me, especially in the second half. Fall kept goal splendidly, and I should think he had three shots to stop to McQueen's one. The defeat can in no way be attached to him, for he cleared and kicked well, but I suppose one team has to win, and on the day's play Liverpool fully deserved their victory. The only regret is that while Liverpool can boast of two First Division clubs Manchester, notwithstanding its ship canal, will have to be content with second class football unless the League is extended and Newton Heath admitted.

RESULT: Newton Heath 0 - Liverpool 2

LIVERPOOL: M. McQueen (goal); Hannah and McLean (backs); McCartney, McQue and McBride (halves); Gordon [1], McVean, Henderson, Bradshaw [1] and H. McQueen (forwards).
NEWTON HEATH: Fall (goal); Mitchell and Errentz (backs); Perrins, McNaught and Davidson (halves); Clarkin, Farman, Donaldson, Hood and Peden (forwards).

This and other accounts of the match make it clear that the "Heathens" put up a strong fight in the opening stages when the game showed promise of being a fast, furious and exciting encounter. This was indeed the case until Liverpool's opening goal which, however, seems to have then knocked all resolve out of the Mancunians, whilst the second, a short time after, brought about a complete capitulation. There was plenty of time remaining at this point, it must be said, for the "Heathens" to have fought back and turned the game around - had there been any fight left in them! But the game had then degenerated into a lack-lustre affair with Liverpool, confident of victory, simply biding their time until the final whistle, and Newton Heath making little attempt to upset their nonchalance. Indeed this was fairly typical of Liverpool's play throughout that entire season. All too often the forwards had built up a two or three goal lead and then rested on their laurels, leaving the bulk of the work from then on to the backs and goalkeeper to protect that position. Luckily Liverpool had been outstandingly well served in those departments throughout the season, so that several near disasters had been averted. On this occasion, however, no such near disaster was ever threatened.

The last match of the season was the Final of the Liverpool Senior Cup, Everton and Liverpool replaying the previous year's final.

30/04/1894 LiSC-F: Everton v. Liverpool
Liverpool Mercury - Tuesday 1st May, 1894

This tie was fought out last evening on the Police Athletic Ground. Both clubs were represented by their reserve teams. As will be noticed, the Liverpool team was, with the exception of Rennie, wholly composed of local players.

The first half was mostly in favour of Everton, but owing to the really excellent defence of Millett, Hughes, and Duckers they were kept from scoring, while some meritorious work by the Liverpool right wing on several occasions almost brought about the downfall of Williams charge.

Immediately on resuming **Storrier** scored for Everton, who incessantly attacked Liverpool's goal, but so finely did they defend that Liverpool kept their goal intact for some time. Then **Hartley** and **Storrier** again scored, and Everton won by three goals to nil.

RESULT: Everton 3 - Liverpool 0

LIVERPOOL: Rennie (goal); Millett and Duckers (backs); Kendrick, Hughes and Newall (halves); Powell, Crawford, Travis, Braniff and Bicknell (forwards).
EVERTON: Williams (goal); Parry and Arridge (backs); Walker, Jones and Coyle (halves); Reay, Murray, Hartley [1], Storrier [2] and Elliott (forwards).

For The Record – Season 1893/94

List of Fixtures - Results

Date	H/A	Comp	Opponent	Result	Score
02/09/1893	A	FL:01	Middlesbrough Ironopolis	W	2-0
06/09/1893	H	OM	NEWTON HEATH	W	1-0
09/09/1893	H	FL:02	LINCOLN CITY	W	4-0
16/09/1893	A	FL:03	Ardwick	W	1-0
20/09/1893	A	OM	Newton Heath	W	3-0
23/09/1893	H	FL:04	SMALL HEATH	W	3-1
30/09/1893	A	FL:05	Notts County	D	1-1
03/10/1893	A	OM	Darwen	W	3-1
07/10/1893	H	FL:06	MIDDLESBROUGH IRON.	W	6-0
14/10/1893	A	FL:07	Small Heath	W	4-3
16/10/1893	A	OM	Preston North End	L	0-3
21/10/1893	A	FL:08	Burton Swifts	D	1-1
28/10/1893	A	FL:09	Woolwich Arsenal	W	5-0
04/11/1893	H	FL:10	NEWCASTLE UNITED	W	5-1
11/11/1893	A	FL:11	Walsall Town Swifts	D	1-1
18/11/1893	H	FL:12	NOTTS COUNTY	W	2-1
25/11/1893	A	FL:13	Newcastle United	D	0-0
02/12/1893	H	FL:14	ARDWICK	W	3-0
09/12/1893	H	FL:15	WALSALL TOWN SWIFTS	W	3-0
16/12/1893	A	OM	Nottingham Forest	W	3-0
23/12/1893	A	OM	Ardwick	W	6-2
25/12/1893	A	OM	Accrington	L	0-1
26/12/1893	H	OM	CORINTHIANS	W	2-0
28/12/1893	A	FL:16	Crewe Alexandra	W	5-0
30/12/1893	H	FL:17	GRIMSBY TOWN	W	2-0
01/01/1894	H	FL:18	WOOLWICH ARSENAL	W	2-0
06/01/1894	A	FL:19	Rotherham Town	W	4-1
08/01/1894	H	OM	BURNLEY	W	2-0
13/01/1894	H	FL:20	ROTHERHAM TOWN	W	5-1
20/01/1894	A	LSC-R1	Blackburn Rovers	L	3-4
27/01/1894	H	FAC-R1	GRIMSBY TOWN	W	3-0
03/02/1894	H	FL:21	NORTHWICH VICTORIA	W	4-0
10/02/1894	H	FAC-R2	PRESTON NORTH END	W	3-2
24/02/1894	A	FAC-R3	Bolton Wanderers	L	0-3
01/03/1894	H	OM	NEWTON HEATH	W	3-0
03/03/1894	H	FL:22	BURTON SWIFTS	W	3-1
10/03/1894	H	PL:1	PRESTON NORTH END	W	2-0
12/03/1894	A	PL:2	Burnley	L	2-4
17/03/1894	A	FL:23	Lincoln City	D	1-1
20/03/1894	H	LiSC-R1	BOOTLE ATHLETIC	W	4-1
23/03/1894	H	PL:3	DARWEN	D	1-1
24/03/1894	H	FL:24	CREWE ALEXANDRA	W	2-0
26/03/1894	H	OM	ACCRINGTON	W	8-0
28/03/1894	A	FL:25	Northwich Victoria	W	3-2

Date	H/A	Comp	Opponent	Result	Score
31/03/1894	A	FL:26	Grimsby Town	W	1-0
02/04/1894	A	OM	Newton Heath	L	0-2
04/04/1894	H	OM	DARWEN	W	4-2
07/04/1894	A	FL:27	Burslem Port Vale	D	2-2
09/04/1893	N	LiSC-SF	White Star Wand. (at Bootle)	W	2-1
11/04/1894	H	PL:4	BURNLEY	L	0-2
12/04/1894	A	PL:5	Blackburn Rovers	L	0-5
14/04/1894	H	FL:28	BURSLEM PORT VALE	W	2-1
16/04/1894	A	PL:6	Preston North End	L	0-3
21/04/1894	A	PL:7	Darwen	L	1-8
23/04/1894	A	OM	The Wednesday	L	0-4
24/04/1894	H	PL:8	BLACKBURN ROVERS	L	1-3
28/04/1894	A	FL:TM	Newton Heath	W	2-0
30/04/1894	N	LiSC-F	Everton (at Police Ath. Grnds.)	L	0-3

Table of Player Appearances (1ˢᵗ Team Competitive Matches)

Appearances	Pos	LL	FAC	LSC	PAL
McOwen	G	23	3	1	6
(McQueen M.)*	G	5:1			
Rennie	G				2
McLean	FB	28(5):1	3	1	3
Hannah	FB	24(1):1	3	1	3
Hughes	FB	1			3
Mellett	FB				2
Kellett	FB				1
Killip	FB				1
Mullett	FB				1
McQue	HB	26(2):1	3(1)	1	4
McBride	HB	25(3):1	2	1	5
McCartney	HB	16(1):1	1		3
Trevis	HB				3
Crawford	HB				2
Newall	HB				2
Hendrick	HB				1
Preston	HB				1
Stevens	HB				1
McQueen H.	FW	27(11):1	2	1(1)	5(1)
McVean	FW	22(9):1	3(1)	1	4(1)
Gordon	FW	21(6):1(1)	3	1	6
Henderson	FW	21(10):1	2(2)	1(1)	5
Stott	FW	16(4)	2		4
Bradshaw	FW	14(7):1(1)	3(2)	1(1)	2(1)
Dick	FW	10(2)			1
Givens	FW	5(3)			5(1)
Worgan	FW	1(2)			2(1)
Dewhurst	FW	1			
Duckers	FW				2
Clarke	FW				1(1)
Braniff	FW				1
Dies	FW				1
Nelson	FW				1
Stringer	FW				1
McQueen M.*	UT	22(1)	3	1	2

* goalkeeping appearances shown separately.

LL = Lancashire League. FAC = F.A. Cup, LSC = Lancashire Senior Cup, PAL = Palatine League.

Football League Division Two Standings – Month by Month
(Table positions after last major round of matches in each month)

30/09/1893	Pld	W	D	L	For	Agst	Pts	Avge
Burslem Port Vale	7	7	0	0	30	7	14	4.29
Small Heath	7	5	0	2	19	13	10	1.46
Liverpool	5	4	1	0	11	2	9	5.50
Notts County	5	4	1	0	9	3	9	3.00
Grimsby Town	6	4	0	2	20	11	8	1.82
Burton Swifts	6	4	0	2	18	11	8	1.64
Woolwich Arsenal	6	2	1	3	11	12	5	.92
Crewe Alexandra	5	2	0	3	10	12	4	.83
Walsall Town Swifts	7	2	0	5	11	22	4	.50
Newcastle United	3	1	1	1	9	5	3	1.80
Lincoln City	4	1	1	2	6	8	3	.75
Rotherham Town	6	1	1	4	9	17	3	.53
Ardwick	1	1	0	0	9	18	2	.50
Middlesbrough Iron.	6	1	0	5	8	17	2	.47
Northwich Victoria	5	0	0	5	6	22	0	.27

28/10/1893	Pld	W	D	L	For	Agst	Pts	Avge
Liverpool	9	7	2	0	27	6	16	4.50
Notts County	10	7	2	1	23	10	16	2.30
Burslem Port Vale	11	8	0	3	30	20	16	1.50
Small Heath	11	8	0	3	35	24	16	1.46
Burton Swifts	10	6	1	3	28	17	13	1.65
Grimsby Town	10	5	0	5	29	25	10	1.16
Lincoln City	7	3	2	2	13	12	8	1.08
Crewe Alexandra	8	3	1	4	15	15	7	1.00
Walsall Town Swifts	9	3	0	6	12	18	6	.67
Ardwick	10	2	1	7	14	14	5	1.00
Woolwich Arsenal	7	2	1	4	19	22	5	.86
Rotherham Town	8	2	1	5	12	20	5	.60
Newcastle United	7	2	1	4	12	23	5	.52
Middlesbrough Iron.	8	2	0	6	5	25	4	.20
Northwich Victoria	9	1	0	8	8	31	2	.26

25/11/1893	Pld	W	D	L	For	Agst	Pts	Avge
Liverpool	**13**	**9**	**4**	**0**	**35**	**9**	**22**	**3.89**
Notts County	15	9	2	4	34	16	20	2.13
Small Heath	13	9	0	4	38	25	18	1.52
Burslem Port Vale	12	9	0	3	35	24	18	1.46
Burton Swifts	12	8	1	3	39	21	17	1.86
Grimsby Town	11	6	0	5	35	27	12	1.30
Lincoln City	9	4	2	3	17	18	10	.94
Woolwich Arsenal	10	4	1	5	18	27	9	.67
Crewe Alexandra	8	3	1	4	15	15	7	1.00
Ardwick	12	3	1	8	22	23	7	.96
Walsall Town Swifts	11	3	1	7	13	27	7	.48
Newcastle United	10	2	2	6	18	24	6	.75
Middlesbrough Iron.	11	3	0	8	10	34	6	.29
Rotherham Town	10	2	1	7	14	28	5	.50
Northwich Victoria	11	2	0	9	14	40	4	.35

30/12/1893	Pld	W	D	L	For	Agst	Pts	Avge
Liverpool	**17**	**13**	**4**	**0**	**48**	**9**	**30**	**5.33**
Small Heath	19	14	0	5	63	31	28	2.03
Notts County	19	11	3	5	42	21	25	2.00
Burslem Port Vale	18	11	1	6	48	38	23	1.26
Burton Swifts	17	8	2	7	43	35	18	1.23
Grimsby Town	16	8	0	8	44	40	16	1.10
Newcastle United	16	6	4	6	32	29	16	1.10
Lincoln City	14	6	3	5	34	31	15	1.10
Woolwich Arsenal	14	6	2	6	25	33	14	.76
Middlesbrough Iron.	17	5	3	9	22	41	13	.54
Ardwick	16	5	1	10	29	30	11	.97
Walsall Town Swifts	16	4	3	9	19	34	11	.56
Crewe Alexandra	14	3	4	7	20	35	10	.57
Rotherham Town	14	3	1	10	24	49	7	.49
Northwich Victoria	15	2	1	12	20	58	5	.34

27/01/1894	Pld	W	D	L	For	Agst	Pts	Avge
Liverpool	**20**	**16**	**4**	**0**	**59**	**11**	**36**	**5.36**
Small Heath	21	16	0	5	75	34	32	2.21
Notts County	21	13	3	5	48	23	29	2.09
Burslem Port Vale	21	12	1	8	54	46	25	1.17
Newcastle United	21	10	4	7	49	36	24	1.36
Burton Swifts	19	10	2	7	52	41	22	1.27
Grimsby Town	18	9	1	8	52	43	19	1.21
Lincoln City	17	7	4	6	38	34	18	1.12
Middlesbrough Iron.	21	7	4	10	29	49	18	.59
Woolwich Arsenal	16	6	2	8	27	37	14	.73
Ardwick	19	6	1	12	34	39	13	.87
Crewe Alexandra	18	4	5	9	28	45	13	.62
Walsall Town Swifts	18	4	3	11	22	40	11	.55
Rotherham Town	19	4	1	14	30	65	9	.46
Northwich Victoria	19	2	1	16	22	75	5	.29

24/02/1894	Pld	W	D	L	For	Agst	Pts	Avge
Liverpool	**21**	**17**	**4**	**0**	**63**	**11**	**38**	**5.73**
Notts County	25	15	3	7	60	25	33	2.40
Small Heath	22	16	0	6	76	37	32	2.05
Newcastle United	24	12	5	7	58	37	29	1.57
Burslem Port Vale	24	12	3	9	58	51	27	1.14
Grimsby Town	22	12	1	9	63	48	25	1.31
Burton Swifts	21	11	2	8	61	49	24	1.24
Lincoln City	21	9	5	7	46	48	23	.96
Woolwich Arsenal	22	10	3	9	43	47	23	.91
Middlesbrough Iron.	23	7	4	12	32	57	18	.56
Ardwick	21	7	2	12	39	41	16	.95
Crewe Alexandra	21	4	6	11	32	58	14	.55
Walsall Town Swifts	22	5	3	14	32	54	13	.59
Rotherham Town	23	5	2	16	35	79	12	.44
Northwich Victoria	22	2	1	19	23	84	5	.27

31/03/1894	Pld	W	D	L	For	Agst	Pts	Avge
Liverpool	**26**	**21**	**5**	**0**	**73**	**15**	**47**	**4.87**
Small Heath	27	20	0	7	100	44	40	2.27
Notts County	27	18	2	7	70	28	38	2.50
Newcastle United	27	15	5	7	66	39	35	1.69
Burton Swifts	26	13	3	10	68	57	29	1.19
Grimsby Town	26	14	1	11	68	57	29	1.19
Burslem Port Vale	26	13	3	10	68	60	29	1.13
Lincoln City	27	11	6	10	59	56	28	1.05
Woolwich Arsenal	27	12	4	11	52	53	28	.98
Middlesbrough Iron.	26	8	4	14	34	66	20	.52
Walsall Town Swifts	26	7	3	16	44	59	17	.75
Ardwick	26	8	2	16	44	64	18	.69
Crewe Alexandra	26	4	7	15	36	71	15	.51
Rotherham Town	26	5	3	18	39	86	13	.45
Northwich Victoria	27	2	3	22	28	97	7	.29

FINAL	Pld	W	D	L	For	Agst	Pts	Avge
Liverpool	**28**	**22**	**6**	**0**	**77**	**18**	**50**	**4.28**
Small Heath	28	21	0	7	103	44	42	2.34
Notts County	28	18	3	7	70	31	39	2.26
Newcastle United	28	15	6	7	66	39	36	1.69
Grimsby Town	28	15	2	11	71	58	32	1.22
Burton Swifts	28	14	3	11	80	61	31	1.31
Burslem Port Vale	28	13	4	11	66	64	30	1.03
Lincoln City	28	12	6	10	61	56	30	1.09
Woolwich Arsenal	28	12	4	12	52	55	28	.95
Walsall Town Swifts	28	9	3	16	49	65	21	.75
Middlesbrough Iron.	28	8	4	16	36	72	20	.50
Crewe Alexandra	28	6	7	15	42	73	19	.58
Ardwick	28	8	2	18	47	71	18	.66
Rotherham Town	28	6	3	19	44	91	15	.48
Northwich Victoria	28	3	3	22	30	98	9	.31

Palatine League Final Table

FINAL	Pld	W	D	L	For	Agst	Pts	Avge
Burnley	8	6	1	1	18	19	13	.95
Preston North End	8	5	1	2	21	9	11	2.33
Blackburn Rovers	8	4	0	2	16	14	8	1.14
Darwen	8	3	1	4	16	18	7	.89
Liverpool	8	1	1	6	7	26	3	.27

What Happened Next

Liverpool gained a creditable point in a 1-1 draw at Blackburn Rovers in their opening Division One fixture on September 1st, 1894, repeating the feat in a 3-3 draw at Burnley two days later. That was followed by a run of defeats, however, and by the end of the year Liverpool had obtained only 11 points from 20 League fixtures. Things improved significantly, however, after the new year was begun with a 4-0 win against West Bromwich Albion. In all, five of seven games from the start of the New Year were won, and by the end of March it seemed Liverpool were on the verge of escaping the relegation danger zone. At the very end, however, while the other teams around them finished strongly Liverpool relapsed, dropping back to the foot of the table.

In the test matches, Liverpool were pitted against Second Division champions Bury, losing 0-1 at Blackburn and so forfeiting their position among the elite after only one season. Liverpool were not to be so easily denied, however, winning the Championship of the Second Division again the very next season, and fighting their way back into the top flight through the test matches (by this time, a mini-League having supplanted the one-on-one sudden death system).

Remarkably no less than five players - Matt McQueen, McQue, McVean, McCartney and Bradshaw - who had been prominent in Liverpool's first Second Division championship success also figured in the second. Of these all except Bradshaw had also taken part in Liverpool's Lancashire League campaign.

This time Liverpool cemented their presence in the higher League, and after only five seasons, in 1900/01, had won their first ever League Championship.

The Palatine League

The Palatine League could hardly be deemed a great success, or indeed a success of any sort! At their Annual General Meeting the Secretary of the Blackburn Rovers blamed that club's poor financial returns on the season, despite moderate success on the playing field, on the fact that the Palatine League fixtures had failed to draw!

This however, in hindsight, is easily explained by the fact that most of the clubs involved in the competition habitually fielded largely reserve elevens in Palatine League matches – this included Liverpool, at least after the opening fixtures. This was directly contrary to the objective behind the formation of the League, which was to provide additional first-class fixtures to flesh out the season, and was probably largely due to the games all being played late in the season when the clubs had injury problems to contend with and/or more important matches to prepare for.

Regardless of the reason, if the clubs failed to take the competition seriously, they could hardly blame the supporters, nor indeed the press, for doing likewise. Indeed, after the first few rounds of fixtures the press generally wasted little space in covering Palatine League matches.

The following season Everton withdrew from the competition and Accrington were voted out, leaving four clubs in each division. With Everton's influence removed Liverpool were allotted to the Southern Division with Bolton, Bury and Newton Heath – Blackburn, Burnley, Darwen and Preston made up the Northern Division. The competition ran for one more season before being disbanded.

I hope you have enjoyed this book. If so, watch out for other titles in the Season Scrapbook series.

Printed in Great Britain
by Amazon

LIVERPOOL

Season Scrapbook
1892/93 & 1893/94